American Studies

A tri-annual interdisciplinary journal sponsored by the Mid-America American Studies Association, the University of Kansas, and the Hall Center for the Humanities.

Editors:	**David M. Katzman**
	Norman R. Yetman
Associate Editor:	**William Graebner,**
	State University of New York, Fredonia

Assistant Editor:	Cheryl R. Ragar
Managing Editor:	Ailecia Ruscin
Production Staff:	Pam LeRow, Paula Courtney, and Lynn Porter

ISSN 0026-3079

American Studies

The Library as an Agency of Culture

Guest Editors: Thomas Augst and Wayne A. Wiegand

Articles

Notes on Contributors

Elizabeth Jane Aikin has a master's degree in library science from Indiana University and a Ph.D. in U. S. history from the University of Michigan. She is Senior Academic Advisor in the National Endowment for the Humanities Fellowships Program. Her publications include *The Nation's Great Library: Herbert Putnam and the Library of Congress, 1899-1939* (University of Illinois Press, 1993), and "Valley of the Shadow," *Humanities* 18 (March/April 1997): 18-22.

Thomas Augst is Assistant Professor of English at the University of Minnesota. Some of his essays on American literature and culture have appeared in *American Quarterly* and *Political Theory*. His book, *The Business of Living*, explores literary practices and moral authority in nineteenth-century America and will be published by the University of Chicago Press in 2003.

Juris Dilevko is a member of the Faculty of Information Studies, University of Toronto, Canada.

Jacalyn Eddy is a graduate student in the Department of History at the University of Rochester, where she is completing her doctoral dissertation, "Bookwomen: Creating an Empire in Children's Book Publishing, 1919-1939."

Lisa Gottlieb is at the Faculty of Information Studies, University of Toronto, where her research interests focus on classification theory and library services for children and young adults.

Benjamin Hufbauer received his Ph.D. from the University of California at Santa Barbara, and is currently Assistant Professor of Art History at the Hite Art Institute of the University of Louisville. He is working on a book-length study on presidential com-

(continued on p. 210)

Introduction

American Libraries and Agencies of Culture

Thomas Augst

To think about libraries is to think about the material forms that culture takes within a social landscape. Each essay in this special issue examines some of the agencies by which Americans have invested particular goods and prac- tices—especially printed books and the act of reading—with a diverse array of meanings and documents some of the functions that libraries play in the lives of individuals and communities at particular moments. In the pages that follow, the library is a protean thing. It is a painstaking record of books loaned to neighbors. It is a soaring, marbled space designed to produce silence in a noisy cityscape populated by immigrants. Libraries take historical form in the circulating records of social libraries in the nineteenth century; in the gendered cliché of the female librarian reading aloud to children in the early twentieth-century; in the 1930s, in a collection at the Library of Congress or the plans Franklin D. Roosevelt made for the preservation of his papers; in the 1950s in reading programs at the New York Public Library or state and local tax referendums. At the end of twen- tieth century, the library is an absence from a planned community built by Disney.

Each of these essays proposes that we analyze culture from a particular place within a landscape that is at once social, historical, and physical. It is within these institutional locales of culture where communities broker the ten- sions between the individual and community, the public and the private, the material and the symbolic. As sites where often lofty, ideological claims about

0026-3079/2001/4203-005$2.50/0   American Studies, 42:3 (Fall 2001): 5-22

the value of knowledge collide with seemingly mundane problems of access, management, and technology, libraries allow us to think more fully about the processes of American culture more generally. Historically the library has borne the particular weight of defining culture and devising means for its practical administration, all within a tangible set of problems regarding circulation, cataloging, and storage.

Only when we attend to the seemingly mundane and ordinary ways in which institutions work can we fully appreciate how and why the idea of culture has literally come to matter in the lives of individuals and communities. This becomes palpable and tangible in collecting books, in a bookmobile traveling to rural outposts, and in buildings that haunt the horizon of small towns and large cities across the United States. In the remainder of the introduction, I situate the essays in this special volume of *American Studies* in relation to major issues that have defined the production, dissemination, and consumption of American culture: issues of social access, the construction of public life, and the organization of knowledge. Agencies of cultural formation become newly visible when understood from comparative historical locales. What a library is depends on what it does: it is a social enterprise, a physical infrastructure, a symbolic site of collective memory. In the contests waged within and without the walls of libraries, we see with particular clarity how culture came to be institutionalized as the end of individual and collective lives, at once a powerful symbol of democratic liberty and an effectual safeguard against its excesses.

The Social Enterprise

The modern history of the library has become inseparable from the form and fate of print. In medieval archives manuscripts were chained to desks because they were so costly to produce and difficult to replace. The idea that large numbers of people might remove books they did not own from a shelf or room for days and weeks at a time depended on the industrial production of printed goods. Along with the expansion of literacy, a crucial part of the revolution sparked by the printing press was new modes of access that brought printed books to audiences outside of cosmopolitan circuits of learned elites.

The history of American libraries is distinguished by innovations in the institutional and social forms of reading, beginning with the Library Company of Philadelphia. In 1729, Benjamin Franklin and several of his peers created the first circulating library open to public subscription. In doing so, they helped to invent social libraries, organizations the primary purpose of which was to make reading available to its members, and which operated essentially like joint-stock companies whose members agreed to pool resources for their mutual benefit. Prior to the Library Company, the only libraries in the colonies aside from a few private ones were academic and theological, designed mostly for the training of ministers: collections at Yale, Harvard, and William and Mary, and the several collections established by the Anglican missionary Thomas Bray and the Society for the Propagation of the Gospel.[1] Most of these collections were formed by donations from Britain. By contrast, the Library Company purchased books to meet the tastes of its members, taking a pragmatic rather than ideological approach to the supply of books. It defined culture itself in terms of access, and it drew upon the entrepreneurial energies and managerial strategies of commerce to facilitate the provision of ostensible "public goods." Although one had to own stock in the Library Company to use it, Franklin himself referred to it as the "public library of Philadelphia," and its orientation was self-consciously inclusive and egalitarian. As its eighteenth-century catalogs demonstrate, it had relatively little of the theological literature that dominated most elite libraries, and the only works in Latin and Greek it had were donations rather than purchases; it was increasingly stocked with contemporary literature by Alexander Pope and others, as well as the novels of Henry Fielding and Ralph Richardson.[2]

Like so many reformers, educators, and philanthropists who would follow him, Franklin described the fruits of learning in the explicit language of a civilizing mission. In his *Autobiography* he saw social libraries such as the Library Company as a specifically republican institution that promoted equality and a national consciousness: "These libraries have improved the general conversation of the Americans, made the common tradesmen and farmers as intelligent as most gentlemen from other countries, and perhaps has contributed in some degree to the stand so generally made throughout the colonies in defense of their privileges."[3] The wonder of America, as his own life attested, was that an artisan might become as intelligent as the sons of the gentry, limited only by his own curiosity and ambition. Franklin's comment epitomizes the myth and ideology that would distinguish both the history of the library and the development of what we might call the cultural agencies of liberalism. Here the individual pursuit of self-interest (young men seeking to "improve" through reading) would rebound to the good of the civic enterprise. In the new world, access to cultural goods usually reserved for the well-born would, not only transform "common tradesmen and farmers" into gentlemen—as Franklin's own story so famously attested—but also improve conversation and intelligence, crucial elements in the citizens' defense of their political privileges. At that same time, such liberal agencies of culture were non-coercive, creating opportunities and rewarding individual initiative rather than prescribing lessons or enforcing dogma. Young men were more inclined to recognize the importance of public goods if they had had some material, personal benefit from it, if they catered to their desires as well as their duties.

Social libraries like the Library Company transformed advanced learning from the complacent privilege of inherited status to a symbol of individual freedom and opportunity. Franklin and the thousands of successors who formed these institutions recognized that culture could be rationalized according to democratic agencies of supply and demand, in ways that effaced republican distinctions between public goods and private interests, between citizenship and consumption. Before 1876, over 3,000 social libraries had been founded, largely in the northeast United States. Many were small and short-lived and did not survive the initial enthusiasm of their founders.[4] The most successful of them, such as the New York Mercantile Library, drew on strategies of commercial enterprise, mastering practical strategies of promotion and service to deliver reading matter while "fresh," as annual reports often described it. As private organizations that depended on the satisfaction of dues-paying members, social and "proprietary" libraries had economic incentives to define their market for reading, and to figure out the most effective means of exploiting it.[5]

Limitations of gender, class, ethnicity, and race belied the rhetoric of republican equality, and social libraries helped to institutionalize a more democratic print culture that valued books not as a form of elite property but rather a medium of mass circulation. Instead of enforcing status in educational and social hierarchies dominated by the learned ministry and gentlemen, books acquired social life through exchange and use. The essays that follow document the scope and nature of this social life of books and suggest some of the ways that American culture has been shaped by contests over access. Before the twentieth century, real access to books would continue to be limited by gender, class, ethnicity, and race, in ways that reflected the limits of American democracy itself.

The new social life that books acquired with popular libraries challenged not only the monopoly that traditional elites had on access to books, but also the practices and values through which readers became engaged with them. In her research note on two social libraries in antebellum America, Emily Todd demonstrates how we can use circulating records to specify the nature of readers' engagement. At both the Richmond Library Company and the Lyceum and Library Society of New Orleans, individuals used the intellectual freedom afforded by social libraries to read fiction, as they typically did in social libraries in the nineteenth century, and as they would continue to do in public libraries in the twentieth century. In the pace and the pattern at which readers borrowed the novels of Sir Walter Scott we see the emergence of a compulsive style of emotional and psychological attachment, at once extensive and intensive, that would become endemic to the popular tastes for mass culture. The experience of Scott's novels in the 1830s were, in some rough sense, equivalent to the repeated viewings of *Titanic* or fanatical devotion to Harry Potter novels in the 1990s.[6]

In balancing access to "useful knowledge" and self-improvement, with the social pleasures of leisure and consumption, libraries give shape to emerging communities.[7] The spread of a mass culture of print promoted new kinds of consumption because, as Ronald and Mary Zboray point out in their groundbreaking essay on private libraries in antebellum America, it entailed a profound decentralization of cultural capital from the exclusive colleges and private libraries of gentlemen to the parlors and kitchens of the middle class. As printed goods saturated everyday spaces in nineteenth-century America, the functions of a library were assumed in the domestic habits of collection, preservation, cataloging, and reference. In their analysis, a library ceases to be a particular place and a set of objects, a formal institution built of brick and mortar. It becomes instead a continuity of practices, a complex of habits among family, friends, and neighbors that assimilate books into the rhythms and rituals of housekeeping and sociability. In making these patterns and functions of the library visible in the quotidian practices of everyday life, the Zborays suggest how strongly our ability to see what culture is came to be colored by the large buildings that sprang up in the late-nineteenth century. As informal functions of the domestic library were delegated to public libraries, an entire habitus of culture was overshadowed, if not eclipsed, by forces of centralization and professionalization—by formal protocols of cultural authority that became embedded in bureaucratic institutions.

The Public Infrastructure

In the age of the social library, the major contest was over access, but in the age of the public library, it would be over the boundaries of public and private life, the infrastructure of civic space. Following the innovations in paper production and the steam-powered press, the printed book was the first truly mass medium, one that to social elites and reformers seemed indifferent, if not corrosive, to moral standards and social hierarchies, indeed to the very inheritance of Western learning. The canary in this particular mineshaft was the popular novel, the development of which in the eighteenth century coincided with the spread of social and circulating libraries. At the end of the eighteenth century, Caritat's immensely popular commercial library in Manhattan catered to upper-class tastes with its impressive supply of fiction and its appeal to the genteel conventions of intellectual improvement and moral edification. In his 1804 catalog Caritat included "explanatory" notes and excerpts from critical reviews that argued for the moral propriety and literary worth of some of the hundreds of novels that he rented out.[8] Debates about the value of the fiction in social libraries continued throughout the nineteenth century and persisted well into the twentieth century, as public libraries and the library profession struggled to define acquisition and circulation policies. These debates reflected larger anxieties about the moral consequences of mass culture and marketplace values for the democratic polity.

Few institutions were more important in making a new ideal of public culture palpable and visible in the material and social landscape of nineteenth-century America than the public library. In their first annual report, the Trustees of the Boston Public Library paid homage to the Gutenberg Revolution as having produced "the great intellectual revival of the modern world" by making books cheap and abundant. But what good was the invention of printing and the spread of literacy without the means to put these books in the hands of a reading public? The trustees admitted the presence of many libraries in Boston, and pointed out that two-thirds of Massachusetts towns that had social libraries were "languishing." Despite all the other libraries in Boston, "multitudes among us have no right of access to any one of the more considerable and important of these libraries." The brilliant strategy of the advocates of public libraries was to redefine the agency of culture in terms of progress and abundance. Like canals and turnpikes and railways, or the modern freeway system, libraries should be seen as part of the physical infrastructure and capital improvements by which a society invests in its future. As the Trustees continued:

> The old roads, so to speak, are admitted to be no longer suffi-
> cient. Even the more modern turnpikes do not satisfy our wants.
> We ask for railcars and steamboats, in which many more per-
> sons—even multitudes—may advance together to the great
> end of life, and go faster, farther and better, by the means thus
> furnished to them, than they have ever been able to do be-
> fore.[9]

Since the eighteenth century, the laissez-faire philosophy of liberal capitalism had equated the free traffic in goods with the spread of knowledge and the diffusion of cosmopolitan manners and refined customs that marked a people as "civilized." As new modes of transportation and communication fed the growth of markets and commerce, so too libraries would make the trade in ideas more efficient, taking us "to the great end of life" in a way that is "faster, farther, better" than by previous means available.

The existence of thousands of libraries in towns and cities across nineteenth-century America—in common with Sunday schools, lyceums, hospitals, and prisons—was not enough. Libraries had to become permanent fixtures in the civic landscape. Already by 1869, when Edward Edwards made his comparative study of free town libraries in Europe and America, he was struck by the greater enthusiasm in the United States for tax support of libraries and other educational institutions: "In the course of the rapidly increasing attention bestowed, throughout almost all parts of America, upon public libraries as powerful and indispensible instruments of civilization" attention soon fastened "upon the municipal action of incorporated towns, as offering the best of all machinery for making Free Libraries thoroughly progressive and truly permanent."[10]

The most persuasive and influential argument for how public libraries served this civilizing function and why they needed tax support to be "thoroughly progressive" came from their partnership with public school systems. What good was education if, in fitting students with the equipment for learning, it left them without a "right of access" to the universe of knowledge? "It awakens a taste for reading, but it furnishes to the public nothing to be read. It conducts our young men and women to the point, where they are qualified to acquire from books the various knowledge in the arts and sciences which books contain; but it does nothing to put those books within their reach." The "public makes no provision whatever" by which young people "can carry on their education and bring it to practical results by private study."[11] Republican ideology of education allowed reformers to justify the enormous "provision" that, in the following century, would be made by the "public" for libraries in cities and towns across the nation. Indeed, prior to the cascade of library legislation later in the century, most nineteenth-century towns already had libraries attached to their local schools. Legislation in the late-1830s permitted school districts to levy taxes for school libraries. By 1850 Massachusetts had 2,084, while New York schools had some 1.5 million library books.[12]

As with the huge public investments in internal improvements, the public library became a fixture in the urban landscape. Aggressive campaigns by urban reformers and private philanthropists effected a profound transformation in the social habitat of the modern liberal state. A new public culture emerged from the partnership of private philanthropy and tax-supported agencies of local and state government. John Jacob Astor left $400,000 for a library because, as his will stated, he wished "to render a public benefit to the city of New York, and to contribute to the advancement of human knowledge and the general good of society. . . ."[13] In the early-twentieth century Andrew Carnegie's benevolence was especially important in spreading the library as a public agency across the United States. Carnegie's money built 1,679 libraries in the United States, and perhaps more important, extorted public commitments to libraries from communities, since the gifts came with the obligation that communities pay for their maintenance and support in perpetuity. Built in more than 1,400 communities between 1880 and 1920, Carnegie libraries were often the only government buildings besides the county courthouses. Today, more than 1,000 of them are still being used as libraries.[14]

In striking contrast to state sponsorship of arts and letters in other nations in the developed west, much of the infrastructure for public culture in cities across the United States was initiated by private philanthropy. As Peter Dobkin Hall has argued, this may have been a result of the historic openness of the American political system. As the franchise was opened to white males in the early-nineteenth century, elites in the northeastern United States made innovative use of non-profit corporate charters to develop a network of non-profit institutions that afforded them new channels of leadership, new agencies of social control. As Anglo-American Protestants lost their dominance at the ballot box, they made philanthropic institutions such as the library a preferred mode of politics by other means.[15] In this regard, the magnates who forked over the enormous sums made no bones about their motives. As Carnegie, who gave away more than $50 million for libraries, declared in 1900: "I choose free libraries as the best agencies for improving the masses of the people, because they give nothing for nothing. They only help those who help themselves. They never pauperize. They reach the aspiring, and open to these the chief treasures of the world—those steeped up in books. A taste for reading drives out lower tastes."[16] As Carnegie's comment succinctly summarized, the "agency" of the public library was moral uplift and social control, not a system of welfare that would "pauperize" steel workers by robbing them of their initiative and independence. It was an agency of self-help that would reward the "aspiring" of talent and will, substituting baser instincts for drinking, dancing, and sex with the "higher" taste for books. Such benevolence invited the working classes to think about abstract "treasures of the world" rather than their wages, to focus on opening up their minds rather than the sensate pleasures of their bodies or their impoverished living conditions. For Carnegie, Pennsylvania steel workers would rise above the working classes by trusting their futures to individual ambition instead of collective organization.

These public libraries were not only "instruments" of social control, but also the nineteenth century's most impressive symbols of what Astor termed the "general good of society," of liberal capitalism's capacity to create "civilization." Franklin's biography, after all, traced the movement of a self-made man into public obligation: it was an advertisement of how the pursuit of self-interest could produce public goods. No idea became more central to liberal ideology than the opportunities for social mobility afforded by education, the freedom realized through access to books. As they looked back to modest beginnings, figures as diverse as Franklin, Carnegie, Frederick Douglass, and countless others celebrated the miraculous power of reading to transform one's material and social circumstances. Just as the blighted social and economic landscape of industrial capitalism was putting the power of the individual in question, this liberal ideology was propagated with missionary zeal by a new cadre of professional librarians and educators. As they spread the gospel of public culture to small towns across the United States, public libraries would acquire status as a public good, worthy of tax support, by giving the unwashed or provincial masses the chance to worship the civil religion of liberal individualism. Ushered into these ornate temples of self-improvement, educated citizens were assumed to become more capable of assuming the duties and enjoying the fruits of liberty and less likely to challenge the social inequalities that grew with each decade.

The early campaign for tax support of libraries coincided with a comprehensive effort to define librarianship as a professional mode of civic service. The passage of the Pendleton Civil Service Reform Act in 1883 sought to give government service a more "professional" character, at a moment when professionalism was increasingly defined by positivist and managerial norms of objectivity, efficiency, and expertise. While political appointees would occupy the upper tiers of government agencies, the machinery of governance would remain relatively undisturbed by the tides of popular whim and the political corruption that seemed to have compromised the integrity and quality of civic life. Like the post office or other departments of an expanding network of municipal and state bureaucracies, the modern library specialized in "services" that could be evaluated and standardized according to rationalized, bureaucratic methods. The smooth, continuous operation of municipal administrations—like the monolithic buildings that housed them—became powerful symbols of democracy's ability to survive the winds of political fashion. The major argument for this extraordinary expansion of state sponsorship of "instruments of civilization" such as the public schools and libraries in the Progressive era was the influx of millions of immigrants and the social havoc wrought by industrialism in the late-nineteenth and early-twentieth centuries.

Like the urban settlement houses that sprang up at the turn of the century, public libraries helped give new institutional forms to civic life. They did this in large part by challenging the gendered meanings that had defined roles and responsibilities of public life. In "'We Have Become Too Tender-Hearted': Gender and the Language of Negotiation in the Public Library," Jacqueline Eddy examines the language in which library professionals employed the rhetoric of gender to claim cultural authority for the library and enhance the status of their profession from 1880 through 1920.[17] Eddy analyzes the "official" language of the library movement, primarily drawn from the American Library Association and (until 1906) its primary organ, *The Library Journal*, as they addressed professional education, the admittance and segregation of children, the new strategies of community outreach, and other issues. The library became a fixture in the public landscape during the decades when the very shape of the civic sphere and the limits of private life were being profoundly transformed by modern conflicts over gender roles. In issues relating to poverty, education, and children, thousands of women occupying the rank and file of progressive reform sought to bring moral conscience and practical skills associated with Victorian domesticity into the urban landscape. At Hull House, Jane Addams and her colleagues literally set up house in an immigrant ghetto, applying their own expertise with the "home economics" of hygiene, nutrition, and maternal care to problems of urban life. These problems could no longer be managed by male-dominated political systems that, like so many fathers in Victorian melodrama, had become incompetent, corrupt, or derelict in their public duties. With the entrance of women into education and social work, the rise of the "new woman" and networks of women's clubs, the grass roots mobilization against drinking and other social pathologies, and the struggle for the vote, questions about the social status and moral authority of women became integral to every aspect of municipal, state, and national reform. One wonders whether massive investment in public libraries would have been possible without the moral authority that women brought to bear in their new roles. As public libraries opened children's reading rooms and offered counsel to immigrants, women came to play new roles in public life without challenging Victorian proprieties, and they did so at a lower cost to municipal taxpayers.

The institutions of public culture built by private philanthropy and the state brought the "advancement of human knowledge" to otherwise dark provinces of American life, outposts in an expanding national culture in the twentieth century. Two essays offer contrasting perspectives on the diffuse process by which libraries became enmeshed in larger contests over the meaning and form of American culture during the middle of the twentieth century. If in the nineteenth century freedom had been a largely moral category—freedom from lower tastes, as Carnegie put it—it became, with the emergence of the United States as a military and economic superpower, an increasingly political category. Jean Preer offers a case study of how the New York Public Library came to develop a new kind of service called "Exploring the American Idea" (EAI). Like the Great Books Program, EAI was an adult education program designed to foster an awareness of democratic values, at the same moment when agencies such as the Voice of America or the Unites States Information Agency were seeking to spread the empire of American liberalism abroad.[18] Through reading lists and discussion groups sponsored by the program, popular audiences gained access to an emerging canon of literary works that, like the first academic programs in American Studies or influential studies such as F.O. Mathiessen's *American Renaissance* (1941), expressed a cohesive and exceptional cultural identity. As Preer reconstructs the particular history of Exploring the American Idea, however, its ideological meaning becomes less cohesive and certain once we see the complex negotiations between individuals and groups, elites and popular audiences—from which cultural agencies develop in complex social and institutional environments.

What then can the case of the library teach us about otherwise familiar episodes in the development of liberal hegemony? As libraries and other institutions became quasi-governmental agencies, processes of cultural formation became increasingly contested and more diffuse than scholars have sometimes imagined. In "Reading versus the Red Bull," Christine Pawley tells the story of the Door-Kewaunee, Wisconsin Regional Library Demonstration Project, which between 1950 and 1953 established rural bookmobile service, expanded small-town library collections, and introduced cooperative cataloguing and book selection. Focusing on an electoral referendum in 1952 about whether the county would continue funding the initiative, Pawley demonstrates how political abstractions playing out nationally became palpable at the grass roots level as a conflict over taxes, pitting liberal/progressive views of the civic role of libraries against forces of social and cultural conservatism. As library advocates and local politicians manipulated rhetoric of the Cold War to their own ends, their arguments were in large part resisted by the patrons of bookmobiles, who continued to be interested mainly in reading fiction. Whatever the national and global meanings that elites attach to them, cultural agencies are constituted in practices and uses, within particular communities and local lives. No less than Ben Franklin and his fellow artisans, the ordinary people who gathered in reading groups at the New York Public, or took books from the bookmobiles in rural Wisconsin were using institutions to their own purposes. To understand the role of the library in American life requires that we understand agency itself in terms of appropriation. To read a book is to borrow from established forms of cultural authority and to refashion that authority within personal and communal contexts of meaning and practice.

As the funding and administration of libraries was transferred from philanthropy to the public purse, libraries became as integral to the local infrastructure of civic life as roads and bridges were to transportation networks. As programs such as "Exploring the Idea" or the Wisconsin Library Demonstration suggest, these municipal agencies of American culture would develop according to bureaucratic imperatives that accompanied the enormous post-War expansion of the scope and complexity of government at the local, regional, and national levels. Professional initiatives such as the Public Library Inquiry, published by the Social Science Research Council in 1950, found that the nation had a "multitude of libraries, some of them magnificent institutions, but it has no library system," and recommended an "integrated or interrelated machinery" of management that has now become commonplace in services such as interlibrary loan and on-line catalogues. The federal government became involved in expanding the infrastructure of public library service with The Library Services Act in 1956 and the Library Services and Construction Act of 1964, perhaps in response the report's observation that "communist countries have been most active in promoting public library growth within their borders."[19] In the mid-1990s, there were over 16,000 public library buildings in 9,000 library systems, with more than half part of a municipal government. Almost 80 percent of the total operating income of $5.9 billion came from local sources, with 12 percent coming from the state and 1 percent from the federal government.[20] The "machinery" of library service had indeed become more centralized as well. More than 71 percent of the population was being serviced by only 11 percent of the public libraries, and almost 70 percent of public libraries were members of a system, federation, or cooperative service.

Public libraries and other institutions established boundaries between public and private life that have become crucial to the modern meaning and experience of community. In their comparison of two libraries in Florida, Gottlieb and Dilevko open a window on the fate of the community at the end of the twentieth century, in a social landscape increasingly shaped by the private forces of global capitalism, and mass consumption. When the Disney Corporation first built the private residential development of Celebration, it made no provision for a town library. We might see this initial omission as a symptom of the corporate takeover of public life occurring at every level of education. The public library in Celebration eventually differed from the one next door in neighboring Osceola County in an emphasis on therapeutic self-help books that, as Dilevko and Gottlieb argue, reflects a profound shift in the ideology and social fabric of community. In its residents' desire for a library, one can see nostalgia for an image of small town life, the same fantasy of Main Street U.S.A. that Disneyland has sold for generations. For those who can afford it, this fantasy entails standardization, homogeneity, and control of the social environment that ethnic and class diversity make impossible elsewhere. As the case of Celebration suggests, the privatization of community is eroding the infrastructure of civic life that allowed earlier generations of Americans to recognize collective goods as distinct from goods in the marketplace. Community in postmodern America has itself become a function of niche marketing, in which "culture" has become synonymous with leisure and consumption.

Sites of Memory, and the Memory of Technology

Libraries enlarge our understanding of agencies of culture from two perspectives: the competition for goods and status and the construction of an infrastructure for public and national culture. In both regards, the history of libraries exemplifies conflicts—between individualism and community, between private and public—that are endemic to the process of cultural formation in the modern United States. But as the essays in this volume also demonstrate, the library itself has a more specific history as a unique kind of agency, related to the storage, retrieval, and organization of knowledge. All cultures, of course, develop tacit and formal means for preserving the past for the benefit of future generations. From the campaign of ancient rhetoricians to devise "places of memory," to the modern campaigns to devise a universal standard bibliography, the Western ideal of the library has represented not merely a collection of books gathered for some purpose but also arguments about the location, form, and power of knowledge in particular social and historical contexts. As a symbolic space, a type of collection, a kind of building, the library gives institutional form to our collective memory.

This can be seen in the case of Presidential libraries, which as Benjamin Hufbauer demonstrates in "A Shift in Commemoration," was invented by Franklin D. Roosevelt. By naming his memorial a "library," Roosevelt sought to be remembered for posterity by trading on the prestige and good will associated with libraries. And yet, in its pragmatic organization and architectural form, the complex was meant to operate as a popular museum as well as archive, appealing to a general public of tourists rather than a coterie of scholars. Such institutions intervene in our collective memory less through the functional preservation of documents and archival material, than through the production of national history as an locus of symbolic imagination. Through his analysis of the physical design and layout of the library, Huftbauer demonstrates how the institution creates "narrative circuits of settings and objects" that conflate an individual's life with a national past, shrouding public history in the aura of the sacred. We have no kings in America, but the growth of the imperial presidency in the twentieth century has helped to satisfy a thoroughly aristocratic desire to elevate particular objects and individuals above the democratic horde—to worship at the tomb of presidents grown Pharaoh-like in their cultural stature.

Libraries not only create access to the cultural goods, but they also institutionalize through their collections and policies changing ideals of culture. The creation of large national libraries throughout the early modern period were coincident with the invention of traditions that helped to legitimize the modern nation-state. Along with museums, monuments, and other public places, libraries and their collections helped to locate a disembodied historical consciousness in physical and symbolic sites of what Pierre Nora has diagnosed as the realms of national memory.[21] In narrating the development of the Archive of American Folk Culture in the Library of Congress, Jane Aikin helps us to understand the process of institutional innovation and adaptation that helped to shape our collective heritage in the modern era. In the nineteenth century, Charles Jewett's advocacy for making the Smithsonian institution a national library depended on a moralistic distinction among the objects of culture. "Standard" books in research libraries demanded the gravity and intensity of "study," unlike the "ephemeral works" and cheap publications that were piled up like so much lumber on the shelves of circulating libraries, athenaeums, book auctions.[22] It was only in the twentieth century that folk music and other ephemeral pieces of the vernacular past came to have a value for scholars. Aikin describes the efforts of Herbert Putnam and Robert Winslow Gordon to expand the scope of the Library of Congress' mission and function, given its unique legislative status, and given the low status of music as an object of scholarly and historical inquiry. Aikin reminds us of the contingent, pragmatic process by which popular "culture" came to be discovered in the 1920s and 1930s, newly visible pieces of a rapidly evolving national patrimony.

Like the Smithsonian and the Library of Congress, large public institutions founded in the nineteenth century made historical arguments about the meaning and purpose of "culture" in the modern world. Adorned with imposing and classical proportions of the Beaux arts tradition and the "City Beautiful" movement, huge edifices such as the New York Public Library were designed to promote and protect a traditional ideal of civilization from the anarchic, benighted modern urban life. In "The Sound of the Civic: Noise and Urban Subjectivity at the New York Public Library," Ari Kelman takes the silence of libraries as the occasion for thinking about the phenomenology of civic life. The immigrants who sat quietly awed by the majestic splendor of the Public Library's reading room in the early twentieth century found refuge from an urban social life that, as Kelman argues, is always noisy. Seeking to control and regulate this noise of the modern city, the philanthropists and reformers who agitated throughout the later nineteenth century on behalf of libraries and other municipal institutions (the art museum, the concert hall, the opera house, the park system, etc.) saw themselves as what Dee Garrison once termed "apostles of culture."[23] In sharing the British educator Mathew Arnold's definition of culture as the "best that has been thought and said," their efforts were motivated by a moralistic, if not spiritual, quest to create a space for tradition, proportion, and reverence in a modern social landscape grown crowded and noisy with mass consumption and ethnic pluralism. Their elitist ideal of civic life was embodied in the cold, imposing, silent spaces because the hustle of work and leisure in the highly commercial and industrial spaces of the city were seen as alienating to ordinary peoples' capacity for thinking and acting as citizens. Whatever their efficacy in "improving" or "controlling" the masses, these buildings allowed Americans literally to hear the sound of the civic, to develop a sensory and corporeal attachment to a symbolic ideal of democratic culture and a Victorian creed of liberal individualism.

With their granite and limestone walls, with the echo of one's footsteps on their polished marble floors, these large edifices have become monuments to a moral ideal of learning that now seems obsolete. These libraries are mausoleums for the bounded "corpus" or unified "body" that knowledge seemed to have, prior to its virtual decomposition in the digital age. In the mid-twentieth century, librarians embraced an alternative epistemology subsumed in the term "information," with its connotation of "scattered disjunct fragments of fact."[24] As federal defense and intelligence agencies sponsored research and technology in information systems and data analysis, schools of librarianship expanded their discipline to include "information science." Increasingly, the agency of the public library would be identified less with buildings and the lending of books, than with centralized, cooperative systems of information classification, storage, and retrieval. As early as 1940, an early prophet of information systems, Vannevar Bush, imagined a "memex," a "sort of mechanized private file and library" using microfilm to store books, records, and communications on a device that resembled a desktop computer. New technologies would dispense with the cumbersome "artificiality of systems of indexing" that had been designed for books, operating in a more organic or natural way by "the association of thoughts," as "an enlarged intimate supplement" to memory.[25] As Bush predicted, the computer age would help to make private and virtual those agencies of knowledge that the libraries of the nineteenth century had made so insistently public.

In twentieth-century America, the agencies of culture became identified with "progress" in media and technology in ways that fundamentally challenged the public function of the library. In the 1957 film comedy *Desk Set*, we find an acute parable about the potential anachronism of the library as a human institution, in a universe of knowledge grown inhuman in scale and esoteric in its particulars. Spencer Tracy plays a "methods engineer" who installs an " electronic brain" in the "Research and Reference" office of the Federal Broadcasting Corporation, threatening to replace the entire office. As it is imagined in the film, the library became the province of a group of eccentric and endearing office "girls" adept at the recall of trivia and the intuitive solution of brainteasers. Amidst the dusty piles of books and the clutter of corporate office, the library's traditional challenges of storing and retrieving knowledge are dramatized in the spectacle of Katharine Hepburn reciting verses of Longfellow and naming all of Santa's reindeer. The comic premise of the movie is that technological progress and corporate efficiency cannot do without the quirky charm of a librarian, no less than a work-obsessed engineer can do without a gal.

Marrying off the spinster to the computer geek, the film manages reconciliation between the traditional form of the library and new technology that has proved more problematic in real life. Reduced to its functionality for "reference," that "knowledge" long idealized as the humanist end of civilization has been rationalized as information. It has ceased to represent a public good, a means to developing one's capacity for enlightened reason and furthering the collective inheritance of "culture," and has become instead a commodity within the all-encompassing world of the multinational media corporation. Decorated in the steel shelving and desks that would become ubiquitous in administrative offices throughout the 1950s and 1960s, the library depicted in the film is a vestigial artifact in the evolution of media technology and the social institutions under corporate capitalism. The feminized images of the library and librarians in *Desk Set* or in Sinclair Lewis' *Main Street* have become part of our collective memory. They recall social and institutional forms that have been bypassed by what came, in the late-twentieth century, to be called the information superhighway.

Managed from the offices of IBM, Disney, AOL-Time Warner, and other centralized, hierarchical corporate agencies, culture is not about prized goods, gaining their value from the social distinctions they enforce between gentlemen and plebians, the values they negotiate between learned and popular tastes, but about systems and processes—or what has, with the digital age, increasingly come to be called "networks." Culture is a pathway, or what the Trustees of the Boston Public Library termed in 1852 a "right of access": it is a set of relationships or links by which individuals become more effectively integrated into the production and exchange of information. Or, to put it in contemporary terms, any library is merely a portal to a network. From this perspective, the buildings and books they hold become secondary to the amorphous potential and magical promise of distributed systems in the postmodern organization of the information economy. When San Francisco built its new flagship public library in the 1990s, it engaged in wholesale "book dumping" because its director saw physical books as peripheral to its mission in the information age.[26] And, indeed, although libraries today receive more visitors than ever, it often seems that their most crowded spaces are where people sign up and patiently wait their turn at the computer terminals made available for public use.

The essays that follow help us to understand the social and historical life of print culture that libraries helped to institutionalize over the last two hundred years, and to appreciate the genealogy of an essentially Victorian symbol of public life. They also help us to see more clearly what the potential disappearance of the library from the local landscape of Celebration and elsewhere portends for the processes of cultural formation in the twenty-first century. Where exactly is culture, in a world where the forms of knowledge have been reorganized by new media and digital technology, where the experience of public life is increasingly realized through private acts of consumption? With the development of new media and the gradual usurpation of state sovereignty by the multinational corporation, agencies of culture have shifted from particular objects and local sites, to institutional systems and networks on a regional, national, and increasingly global scale.

Notes

1. On Bray and his legacy, see Charles T. Laugher, *Thomas Bray's Grand Design: Libraries of the Church of England in America, 1695-1785* (Chicago, 1973).

2. Edwin Wolf II, *Catalogue of the Library Company of Philadelphia: a facsimile reprint of the edition of 1741, printed by Benjamin Franklin* (Philadelphia, 1956). Franklin referred to the Library Company as "Philadelphia Public Library" while others referred to it as city library or the Philadelphia library (v,vi). Many of the Library Company's texts were "standard," available at Harvard and Yale, and subsequently in the New York Society Library. From a total of 375 books in 1741, it had 114 in the area of history, 69 in literature, 28 in science, 38 in theology, 33 in philosophy, 28 in the social sciences, 13 in the fine arts, 10 in linguistics, and five others. Tradesmen did not view Latin and Greek as necessary to their advancement up the social ladder, and the Company's collection avoided books in foreign languages. It had only 13, while half the books at Harvard were in Latin. "As in the scheme of the library I had provided only for English Books, so in this new scheme my ideas went no farther than to procure the means of a Good English Education," Franklin later said about the Academy of Philadelphia in 1789. So too, the Company was noticably light in theology, which filled two-thirds of Harvard's library in 1723 and half of Yale's in 1843. The literature collection was mainly contemporary and Augustan, with no Chaucer or Shakespeare. The only editorial comment in the entire 1841 catalogue is about *Locke's Essay Upon Human Understanding*, "Esteemed the best Book of logick in the world." Except for Pope and Vertot, there were more books by Locke than by any other author (xi). On the eighteenth-century context of the Library Company, see Hugh Amory and David D. Hall, eds., *The Colonial Book in the Atlantic World* (Cambridge, Mass., 2000), and Edwin Wolf II, *The Book Culture of a Colonial American City: Philadelphia Books, Bookmen, and Booksellers* (Oxford, 1988). On social libraries within the context of colonial networks of book publishing and distribution, see James Raven, *London Booksellers and American Customers: Transatlantic Literary Community and the Charleston Library Society, 1748-1811* (Charleston, S.C., 2001).

3. J. A. Leo Lemay and P. M. Zall, *Benjamin Franklin's Autobiography* (New York, 1986), 57.

4. Haynes McMullen, *American Libraries Before 1876* (Westport, Conn., 2000). Also see David Kaser, *A Book for Sixpence: The Circulating Library in America* (Pittsburgh, 1980).

5. Thomas Augst, "The Business of Reading in Nineteenth-Century America," *American Quarterly* 50 (June, 1998) 267-305.

6. On intensive and extensive reading patterns, see David D. Hall, "The Uses of Literacy in New England, 1600-1850, in *Printing and Society in Early America*, ed. by William Joyce et al. (Worcester, Mass., 1983), 1-47.

7. For studies that situate nineteenth-century print culture in a rich context of social practices and institutions, see Gilmore, *Reading Becomes a Necesssity of Life: Material and Cultural Life in Rural New England, 1780-1835* (Knoxville, Tenn., 1989); Ronald Zboray, *A Fictive People: Antebellum Economic Development and the American Reading Public* (New York, 1993); Christine Pawley, *Reading on the Middle Border: The Culture of Print in Late Nineteenth-Century Osage, Iowa* (Amherst, Mass., 2001).

8. George Gates Raddin, Jr., *An Early New York Library of Fiction, with a checklist of the ficiton in H. Caritat's Circulating Library, No. 1 City Hotel, Broadway, New York 1804* (New York, 1940).

9. *Report of the Trustees of the Public Library of the City of Boston, July 1852* (Boston, 1852) 5, 15, 12-13. The history of public libraries was for decades aligned with the progress of liberal democracy. See Sidney Ditzion, *Arsenals for a Democratic Culture: A Social History of the American Public Library Movement in New England & the Middle States from 1850 to 1900* (Chicago, 1947), and Samuel Swett Green, *The Public Library Movement in the United States, 1853-1893* (Boston, 1913).

10. Edward Edwards, *Free Town Libraries: Their Formation, Management, and History in Britain, France, Germany, and America* (New York, 1869), 273.

11. *Report of the Trustees*, 7.

12. Michael Harris, *History of Libraries in the Western World*, 4th ed., (Metuchen, N.J.,1995), 190. In *Third Annual Report for the Massachusetts Common Schools,* Horace Mann put forward the same argument as the Trustees of the Boston Public Library, summarized the credo for school district libraries, which were another significant forerunner of the public library system, in similar terms as the Trustees of the Boston Public Library. After the rising generation has acquired "habits of intelligent reading in our schools what shall they read? For, with no books to read, the power of reading will be useless; and with bad books to read, the consequences will be as much worse than ignorance as wisdom is better." It was up to educators, intellectuals and legislators to decide for the "great mass of children in the State" what books are "moral and intellectual wants, and fitted to nourish their minds with the elements of uprightness and wisdom." Cited in Harris, *History of Libraries*, 189. Sunday school libraries were probably the most numerous and least known type of library in nineteenth-century America. Every church in north and west had a collection designated as Sunday school library—at times large general collections, but often only religious and inspirational texts; especially in areas without other libraries, they were consulted by children and adults alike. See McMullen, *American Libraries*.

13. Edwards, *Free Town Libraries*, 312.

14. On the construction and funding of public libraries since the late nineteenth century, see Donald Oehlerts, *Books and Blueprints: Building America's Public Libraries* (Westport, Conn., 1991).

15. Peter Dobkin Hall demonstrates "the reorientation of the Old Standing Order," "from an elite with public responsibilities to a group whose influence was mediated through private institutions," which included colleges, museums, libraries, hospitals, and other benevolent institutions. Only 12 percent of donations given for such institutional benevolence in Boston between 1800 and 1860 went to publicly controlled charities. Fundraising shifted towards larger donations by smaller numbers of donors who wielded greater influence over the institutions as a result. Donations from the private sector depended increasingly on the insulation of privately chartered institutions from public oversight: "The development of a national culture became the peculiar task of a small set of privately funded institutions in states in which public interference in the affairs of private corporations was minimal." Peter Dobkin Hall, *The Organization of American Culture 1700-1900: Private Institutions, Elites, and the Origins of American Nationality* (New York, 1984), 110, 122.

16. Cited in Harris, *History of Libraries*, 246-7. For an excellent study of Carnegie libraries in their social and cultural context, see Abigail Van Slyck, *Free To All: Carnegie Libraries and American Culture, 1890-1920* (Chicago, 1995). For essays on the refusal of Carnegie libraries, see Robert Sidney Martin, *Carnegie Denied: Communities Rejecting Carnegie Library Construction Grants 1898-1925* (Westport, Conn., 1993).

17. For the best history of the emergence of librarianship as a profession, see Wayne Wiegand, *The Politics of an Emerging Profession: The American Library Association, 1876-1917* (Westport, Conn., 1986). On development of library ideology as it related to censorship and the freedom to read, see Evelyn Geller, *Forbidden Books in American Libraries, 1876-1939* (Westport, Conn., 1984).

18. On the international role of the libraries preceding and during the cold war, see Gary Kraske, *Missionaries of the Book: The American Library Profession and the Origins of United States Cultural Diplomacy* (Westport, Conn., 1985). For another analysis of professional ideology, see Michael F. Winter, *The Culture of Control and Expertise: Toward a Sociological Understanding of Librarianship* (Westport, Conn., 1988). For broader perspectives on liberal consensus and American culture during the 1950s, see Lary May, ed., *Recasting America: Culture and Politics in the Age of the Cold War* (Chicago, 1989).

19. Robert Leigh, *The Public Library in the United States* (New York, 1950) 73, 7. The report summarized the principles that should govern the modernization of library service: 1) Democratic opportunity to learn; 2) Freedom of communication; 3) Popular control and expert direction: Public institutions carrying on specialized activities are properly subject to expert direction; 4) Institutionally represent the interaction of "expert and lay judgement"; 5) Special groups and the mediating function—need to serve the whole, "constituting an effective symbol of communal fraternity" ; 6) Centralization and local participation; 7) Technological change and institutional tradition. For a parallel assessment of the national situation of libraries made in the 1980s, see *Alliance for Excellence: Librarians Respond to A Nation at Risk* (Washington D. C., 1984).

20. See Adrienne Chute and Elaine Kroe, *Public Libraries in the United States: FY 1996* (National Center for Education Statistics, February 1999), iii.

21. Eric Hobsbawm, "Introduction: Inventing Traditions," in *The Invention of Tradition*, ed. by Eric Hobsbawm and Terence Ranger (Cambridge, 1992); Pierre Nora, ed., *Realms of Memory: Rethinking the French Past*, trans. by Arthur Goldhammer (New York, 1996). Also see Eric Hobsbawm, *Nations and Nationalism Since 1780* (Cambridge, 1996).

22. Charles C. Jewett, "Report of the Assistant Secretary, Relating to the Library," *Third Annual Report of the Smithsonian Institution* (Washington, D. C., 1849), 39.

23. Dee Garrison, *Apostles of Culture: The Public Librarian and American Society* (New York, 1979).

24. Thomas Richards, *The Imperial Archive* (New York, 1995) 5.

25. Vannevar Bush, "As We May Think," *Internet Dreams: Archtypes, Myths and Metaphors*, Mark Stefik, ed. (Cambridge, Mass., 1996) 16, 17. For an analysis of the technological, practical, and spatial issues faced by libraries in the electronic era, see R. Howard Bloch and Carla Hesse, eds., *Future Libraries* (Berkeley, 1995).

26. See Nicholson Baker, "The Author vs. the Library," *The New Yorker* (14 October, 1996); Nicholas Basbanes, *Patience & Fortitude: A Roving Chronicle of Book People, Book Places, and Book Culture* (New York, 2001). Also see Baker's essay on the destruction of old card catalogues: Baker, "Discards," *The New Yorker* (4 April 1994). More recently, Baker has questioned the microfilming by libraries, which has led to the destruction of historical newspapers and periodicals. Nicholson Baker, *Double-Fold: Libraries and the Assault on Paper* (New York, 2001).

The Sound of the Civic: Reading Noise at the New York Public Library

Ari Kelman

> In a certain way, identity, then, is a noise that interferes with
> the messages that we transmit and receive. It's hardly audible
> to others, but we hear it loud and clear. Yet it's not the kind of
> noise that bothers us; on the contrary; it gives us a sense of
> reality, a measure of empowerment: it adds "room-tone" to
> the otherwise hyper-real world around us.
> —Anton Shammas[1]

This city is loud. Too loud. That incessant rumble that seems to come from below the ground and above our heads; that sound that comes creeping and screeching and pounding; that sound that is utterly omnipresent, yet defies precise representation; that noise that, no matter how hard I listen I cannot ever quite manage to render comprehensible as if it slips out from meaning like it slips in through windows. That noise disturbs, awakens and exposes. It is caked on the walls of my building and is always crawling beneath doors and sliding through open windows. You can't turn it off, and you can't escape it. It simply is. It is one of the most blaring facts of city life. But how does the city make so much noise? And what does this noise mean?

Commonly understood, noise is defined as either incomprehensible or unwanted sound. The New York City noise statute, adopted in September of 1972, defines noise as the production of any sound which, when measured at a dis-

0026-3079/2001/4203-023$2.50/0   American Studies, 42:3 (Fall 2001): 23-41

tance of 3 feet from an open window exceeds 45 decibels or, when measured in an open area at a distance of 50 feet, exceeds 80 decibels.[2] Until it seeps out of a window or disturbs someone across a public plaza, it is only sound. In New York City, noise is, by legal definition, disturbing. It is the by-product of heavy machinery, of busses, air conditioners, and other such mechanized things of urban life. It is cell-phones and car alarms and the metal gates of storefronts slamming. These elements of urban life are only sound until they enter into spaces they ought not. Only then do they become noise. Noise is what you hear when you don't want to hear anything at all. Alternatively, it is what you hear when you would rather hear something else. Or, when you would rather hear nothing at all. French philosopher Jacques Attali has written that noise possesses the potential for liberation for the ways it challenges established codes of symbolic communication.[3] Noise, for Attali, scrambles intentional meaning and therefore opens spaces for radical practice or interpretation. While Attali's definition is appealing, there's little in the way of semiotic redemption when a car alarm keeps you up between 2:00 and 4:00 a.m.

Intention and liberation aside, noise is the unintentional and uninvited output of a subject (mechanical, biological, or otherwise) involved in some other activity. He/She/It does not necessarily intend to be noisy, it just is. It is one of the definitive characteristics of life in New York City. The noise of the city is a mad amalgam of busses, cars, sirens, radios, conversations, and airplanes, all of which is underwritten by the more subtly diffuse and ever present hum of radiators and water pipes, air conditioners, and countless other infrastructural elements in the sound of the city. Even abstractly, the city itself seems to buzz or hum without pause. Life in the city is practically unimaginable without noise. Inescapable as it is during the day, by night it is somewhat reassuring, suggesting the safe presence of other people on or near the street—close enough to offer a subtle security for walking alone, but not too close that they themselves become threats. By that same logic, if the street is too quiet, there is certainly something wrong. The ambient noise of the city as it trickles out of passing cars and partially open windows actually communicates something discreet. Rather than confounding intended meaning, as Attali concluded, in the city, noise itself takes on a whole set of meanings of its own. Noise itself means.

Technically, noise exists in any communication loop. Static on radio broadcasts, pixillation of digital images, melted chocolates on Valentine's Day, any unintended accompaniment to the transmission of information would constitute noise.[4] Noise emerges between the sender and the receiver of a given message during the act of communication, but is not necessarily introduced by either party. It is a necessary by-product of the system. Sometimes it obfuscates the intended meaning, sometimes it enhances it. It is neither absolutely disruptive, nor necessarily unpleasant. Noise is not something that is produced either intentionally or accidentally by anyone. It cannot be produced at all, but only ever received. "Anything that arrives as part of a message, but that was not part of the message when sent out, can be considered as noise introduced in transmission."[5] Noise works against any total and discreet production of meaning by adding unintended dissonance to it; noise is the part of the message that is unintended, unmentionable. Noise is (what is) heard even when it is not meant (to be). It is what escapes in the transmission of information, yet, when consumed, is often (mis)understood as part of the intended message.

Insofar as any system of communication is constructed between social subjects, nobody is necessarily responsible for the noise produced. In materialist terms, noise is consumed but never produced. You can't make noise, you can only hear it. In this way, noise ends up sounding a lot like silence, as silence, too, can be heard but never emitted, consumed but never produced. To produce silence fills it with all kinds of communication, which is always noisy, even if it is not always noise. Yet, by definition, pure silence cannot communicate. It can only be heard, most poignantly, in a vacuum, in the absence of a social(ized) space; once space is socialized, it's too late, too informative, too informed, too noisy. Noise, on the other hand, must accompany information. It is necessarily social. Noise is produced in and by communication. It is communicable, communal. The listener attributes it to the speaker, and the speaker attributes it to the listener. Given the inadequacies and inaccuracies of language, noise is about the only reliable part of the system. It is what you hear when you don't want to, at all. Perhaps it reminds us, like a low-level alarm or a dial tone, that a given communication loop is functioning. If not for the disruption, how can we be sure that the system is working? Like the sound of an urban street late at night, noise in communication threatens to disrupt the system, but ultimately holds the system together. Without noise how would we know what silence was? Music? Communication? Without noise, the system might perform too well, too purely, and, like oxygen, could become toxic. If noise is consumed but never produced, then perhaps the issue at stake in this discussion is not about the production of noise, but its productivity. In other words, how does noise produce the city?

Reading Room

In the heart of New York lies the main branch of the New York Public Library. It was built to be a great storehouse and disseminator of information, and it daily stages struggles against noise while actively participating in the production of New York City for everyone from tourists to scholars. The main branch is a public space, but it is not a free space. Anyone who would like to may enter the library, but once inside, behavior is quietly regulated and carefully choreographed. Although it is probably the most demographically diverse space in New York City next to the subway, the social interactions within the library must be quiet ones, so as not to disturb the library and its patrons at work. By staging, scripting, and silencing encounters between people and people, and between people and texts, the main branch of the New York Public Library becomes powerful and deeply productive of a civic, if eternally noisy, city. As a public building and a potent symbol of New York's status as a global capital of culture, the main branch speaks volumes even when its visitors read only temporary exhibitions or tourist guides. The building speaks because, as a library, it has to. How and what the building speaks—and whom it permits to speak—is part of an ongoing struggle between noise and information, books and people, civility and the city.

In *The Death and Life of Great American Cities*, Jane Jacobs criticized city planners for underestimating the power of public spaces to engender civic interaction. Jacobs asserted that the activity and interactivity of people in these spaces—like sidewalks or parks—guarantee both safety and social interaction that, in turn, would raise the quality of life for urban residents.[6] In a similar vein, Richard Sennett called for the planning and development of "disordered" spaces in which the urban population would be able to freely interact and create its own meanings of and for urban space and life.[7] Although both authors have different ideas about what those spaces ought to look like and how municipalities ought to go about enabling them, both agree that these spaces are going to be noisy. In particular, Sennett's notion of "disorder" suggests a space that would not only tolerate but encourage mis-pronouncements, misinterpretations, and public clamor. Disorderly space is space that surprises and encourages unpredictable activity. Disorderly interactions are more susceptible to noise as they occur between people who are not necessarily familiar with one another. Practically, arguments and conflicts in and over public spaces—park benches, subway seats, sidewalks—are elements of public discourse that are nearly always noisy. In New York City, public interactions are flavored by accents, entitlement, linguistic differences, contrasting notions of inflection, gesticulation, personal space, and public responsibility. As much a city of immigrants as any other city on earth, public space in New York is necessarily fraught with misinterpretation and often underwritten by total linguistic incommunicability. The sounds in these interactions are always noisy, and the noise of these miscommunications, in turn, escalates the sound. As an ever-present part of the public networks of communication, these noisy interactions define public space and behavior at least as much as the public defines the interactions themselves.

These noisy interchanges are literally the stuff of urban life; they simply cannot take place elsewhere. This is not to suggest that suburban or rural spaces can't foster public discourse, but instead that the density of urban life conditions certain kinds of public encounters. These noisy interchanges—which Sennett and Jacobs would like to see expand and increase—are part of public discourse. Whether or not they are explicitly political or well-reasoned, these discussions are always negotiations within which the very terms of the public are at stake: who sits where, who gets what, who did what to whom and when. Often, their very public staging puts the discussion at risk through the introduction of passing traffic, subway cars, or sirens. The publicity of the exchange and the publicity of the noise it produced, in turn, produce a public that is involved in its social and spatial environment. The public is produced both by and in spite of the noise. Like Shammas' "room-tone" or the sound of the street at night, noise keeps urban subjects mildly aware of the public of which they are always a part. As a result, the inevitable noise of miscommunication may open up rather than foreclose avenues of conversation. Jurgen Habermas would consider these moments to be threatening to a public-in-formation, to public information. For Habermas, communication that is going to produce a public must be noiseless. Habermas has written that the creation of social bonds within the bourgeois public sphere relied on the unfettered expression of individual opinion. Such communicative moments were born in salons and coffee houses and fed the nascent notion of a public that was relatively autonomous within the state. During the heyday of the public sphere, debate circulated fluidly and freely among men of the bourgeoisie, unfettered by connections either to commerce or to government. The rarefied air of these discussions must have been noiseless, as noise would have meant miscommunication and therefore threatened the free and equal exchange of ideas. Moreover, noise would have threatened the unity of the public due to differences in definitions of the very public that any given discussion was creating. To be sure, Habermas does permit disagreement, but it is a very understanding kind of dissent, in which each party, it seems, understands the position of the other, and both agree to disagree. Even the most public of discourse is not necessarily organized around consent.

Behind the scenes of Habermas' public sphere were individuals that were actively reading. Fed by the commercial novel and the popular press, these individuals were consuming common texts that enabled greater moments and loci of discourse and commonality. Shared texts would create shared experiences and shared discourse, which would feed a common notion of a relatively autonomous public that took root within the private realm. To be public meant operating under the authority of the state, and effectively limiting the ability of individuals to freely engage in political discussion. Thus, the public sphere was staged privately. The "transformation," or decline, of Habermas' public sphere occurred when discussion began to assume "the form of a consumer item."[8] Books, theater tickets, and museum admissions, as the cultural items that fed discussion in the public sphere, could be bought and sold without challenging the independence of the public sphere. Conversation, as the site of public discourse, had to remain a non-commodity for it to retain its power within the public. The central relationship here was between reading materials and conversation and the alchemy that would transform the former into the latter. Central to the success of the public sphere was that readership, even as it imagined itself on a one-to-one relationship between book and reader, fed a broader communal process that was rooted in conversation.[9]

At the main branch of the New York Public Library, people can read or research, but not talk. Moreover, in the library, reading is a public performance; one must not only submit one's request to the librarian in writing, but the tables and carrels are public spaces, that often betray the presence of people who had previously read and worked there. It is also not uncommon to find other people's notes or bookmarks in books.[10] The reading rooms are full of people and books, each in full view of everyone else. For Habermas, the public library is too public to host a properly public sphere. As a space, it is too public to afford the privacy necessary for free, autonomous debate. In fact, both of the key relationships in Habermas' public sphere are reversed in the library; the books are free but conversation is not. This relationship is probably the definitive characteristic of the New York Public Library. As a public institution that attempts to foster private interactions between people and texts, it is simultaneously concerned with the public at large *and* the individuals who have come to read. Whether or not it is successful in producing these relationships relies on its ability to keep conversation between patrons to a minimum. In other words, the success of the library relies on the silence of its patrons. The success of its texts depends on their silent consumption. The success of the civic, however, relies on their noise. The library provides information but it cannot facilitate congregation or conversation— at least not within its walls. Because of its inversion of the key relations in Habermas, the production of an active citizenry cannot take place at the library, but elsewhere. The library is too quiet to permit conversation, even as it is deeply concerned with producing civic subjects who read. As long as it doesn't happen in the library, public discourse can be as loud as, or louder than, its participants want. To keep noise to a minimum, the library—as a reading space—must be actively involved in the production of subjects who know how to read quietly. Built into the space of the library, and into the public "elsewheres" that the library produces itself against and alongside, is a complex technology of silence, necessary for the discipline and cultivation of a quiet public. By introducing noise into Habermas' discussion of public discourse, the privacy of the act of reading is brought into question. Whereas Habermas simply takes reading for granted, the library offers a counterexample that suggests that reading never happens by accident.

To be sure, the kind of reading intended by the individuals, institutions, and forces involved in the formation of the main branch of the New York Public Library shared an understanding of reading that was quite different than the kinds of public reading practices David Henkin found on the streets of antebellum New York.[11] Henkin found evidence that illiteracy was not widespread, and even if people did not have access to novels or longer texts, they could easily navigate the public signage that could be found all over the streets and buildings of New York. Henkin states that he is not concerned with the origin of mass literacy, but with "the process by which reading habits were expanded and democratized in the nineteenth century." Newspapers, money, handbills, billboards, and other textual sites dot the landscape of Henkin's analysis, yet the practices involved in "city reading" were not the studious, civilized practices that the library needed. Lawrence Levine's work on the creation and interplay of cultural hierarchy around the turn of the century might suggest that Henkin's reading practices were the popular precursor to the civilized reading imagined and enforced at the library.[12] The awesome and imposing structure, alongside the enforced silence helped to sacrilize—and thus elevate—the library from an institution merely of books, and into an institution of high-cultural transmission. And culture can't be transmitted to people who don't behave, don't read quietly, and insist on holding side conversations while the library and their neighbors are at work.

The very space of the library, then, is involved in a few simultaneous productions: the production of knowledge, the production of a civilized citizenry that could read quietly, and the production of the city through public discourse that had to happen elsewhere. The library, as an information machine, was built for a population who was not entirely equipped with the skills and practices such a machine demanded. While the masses could read, they could not necessarily perform the *kind* of reading that would result in the production of a public discourse elsewhere. The people, institutions, and ideas that informed upon the construction and consolidation of the New York Public Library were conscious of this and built these into the main branch and its function.

Some fifty years before the main branch was built, city planners, urban critics and social reformers overwhelmingly favored broad, open public spaces as the appropriate settings for civilized social encounters. Around the middle of the nineteenth century, both parks and cemeteries were favored as antidotes to the ills of urban life. It was widely believed that residents of the dark, dirty, crowded city could be healed if they were to spend some leisure time contemplating life while strolling the green pathways and pastures of public space. The operative theory held that the space would naturally condition peaceful (and therefore civilized and elevated) thought, which would, in turn, condition appropriate civic behavior. Frederic Law Olmsted, architect of New York's Central Park believed that the park would reform the city entirely; by bringing space and calm to the urban order, Central Park would bring order to the social world, as well.[13] Just as a park could stem the spread of urban slums, it could educate the masses toward taste and away from vice, as well. The belief in the power of social space to shape civic life was so deeply held that between 1856 and the 1903, New York City purchased land for eleven parks, each occupying more than 100 acres.[14] Despite this belief in the power of the "natural" state of Central Park to cure the ills of the urban, it quickly became clear that the masses were in need of greater instruction as to how to make playing in the park perform the civic work that Olmsted and other reformers believed would "naturally" take place in the space created. By the Civil War, only eight years into the park's existence, some 125 different signs appeared in the park, offering everything from directions to "do's and don'ts."[15] Without the signage, the park was too quiet to perform effectively its civic duty.

Or perhaps the intended purposes of the park were not noisy enough. Without the signage, the ideological intentions of the park were too unclear, too quiet for the masses to understood and abide by them. Without the noise of signage in the park, the park itself could not speak loudly or clearly enough, and the space was imperiled by the actual behaviors that its silence enabled. The signage in the park introduced noise into the serenity of rolling landscapes and panoramas that Olmsted carved into the park. Without this noise, the park could not have performed itself nor could it have contributed to the urban order its creators sought. The park was too quiet to perform properly, and needed some noise upon and through which it could. Without signange, without disrupting its pastoral landscape with obvious urban sign(ification)s, the space could not succeed as its creators had intended. In fact, the fear held that without instructional and directional signs, the park would become a space that would exacerbate rather than eradicate urban ills. What the space lost in silence, it gained in efficiency and functionality. The noise of signage was a rather small sacrifice in the name of civility.

For those still concerned with civility and urban life, the question of space remains: if there are to be "free" spaces, how to best ensure that they—and the people found there—will properly perform? In some measure, the space must be socialized. David Henkin's point about the signage in Central Park is that it only "made sense" to people who were already habituated to reading in public spaces.[16] This begs the question of public spaces designed specifically for that practice, and what and how these spaces were socialized. Henkin is concerned with the publicity of reading, and the ways in which reading in public is itself a kind of spectacle. Henkin is keen in his reading of public reading, but what happens to urban spaces when they are organized around the practice of reading; if reading is "written into" the space itself, what strategies of socialization need be in place in order to make this space perform?

The Sound of the Space

> Obviously, a city does not present itself in the same way as
> a flower, ignorant of its own beauty.
> It has, after all, been 'composed' by people, by well-defined
> groups.
> —Henri Lefebvre[17]

We know from Benedict Anderson that the formation of "imagined communities" is deeply indebted to the dissemination of print material.[18] Although Anderson is specifically concerned with modern nationalism, his observation is valuable to us in the library. He wrote, "[n]othing perhaps more precipitated this search [for a means of linking fraternity, power, and time together], nor made it more fruitful, than print capitalism, which made it possible for rapidly growing numbers of people to think about themselves, and to relate themselves to others, in profoundly new ways."[19] These "new ways" included a consideration of others along national or communal lines that had not existed before the common encounter with a specific text. Reading Anderson through Henkin, the reading practices shared by disparate proto-nationals were, in a sense, awaiting a text that would write them into a nation. The people were readers before they were nationals. The introduction of a text did not produce the nation *ex nihilo* out of populations who shared nothing, but rather it fit into an extant set of shared cultural practices. In a sense, they were already performing a vaguely defined common culture, they merely (literally?) lacked a shared textual experience that would articulate their commonality. By 1900, the masses of New York had already evidenced their voracious appetite for books; that year the New York Free Circulating Library ranked first among the ten largest cities in books circulated, even as New York ranked ninth among per capita municipal funding.[20] In a city as large and ethnically diverse as New York, perhaps no text could shoulder the responsibility that Anderson assumed inherent in them. Instead, the library offered a way to produce the city not on the level of content but on the level of practice. Coordinating reading practices through the library could be a more effective technique for civilizing the masses as it truly enabled linguistic and ethnic particularity to flourish while requiring each individual to conform to a particular pattern of behavior. By valuing practice over content, the library could instruct its patrons without jeopardizing the freedom of information that it sought to house and circulate. It would channel the practice for the masses who, it was imagined, would create a civilized urban public in turn. All of this is not to downplay the significance of content, but to highlight the practice of reading; not everyone in the library is reading the same thing even as they are participating in a collective culture and in the production of a specific space. Spaces, like people, must be socialized as well.

Henri Lefebvre suggested that "social space does not have all the characteristics of 'things' as opposed to creative activity. Social space *per se* is at once *work* and *product*—a materialization of 'social being'."[21] [emphasis in the original] Social space, or the space that enables the staging of social life, is a construction that is at once ideological and concrete. Social space is both a staging ground for exchange, while it also structures those very exchanges. Social space is not a passive vessel, but a medium that acts upon the subjects and objects that circulate within it. Further, social space "contains a great diversity of objects, both natural and social, including the networks and pathways which facilitate the exchange of *material things and information*. Such 'objects' are thus not only things but also relations."[22] [emphasis mine] In social space, the exchange of information is as significant as the exchange of material objects. It follows too that the practices or conventions of exchange are as involved or informed by the space, as well. The building was responsible not only for facilitating the exchange of "material things and information," but also it was responsible for spatially informing these exchanges and their resultant social relations.

Prior to 1895, New York City did not have a city-wide public library system. Unlike other leading cities of the day (Boston, Chicago, London, Paris,

Amsterdam), New York's two notable research libraries were private endeavors, independently owned and maintained by two of the city's wealthiest families, the Lenoxs and the Astors. Both were devoted to scholars, bibliophiles, and researchers and neither offered a circulating collection. Although they were open to the public neither operated under the pretense of being a "public" institution, favoring and catering to the city's elite. The remainder of the city's population, which was growing rapidly due to a massive influx of new immigrants, did not have an organized lending library until 1878 when the endeavors of a handful of teachers at Grace Church were finally realized in the establishment of the New York Free Circulating Library.[23] The NYFCL was housed in small libraries and reading rooms throughout the City of New York and operated without a main branch. It, too, was privately funded, yet the distinction between the Astor and Lennox libraries and the NYFCL was quite sharply drawn on the basis of class and ethnicity. This was keenly articulated in the formal announcement of the incorporation of the NYFCL, published in the *Evening Post* of March 18, 1880. It read:

> The Astor Library supplies in a great measure all the requirements of a reference library. The Mercantile Society and other libraries satisfy the wants of the class of readers who can afford to pay a small annual sum for their privileges, and the Apprentices' and Young Men's Christian Association libraries furnish books to persons who belong to the classes which they represent. Only one class of people in our city are unprovided for in the matter of reading—that is the very poor, some of whom cannot afford to pay annual dues to procure their reading, and are not eligible for the free libraries.[24]

Audible here is the rhetoric of "improvement" that was so popular some 30 years earlier and could be widely heard and read in the parks movement. "The intellectual elevation of the masses" seemed to be the popular philanthropic aim of the day, whether it come by brook or by book.[25] What is even more striking about this document is its recognition of the ethnic divisions that striated the city. These different libraries not only served different populations, but also symbolically represented the numerous publics that lived in the city of New York but who did not yet engage in a common text or even a common space. To be sure, economic forces and residential necessity provided ample room for the city's ethnic communities to mix, and very few neighborhoods were so mono-ethnic so as to provide insularity against the city's other ethnic groups.[26] While the various populations of the city were living a coordinated if not cacophonous existence, the Trustees of the Lenox and Astor libraries had consolidated their efforts and were courting the city in an attempt to establish a state funded public library system that would also house and maintain the existing collections of both families. For the Trustees to produce a "civilized capital" rather than a disorganized metropolis necessitated an elaborate production of the city in a way that would convince New York City government that a unified, publicly supported library would benefit the city at large. The carefully crafted proposal would follow on the consolidation of the Astor and Lenox libraries under the guidance of John Bigelow, an attorney and trustee of the Tilden foundation.[27]

The formal proposal for the NYPL, presented to New York Mayor William L. Strong on March 25, 1896, is as much about the building (as a noun and a verb) of the main branch as it is about justifying the library's establishment. The success of the library project was reliant on the symbolic conflation of the building itself and the civic function of the library. Both the physical building and the civic benefits were projected on the bodies of the citizenry, who were become the agents for the noisy transmission of information and the "imagineers" of New York.

> Indeed, a popular public library, bringing sound litera- ture within the reach of every man's home, is in a very real sense a part of the educational system of the State. Education ought not to stop with the public school, nor even with the high school. It is necessary also to provide the higher school which a well-equipped popular library can alone afford. More- over the State has a profound interest in aiding the circulation of ideas that are not ephemeral. The best influence of a popu- lar press must largely depend on its having within reach a com- plete storehouse of scientific, economic and historical facts, with which to correct the crudeness of hasty judgments of great social and national movements.[28]

The State will benefit from the spread of ideas, and will improve the lot of the popular press and the citizens who read it. In other words, good libraries breed good institutions that make good citizens who, in turn, make a good city that deserves to be considered among the capitals of the world (long before that became New York City's tourist slogan for the summer of 1995). The beckoning agent of civic interpolation is the information captured by "sound literature," the sound of literature, the call of literature, the response of the literate. The circula- tion of information is, necessarily, a noisy process, even as its civic agents are compelled to be silent. The silence of the agents, however, is an indication of the success of the library project; if the masses are to be civilized, the transmission of information cannot be obfuscated by noise in the system or in the library. Participation in the active improvement of the State, then, is imagined here to be saturated with noise, yet it is to be carried out by a silent and studious popula- tion. There is no room for noise in either the library or the city.

The public, however, was given a voice in the popular press: all of the major New York papers supported the construction of a central branch of the public library.[29] The question as to its location remained, however. Both Seth

Low, President of Columbia University in Morningside Heights and Henry M. MacCraken, chancellor of the University of the City of New York on Washington Square approached the Tilden trust with offers for partnerships for building the library. However, neither the uptown nor the downtown locations befit the new building. Other locations were discussed before the Coroton Reservoir on Fifth Avenue and 42nd Street emerged as a front runner. It was centrally located near the tonier neighborhoods in the East 50s and above, and between the new Metropolitan Opera House on 40th Street and the hub of mass transportation, which converged at 42nd street. As well, this location would provide access to the immigrants who had begun to settle in the Bronx and Brooklyn. Although public opinion supported the reservoir site, the Trustees needed more convincing. The Board of Aldermen took no official position on the matter, beyond a statement that they supported the selection of "a proper site" for the main branch.[30] On April 16, 1895, Alderman Frederick A. Ware pronounced the reservoir "an eyesore" that "should be devoted to some public and beneficial use." He added that the absence of a library ought to be remedied with the construction of one "worthy of the name . . . and commensurate with the wealth and dignity of New York," and that such a "library centrally located . . . would be worthy of the city both from an architectural and literary standpoint."[31] Ware, though not speaking on behalf of his colleagues, voiced a notion of urban reform and improvement that was gaining in popularity among urban planners and politicians of the day.

Ware's linkage between "wealth and dignity" and the "architectural and literary" bespeak some of the ideals of an urban planning movement known as "city beautiful," which held that urban ills could be cured through the planning and construction of monumental buildings that would inspire the "lower classes" to civic greatness. This was an outgrowth of the parks movement, in which taste and recreation were two of the guiding ideals. If beauty and civility could be inculcated through encounters with landscaped parks and "breathing spaces," then the same ought to be true of properly urban spaces. The construction of such spaces would make them, in the words of Lefebvre, both work and process, as such spaces would stand for a particular ideal, while also giving shape to its performance among and upon urban residents. Urban studies scholar M. Christine Boyer has written:

> The municipal art, city beautiful and civic improvement crusades grew as piecemeal efforts, movements that aimed to convert a city built primarily for utility into an ideal form through artistic street signs, well-designed municipal bridges, using color in architectural elements, and improving public squares and buildings. In a similar manner, these crusades were aimed to express the fullness of the human spirit . . . so that the better impulses of the most elevated men would soon become common to all. These lofty attempts at city decoration

sought a new conception of public life and civic loyalty, a restoration of a lost community ethic through the enhancement of public spaces, decorating them with monuments, beautiful street vistas, majestic and classical architecture for public buildings, and allegorical murals in public places.[32]

The city beautiful movement falls closely in line with Lawrence Levine's analysis of American cultural hierarchy in its assertion that beautiful cities would create a beautiful citizenry. A crucial part of a beautiful citizenry was its ability to behave according to the rules of decorum handed down by "the most elevated men." In museums and theaters, that meant paying quiet attention. It meant proper dress and hygiene. In public space, it meant controlling one's bodily functions and the volume of one's voice.[33] In the library, that would come to mean silent reading and mandatory productivity (no loitering in the library). If the key to controlling public behavior was through the creation of beautiful public spaces, then the library was no exception.

Upon its opening in 1911, the building received some criticism because its internal plan was not considered classical enough, although the façade and landscaping were widely praised in the popular and professional press for their "beauty and purity." Reviewing the furnishings, the *American Architect* wrote that they would be "a valuable lesson in decorative art to the hundreds of thousands of people who will annually pass through [its] splendidly equipped apartments . . . to have constantly before them the surroundings in harmony with their serious purposes in seeking the educational benefits of the institution."[34] Externally, the building was praised for standing out in a "city of ugly architecture," and thus raising the cultural cache of the city, even if it were to lay empty. In the press, at least, this monument to truth and beauty was already improving the city's standing among cosmopolitan centers.

The only part of the building that received substantial criticism was the interior floor plan, as it did not conform to the ideals of symmetry and balance so emphasized in classical architecture. The asymmetrical interior space, however, was designed to foster the practical needs of the library. In fact, the Trustees studied the shortcomings of the recently completed Boston Public Library and were careful not to replicate the mistakes made in that library's construction; among the criticisms of that building were that it conformed too stringently to the classical ideals and sacrificed some of the efficiencies necessary for the smooth transmission of information. The trustees of the New York Public Library consulted expert engineers, architects, and librarians so that they could construct both a "convenient store-house for the literary and artistic treasures of the corporation," and "one of the chief monuments of the city."[35] It was going to become the focal point of civic beauty, moral elevation, and high art. Its mere being was to offer a beacon of civic pride through which the city at large would be able to imagine itself as a true cosmopolitan leader on par with European capitals and surpassing its American counterparts. All of this was to be built into the space, but its success relied on the participation of a noisy and unpredictable party: the masses who were both the object and the subject of the library. Like the parks movement illustrated, the multi-ethnic, multilingual, poor, working, largely immigrant masses could not be counted on to willingly perform civility according to the ways in which the planners had imagined. Would the library be any different? Could the uncivilized masses keep their voices down and perform predictably?[36] Once orchestrated, the noise of urban communication was supposed to signify civility, a notion that the city cohered spatially, socially, and sonorously. The main branch was to house and coordinate the information through which the city would be able to noisily imagine itself outside its walls. Inside was a different story.

The production of silence remains a rather noisy business. The great fabricated silence at the heart of the circuit of information, imagination, and production required intense preparation and excruciating regulation. The silence of the building was enforced in the name of the information itself; only when the building was silent could the information speak clearly, without impediment and without noise. Yet this silence was already implicated in the noisy production of information, access, "the public," and the space of the building relative to the city at large. Although the city was to imagine itself around and about this building, the building and all of the information it contained could only speak in terms of the city that lay beyond its walls—the city was produced elsewhere. The library could only signify the city if it could be inhabited, socialized, informative, informed. In other words, the space of the building, this great silent marble space could only anchor the imaginary production of the city if it were noisily narrated by people who lived in the city, provided they narrate elsewhere. Therefore, what became necessary in the production of the main branch of the New York Public Library was an urban subject who would not only listen intently to the sound of civility prompted by the circulation of information, but who would contribute to the silence necessary for the production of the social spaces of the building and the city itself.

Disciplining Noise

> It is not simply at the level of consciousness,
> of representations and in what one thinks one knows,
> but at the level of what makes possible the knowledge
> that is transformed into political investment.
> —Michel Foucault[37]

The building itself was to be "a great central library of reference and exhibit,"[38] not a lending library. It was fully intended, as described in the formal building proposal, to be a place of scholarship and learning, not one of civic congregation nor one of actual circulation. In other words, despite the great amount of information contained therein, the building itself was supposed to be silent. But not mute. In this way, the library can be read (an appropriate methodology for rendering a library) as a disciplinary machine. But machines, too, are noisy things—gears gnashing, motors revving, wheels spinning, doors opening and closing, sirens blaring, pages turning, communities imagining. What kind of noise is heard in the disciplinary machine, and how is this noise productive? In his study of discipline, Michel Foucault draws the correlation between discipline and knowledge, productivity, regimentation and docility. Foucault defines disciplines as "techniques for assuring the ordering of human multiplicities."[39] Insofar as the main branch of the NYPL was charged with the duty of disseminating and coordinating information and people, in order to participate in this exchange and impact the production of space, one was obligated conform to a particular model of civic behavior. If you are too loud, you will be asked to leave the library.

To use the library, one must not only be quiet, but industrious as well. Loitering is prohibited. One must read, research, or produce, but the noise of production must be highly regulated. Not only is noise regulated, but in order to sit and read in the building's main reading room you have to be reading the library's own materials![40] So, not only must you be productive, but you must participate in the production of the library, as well. Regardless of the content or intent of the research, the regulation of noise and the enforcement of productivity serve to channel all library activity into the elaborate staging of itself and the city. If you are going to be in the library, you are going to have to keep your voice down and work. The noise of the civic drowns out the noise of any particular text, and *what* is being read is subordinated to the fact that *anything* is being read *at all*. Remarkably, this notion is made quite explicit in the concluding paragraph of the library proposal. It states:

> When we consider the extent to which an institution of the character proposed may fairly be expected to strengthen the police, diminish crime, raise public standards of morality, attract to our city men from every department of industry and every walk of life, add to the operative power of our people, and extend the influence of our Commonwealth, it can hardly be regarded otherwise than a privilege for the City to share in the work.[41]

Within the library, the quiet activity of reading becomes utterly noisy and social. Reading, no matter how private, is already scripted into the production of the civic, and is therefore a public event. Similar to the noise of the city that keeps us awake at night or calls our attention in the street, the noise of the civic invades the private consumption of information. The free circulation of information would produce disciplined citizens who could efficiently contribute to the moral and economic fabric of the city. The noise of reading overwhelms what is being read; it is consumed but never produced. Only in its consumption is it able to be productive.

Of course, its consumption is easily disciplined. The librarian can always hear you, even when she's not listening. Not panopticism but panauralism. When you enter the library, it does not matter if one is actively being listened to. Instead, those large white marble halls amplify even the smallest sound and betray one's "uncivil" behavior immediately. Civility, however, is never a silent matter. The clatter of keyboards, backpacks, and briefcases all contrast but do not impede the silence of the disciplinary machinery at work. Indeed, these are the sounds of the civic at work in this space. People walking, writing, typing are all involved in the performance and the production of the civic, and therefore these sounds amount to little more than the white noise of the machinery. These audial eruptions are not considered noise in the library because they are expected and even necessary for the machine to function. Were it too silent—no footsteps, no pages turning, no pencils scraping—we could not be certain that the machine was working. Like a heartbeat or the smell that had to added to natural gas to alert us to its presence, these permissible sounds define the space and the behaviors that this space encourages within it and beyond it. In the main reading room patron-citizens are especially conscious of the small sounds they make, and try even to control them, keeping zippering bags and rippling papers to a minimum. In the library, noise will blow the cover of uncivil behavior. Producing the fantasy of always being in the line of sight requires a complicated architectonic scheme. Producing the reality of always being within earshot is a fact of social space. In this way, the most unpredictable fact of social life, the sound that cannot be produced, intended, scripted, becomes the most highly regulated, channeled, and staged.

The noise of civics thus becomes the meta-narrative of the New York Public Library. Participating in the production of the space becomes a civic duty, a public duty, one that is conducted between the individual subject and the city. Communication is highly regulated, controlled, legislated, and must always travel through the circuits of the library. If you are going to talk, you will be asked to step outside. By talking in the library you are already stepping outside the civic circuits of information and communication. You are creating unwanted, uncontrollable, noise that is troublesome to the smooth efficiency of the library and the civic. The disciplined civic subject can hear the difference between the managed silence of the library and the noise of the civic, and she will behave, produce, exchange, and circulate accordingly.

The Noise of the Civic

Tell X that speech is not dirty silence clarified. It is silence
made still dirtier.
            —Wallace Stevens

As the by-product of social exchange (not to be confused with a product of exchange), noise is an inherent characteristic of social space. In this way, noise is always "white"; its omnipresence enables the social to be written, staged and performed in space. Even as it is productive, noise is generally believed to be counterproductive. It disrupts, disturbs, and disables. Countless studies have sought to reduce noise in the workplace and the school because it inhibits productivity.[42] Noise is inherently undisciplined because it can't be controlled in communication. Neither the speaker nor the listener can introduce it, nor can they discipline it. Yet, the struggle against noise in communication has been waged continually from the Radio Act of 1927, which sought to reduce interference between broadcast stations, to noise statutes, to the latest in hi-tech entertainment devices designed for reproducing the clearest sound or the cleanest picture. Noise, with rare exception in the experimental art world, is rarely something striven for, but something to be limited, reduced, erased. At the main branch, this was certainly the case.

If you make noise, you will be asked to leave the library. But both silent civility and a civility of perfect communication are both impossibilities. Participating in the civic order is a noisy business. Engaging others in discourse over books, subway seats, and identity is a noisy business. Anton Shammas mused that identity is noise that shades everything we do while it also grounding us in the world. If this is true, then noise, the very thing that obscures or muddles any message we care to transmit, makes communication possible in the first place. In other words, the very thing that imperils our communications enables them. Like the sounds of the city that remind us that there are lives going on behind the windows and doors of apartment buildings, and that signify safety on New York streets, noise reminds us that the city is there and that we are part of it.

Controlling noise at the library was a critical feature of its civilizing ideals. Proper literary practice was central to the library's conducting of civic subjects and of the city at large. At the library it does not matter quite what one reads, but how. The growth of New York City around the turn of the century begged the question of how the city, the multilingual, multiethnic city that stretched from Far Rockaway to the Bronx, would constitute itself as one city. Separated by class, gender, ethnicity, language, and location, the library was to become the building and the institution that would coordinate these efforts. As an heir of the parks movement and the city beautiful movement, the main branch offered a ripe opportunity for the construction of a beautiful building that would be deeply and intimately involved in the production of an active, urban citizenry. Additionally, the design and construction of a beautiful building that was also functional would succeed in putting New York on par with other capitals of the cultured world.

This was to be a noisy construction, as the people did not know how to read quietly. Literate as they may have been with street signs and handbills, the people did not necessarily know *how* to read. The structure of the main branch was to be instructive on the virtues of beauty, but the silence within it had to be enforced or else the space would get too noisy and would not be able to function.

Noise would obfuscate and blur the intentions of the library both as a space and as an institution. The work of the library was to instruct the masses how to read, not necessarily what to read, and where the power of the space failed to discipline, the librarian could step in. Even if not an overt agent of discipline, the librarian is an agent of production, assisting people in their searches for information, so that their time is not wasted in the library. Productivity and silence, as two critical pieces of the library's function, closely mirror those behaviors of Fordist factory production. The primary difference here is that the products of the library do not necessarily emerge fully formed and ready for market. Rather, they emerge in process, and as elements of urban subjectivity that aid in the performance of these markets, spaces, cities.

Not necessarily interested in producing objects, the main branch of the library is absolutely concerned with the production of subjects. By disciplining noise and attempting to ensure the safe and clear transmission of information from text to individual, the library is deeply involved in productions of the city and the civic subject. These productions go on over and above the noise of public discourse on the street and on the subway. That noise cannot be controlled or limited. Those spaces cannot be silenced or controlled. But the library can and does imagine itself as the silent center of this discourse for all its attempts to encourage a citizenry that knows how to read, and is not afraid to make noise, as long as it is outside the library.

Notes

I would like to thank Professor May Joseph, whose brilliant advice and instruction gave the space for this paper to emerge. Thanks as well to Ben Stewart, Amie Dorman, and to the keen eyes of the anonymous readers of *American Studies*, who saw promise in this paper that I had overlooked.

1. Anton Shammas, "Autocartography," in *The Geography of Identity*, ed. Patricia Yaeger (Ann Arbor, Mich., 1996), 466-475.

2. New York City, NY, Administrative Code §§ 24-201 to 24-269 (1972).

3. Jacques Attali, *Noise* (Minneapolis, 1983), 33.

4. Cited in William Paulson, *The Noise of Culture* (Ithaca, N.Y., 1988), 7.

5. *Ibid.*, 67.

6. Jane Jacobs, *The Death and Life of Great American Cities* (New York, 1992).

7. Richard Sennett, *The Uses of Disorder* (New York, 1970).

8. Jurgen Habermas, *The Structural Transformation of the Public* Sphere (Cambridge, Mass., 1996), 165.

9. *Ibid.*, 161.

10. There's a famous story about a reader at the Lenox library who found a $50 bill tucked into a copy of Shakespeare's *Much Ado About Nothing*, accompanied by a note that read "With it goes my best wishes. From one who has money to spare and is a lover of Shakespeare." Retold in Phyllis Dain *The New York Public Library: A History of Its Founding and Early Years* (New York, 1972).

11. David Henkin, *City Reading* (New York, 1998), 22.

12. Lawrence Levine, *Highbrow Lowbrow* (Cambridge, Mass., 1988).

13. John Sears, *Sacred Places* (Oxford University Press, 1989), 119.

14. M. Christine Boyer, *Dreaming the Rational City* (Cambridge, 1983), 35.

15. Henkin, *City Reading*. 66.

16. *Ibid.*, 67.

17. Henri Lefebvre, *The Production of Space*, Donald Nicholson-Smith, trans. (Oxford, 1984), 74.

18. Benedict Anderson *Imagined Communities* (New York, 1983).

19. *Ibid.*, 36.

20. Dain, *The New York Public Library*, 22.

21. Lefebvre, *The Production of Space*, 101-102.

22. *Ibid.*, 77.

23. Between 1871 and 1880, the United States absorbed over 2.8 million new immigrants, the majority of whom settled in urban areas.

24. Quoted in Harry Miller Lydenberg *History of the New York Public Library* (New York, 1923), 204.

25. Quoted in Dain, *The New York Public Library*, 17.

26. Kenneth Jackson, *The Encyclopedia of New York City* (New Haven, Conn., 1995). Hasia Diner's recent work on the Lower East Side of Manhattan also clearly evidences the Italian community that lived there in numbers at least equal to those of Jews around the turn of the 20th century. *Lower East Side Memories* (Princeton, N.J., 2000).

27. The establishment of the Tilden trust in 1886, which dedicated $2.4 million to the establishment of a "free library and reading room in the city of New York," opened the door for the unification of the two major libraries in the city, and ultimately led to the establishment of the New York Public Library. The New York Free Circulating Library was brought under the administration of the New York Public Library in 1900.

28. Lydenberg, *History of the New York Public Library*, 359

29. Dain, *The New York Public Library*, 152.

30. *Ibid.*, 144.

31. *Ibid.*, 143-144

32. Boyer, *Dreaming the Rational City*, 45-46.

33. Levine, *Highbrow Lowbrow.*

34. Dain, *The New York Public Library*, 337.

35. Quoted in *Ibid.*, 159.

36. Riv-Ellen Prell's work on images of Jewish American women focuses partially on the early twentieth-century stereotype of the "Ghetto Girl," whose primary traits were those of conspicuous consumption and poor manner. Chief among public behaviors frowned upon was loudness. Prell cites a handful of newspaper articles and etiquette books from the 1910's that condemn loudness in speech and laughter, and offer women alternatives for public behavior that do not so apparently signify vulgarity. *Fighting to Become Americans* (Boston, 1999), 44-51.

37. Michel Foucault, *Discipline and Punish*, Alan Sheridan, trans. (New York, 1979), 185.

38. Quoted in Lydenberg, *History of the New York Public Library*, 357.

39. Foucault, *Discipline and Punish*, 218.

40. This was posted on the library's list of rules and regulations, alongside checking your bags and keeping conversation to a minimum.

41. Lydenberg, *History of the New York Public Library*, 362.

42. Numerous studies over the past twenty or so years have indicated that noise inhibits learning and productivity. Schools near Chicago's O'Hare airport have received additional funding for the installation of sound insulation.

High Culture, Low Culture: The Singular Duality of the Library of Congress

Elizabeth Jane Aikin

In 1870, the Library of Congress became the official copyright registry for the books, pamphlets, periodicals, maps, prints, and music published in the United States. It was already the largest library in the country, and as nineteenth-century tradition had it, the nation's chief "storehouse" of knowledge, but with the appearance of massive copyright deposits, the library assumed an equally important, if generally unacknowledged, role in the transmission of culture. By acquiring and retaining the material records of American thought and activity, the library made possible, in theory, the study and perusal of any part of that civilization.[1]

However, no library can collect everything; and even the Library of Congress had to become selective. Its preservation of the cultural record extended much further than the collection of any other library in the country, but necessarily relied on library officials' valuation of particular materials, and their opinions generally conformed to contemporary ideas of what libraries should keep. They did not consider in their planning future needs for materials to be acquired or acquired and later discarded. Neither did they consider changes in the library's role. Nonetheless, during the ensuing decades, several developments helped to redefine the institution.

In 1924, Elizabeth Sprague Coolidge offered the library funds for the construction of an auditorium and for music performances. Four years later, Librarian of Congress Herbert Putnam and Music Division chief Carl Engel created an

0026-3079/2001/4203-043$2.50/0   American Studies, 42:3 (Fall 2001): 43-61

Archive of American Folksong in the library. Coolidge's gift was the first of a series of 1920s bequests and gifts to the library. The folk song archive introduced another "first": the collection of songs, not from books or manuscripts, but from oral culture. Both events were unprecedented, both for libraries in general and for the Library of Congress in particular as a federal agency. But while the Coolidge gift funded primarily activities relating to the library's dominant focus on high culture, the archive introduced not only new materials but new methods of collecting aimed at the capture of the songs of rural people and workers. While historians have commented on the surprising blending of "high and popular culture in unlikely places such as . . . the Library of Congress" early in the twentieth century, a closer look at the "blend" reveals a complex procession of negotiations to define the national collections.[2] Introducing the performance of high culture and documentation of the oral tradition required reducing or removing barriers of critical tastes, congressional opposition, and professional tradition.

Forming the National Collections

Since the mid-nineteenth century, the leaders of the library had aspired to emulate the British Museum's policy of collecting material worldwide. Even though the small appropriations provided by Congress did not allow the purchase of foreign materials on a scale comparable to the accessions brought in by copyright, the Librarians of Congress had through gifts and exchanges been able to build the nucleus of more comprehensive collections. But upon completion of the Jefferson building (1897) and for several years thereafter, Congress provided substantial increases in the appropriations for library materials, thus allowing strategically planned collection development. For American scholars, who had to travel abroad to use the comprehensive collections and unique materials they needed, the impact of such development would be far-reaching. University libraries in the United States at that time could not match continental resources, despite the rapid expansion of higher education, the adoption of the European model of graduate training, and growing institutional emphasis upon original research and publication. But if the Library of Congress assumed the responsibility of serving researchers, the leadership exerted at the national level and supported by federal funds would make domestic scholarship far more feasible—and would provide strong potential for increasing American intellectual output in the sciences, the humanities, and the arts. Herbert Putnam, who became Librarian of Congress in 1899, eagerly undertook the task of creating a national intellectual workshop for scholars as part of his vision for the national library. He was also intent on establishing the library's national authority and securing its recognition as the center for providing cataloging for libraries, bibliographies, answers to reference inquiries, and interlibrary loans. While recognizing that it would take years of patient collecting for the library to amass comprehensive research collections and extend their use to the country at large, Putnam nevertheless worked ceaselessly toward that goal.[3]

His efforts would reflect several important influences on the library. One of these was the fast-growing profession of librarianship; Putnam and many of his division chiefs were among the first professional librarians employed at the library, and they planned to organize and administer the institution in accordance with the highest standards of professional practice as the initial means of establishing the library's national hegemony.[4] Following the lead of their colleagues in libraries throughout the United States, they intended to select "the best reading" on any given subject for the collection. Standards for such decisions remained undefined, however, and librarians in general consulted the opinions of critics, scientists, authors, and scholars when choosing material for their collections, thus employing the cultural authority of experts rather than relying on their own knowledge.[5]

The library profession's caution in defining appropriate collections fitted well with the library's relationship to its chief constituent, the Congress. Librarian Putnam considered maintaining senators' and representatives' confidence his top priority, and his collecting policies therefore adhered closely to standards of taste that Congress could be expected to endorse. Putnam made the final decisions on all purchases himself, and he ordered his division chiefs to review the copyright deposits daily to select only those items deemed suitable for the library's collection. At first the rejected material was simply stored.[6] However in 1909, a new copyright law gave the librarian and the Register of Copyrights the power to dispose of unneeded items by sale, exchange, transfer, or return to the copyright claimant. Putnam then asked the chiefs to develop a formal selection policy. Over time, they selected only about one-fourth or less of the books and pamphlets for permanent retention.[7] Among the types of material they found unsuitable for the national library were advertising matter, patent medicine almanacs, "boys' magazines and books of the Nick Carter and Jesse James type," joke books, illustrated children's books, telephone directories, posters, vaudeville and minstrel music, and comic books. Thus even though a wide variety of material entered the library, it did not necessarily also enter the national collections.[8]

The usual mandate of a national library to amass the literary and cultural output of the nation was one of Putnam's primary concerns, but he planned first to enlarge the library's collection of western European thought and culture, both because of its importance as the background to the formation of the United States and because he considered it the first step toward comprehensive collecting. To build high-quality, authoritative collections, he sought to employ experts in relevant subject fields. When seeking a music division chief, for example, he was fortunate to discover Oscar Sonneck, an American educated at the universities of Heidelberg and Munich, and in Bologna, Florence, and Vienna. Sonneck's knowledge of the classical repertoire fit Putnam's desire for such expertise, but just as important was that he had compiled and was about to publish a pioneering *Bibliography of Early Secular American Music*. Experts in American music were few, and the subject in 1900 remained largely unexplored in the United States.

The lack of recognition of American music and Putnam's determination to build important European collections were not unusual, for during the nineteenth century and well into the twentieth, European cultures were most prominently represented in American library collections. American authors such as Walt Whitman, Ralph Waldo Emerson, Henry Thoreau, and Mark Twain considered American literature too imitative of old world forms, but critics pondered whether a democratic country would be able to produce distinctive work in the fine arts or literature. Some concluded that the United States was too heterogeneous to foster an American culture, but while this cultural inferiority complex dominated domestic criticism, American creativity began to be celebrated abroad. The ragtime melodies of Louis Moreau Gottschalk, largely disdained by arbiters of American musical taste, for example, became popular in mid-nineteenth-century Europe. And even more shocking to American music critics was the growing interest of European composers in drawing on the American vernacular—for example, Antonin Dvorak, whose *New World Symphony* (1893) resonated with the African American and Native American motifs he gathered during a three-year stay in the United States. What composers like Dvorak, Frederick Delius, and Samuel Coleridge-Taylor and continental critics considered most innovative in American forms, in fact, originated chiefly in humble sources similar to the folk origins of European national art.[9]

Aware of European interest in American folk forms, Sonneck nevertheless considered that American music had not yet produced "masters equal to the great European," and that the study of European music would always be important.[10] The library possessed the largest music collection in the country in 1900, with about 320,000 musical works, mostly sheet music, on hand. But the material consisted almost entirely of copyright deposits, and Sonneck thought collection quality poor: the representation of classical composers' scores was meager, and the book collection too small to support research. Buying chiefly European material and initially concentrating on the pre-1800 period and on opera, he worked to complete the classical repertoire while also acquiring the output of American composers in accordance with the library's national mission. His acquisitions budget could not be stretched to purchase either rarities or manuscripts, but as he informed the American music community of the library's need for autograph scores, composers and music companies began to donate their works.

Meanwhile, Putnam had stated in his 1902 annual report that "It seems proper that a national library should contain . . . a reasonable representation of the classical and standard material, both scores and literature, for, whether a science or an art, music has been and is too potent an influence to be omitted from a collection which seeks to exhibit the important factors in civilization."[11] There had been no congressional reaction, but when a few years later the librarian proposed raising Sonneck's annual salary from $2,000 to $3,000, he sought a stronger rationale. Among the library's nonbook materials, maps, prints and photographs posed few difficulties for congressional relations since the former had strategic value and the latter provided historical documentation. Music, however, was another matter, as Sonneck wrote Richard Aldrich, the music critic for the *New York Times*. "The task will be difficult," he explained, "for the mere existence of such a division puzzles Congress, and even very intelligent Members of Congress. They do not understand the need of a collection of musical compositions and they do not appreciate that there is any great body of musical literature entitled to consideration in the Library, or that has scientific or practical interest for the community." Congress would agree, he explained, that copyright music needed to be kept, but

> Our aim on the other hand, as you know from your own inspection, is to build up here a collection of standard and classical compositions and musical literature that shall have interest for the investigator as well as the artist. What is the justification of such an attempt in the National Library? Who will it interest? Who will it benefit? And is the possible benefit one that our National Government can justly promote with public funds?[12]

Putnam also wrote to five more newspaper critics in Chicago, Boston, and New York, and to ten musicologists in prominent music schools, including the New England Conservatory of Music, Northwestern, Vassar, Oberlin, Michigan, Columbia, Yale, and Harvard. He had their answers transcribed (including their high praise for Sonneck) for the House and Senate appropriations committees. In his testimony, the librarian tackled the question of "Why music?" head-on by asserting "Because apart from their use in the *art* (the performance) they [the compositions] are also *literature* and their study is the study of a *science*." He conceded the triviality of much of the music received on copyright deposit, naming ragtime, in particular, and dismissing popular music as "mere parlor songs." But he maintained that folk songs were indispensable to any study of music history, theory, and criticism, and pointed out that such American composers as Edward MacDowell were producing important modern music. Musicians, composers, critics, historians, and teachers, he insisted, needed an authoritative collection, and for only "a slight additional expenditure" the library could provide both "a scientific collection" and "scientific administration." He added that it was the only federal expenditure for encouragement or study of the arts, but the French government spent $100,000 annually solely on grand opera and a like sum on drama; Belgium and Little Saxony provided $100,000 and

$800,000 respectively, and Russia $1,500,000. England donated $500,000 annually for the fine arts in general, and France appropriated an amazing grand total of $3,000,000.[13]

The European references helped convince congressmen who were sensitive to the lack of an American cultural establishment in comparison both to Europe, and more recently, to America's rising status as a great power. They were also accustomed to the argument that other large libraries had less complete collections and that the Library of Congress's support for research collections was consistent with its goal of supplementing other American libraries' resources. Unusual in the appeal were Putnam's use of outside experts and his definition of musicology as a scientific study, but these revealed the growing authority of the national library in commanding expert opinion and Putnam's concern to identify the library with the increasing American respect for scientific methodology.[14]

The hearings accomplished both purposes: Sonneck received a salary increase, and Putnam could be satisfied that the rationale for a comprehensive music collection was acceptable to congress.[15] By the time Sonneck departed the library in 1917, the music division contained nearly 800,000 items, about 720,000 in the form of printed or manuscript music. The collection of American music stretched from the early ballads, psalmodies, and church music to the Civil War songs of both the Union and the Confederacy, to the modern American composers whose scores were prominently represented—Victor Herbert, Edward MacDowell, and Ethelbert Nevin. The division had become the peer of the three or four largest music libraries worldwide.[16]

Putnam did not hire a new music division chief until 1922, when he offered the post to Carl Engel, a native of Paris who had studied at the universities of Strasbourg and Munich and emigrated to the United States in 1905.[17] As music editor for the Boston Music Company since 1909, Engel, like Sonneck, sought to apply the standards of continental musicology to American scholarship. Also like Sonneck, he had little use for copyright deposits. While annual receipts of music fluctuated, they had increased from about 24,500 pieces in 1904-05 to 44,500 by 1919-20, and half to two-thirds of the material was being kept when Engel joined the staff. The new chief thought that the flow of material overburdened the small music division staff, and he observed that a flourishing collection of player piano rolls attracted the attention of too many other staff members. Commenting that copyright deposits included "the good, the bad, and the utterly worthless," he recommended to Putnam that much of the popular material be discarded. Putnam quickly consented, noting that selection rather than wholesale retention accorded with the library's general policies regarding copyright deposits. Thus by the mid-1920s Engel was returning about two-thirds of the deposits to the Copyright Office, and he closed the area housing the piano rolls.[18] The music division remained firmly oriented to the classical tradition.

Soon after coming to the library, Engel was invited to the 1922 Berkshire Festival. Sponsored by a long-time patron of music, Elizabeth Sprague Coolidge, the festivals were held near her home in Pittsfield, Massachusetts, and they were strictly invitational. In a brief letter of thanks, Engel asked Mrs. Coolidge to consider placing in the library her collection of composers' autograph scores for compositions that won prizes at the international competitions preceding the festival, and she later agreed. Moreover, she was seeking a means of perpetuating her concert series through an institution or organization, and consequently proposed that, in connection with the gift, it would be appropriate to sponsor several chamber music recitals in Washington.[19]

The Library of Congress was an unlikely venue for chamber music since it had never mounted cultural events and the federal government had never been a patron of the fine arts. In the fall of 1923, in fact, the library's sole music facility consisted of an old upright piano housed in the basement. As chief of a music division in which no music was played, Engel very much wanted to sponsor performances, and he sketched for Putnam his vision of a division that would "take on a new life" through the concerts. His request seems a natural outcome of Putnam's insistence on hiring experts as division chiefs since such experts might well imagine projects reaching beyond traditional library functions. But on this occasion Engel's ambition conflicted with Putnam's sense of mission; the librarian objected that concerts were beyond the library's scope and that there was no concert hall available to government agencies.[20] He was unyielding until composer Mary Carlisle Howe suggested the Smithsonian's new Freer Gallery of Art as a site.[21] Its use carried two important (and to Putnam, probably advantageous) restrictions: the audience would be limited to 300, and it would be necessary to enlist the Smithsonian as a co-sponsor. Thus negotiations ensued among Engel, Putnam, Freer curator John Lodge, and the Smithsonian. It is likely that Putnam quietly consulted the Joint Committee on the Library as well, and he also contacted the chairman of the Fine Arts Commission.[22]

Mrs. Coolidge envisioned the concerts "for the pleasure and instruction of a select audience," and they would perform the works of living composers. Her musical agenda was one consideration, but the reaction of federal officials was Putnam's main concern, and he insisted that each concert include one composition that was "safe and sound."[23] The invitation list included the White House, Congress, the Supreme Court, the diplomatic corps, music scholars and teachers, newspaper music critics, and as Putnam later explained, "certain others whose aid may be valuable in governmental recognition of such music, and especially in developing the music collection in the Library." Thus, he said, the list was neither "merely social" nor "widely official."[24] Certainly it was both and rigorously select as well. But under his careful management, the concerts, held February 7-9, 1924, were a great success. Praise from Congress and favorable newspaper reports changed Putnam's attitude about involving the library in cultural events, and in his annual report he termed the event "the first notable recognition by our Government . . . of music as one of the finer arts—entitled to its concern and encouragement."[25]

In the fall of 1924 Herbert Putnam attended the Pittsfield Festival, and shortly thereafter Coolidge decided to transfer all her concerts to the Library of Congress. To support the work, in 1925 she offered Putnam $60,000 to build an auditorium at the library plus an endowment with an estimated annual yield of $28,200 for festivals and concerts, awards for original compositions, and an annual honorarium for the chief of the music division.

Putnam was delighted at the gift, particularly since during the post-World War I years Congress had either decreased the library's budget or provided only minimal increases.[26] He immediately conveyed Coolidge's offer of the auditorium to the Speaker of the House of Representatives, and the speaker referred it to the Committee on the Library.[27] Fortunately, although the librarian never mentioned it, the chairman, Robert Luce, had been a college friend of his, and Luce proved a discreet as well as stalwart supporter. Invoking Congress's acceptance of the Smithsonian Institution bequest as a precedent, he stated cautiously that "Your committee on the library has been unable to find any reason why the gift should not be promptly and thankfully accepted," implying that the members had searched hard for reasons to reject the offer.[28] But as Putnam explained, the meeting went smoothly: "As every one of the members had had in advance a personal explanation from me, the statement was chiefly for the formal record (and incidentally for the benefit of the Press Gallery, the superintendent of which was present in person). There was not the slightest demur, but there were various questions designed to elicit facts which might be useful on the floor." Two days later he notified Coolidge that the resolution had passed without question.[29]

Because there was no law allowing a federal agency to accept an endowment, that portion of Coolidge's gift was proposed separately, to enable Putnam and Senator George Wharton Pepper to draft legislation establishing the Library of Congress Trust Fund Board. The bill created a board consisting of three ex-officio members: the Librarian of Congress, the secretary of the treasury, and the chair of the Joint Committee, plus two presidential appointees; it passed both houses unanimously, without debate, and the president approved it the same day: March 3, 1925. It was an unusual departure for the conservative federal establishment of the mid-1920s: acceptance of the board added a new function to the national government as a receiver and administrator of gifts in the public interest, even while President Coolidge was insisting that "The greatest duty and opportunity of government is not to embark on any new ventures."[30] But Congress chose not to examine the ramifications—at least not publicly.

Putnam always attributed the success of the bill to congressional pride in the library, but he quickly moved to integrate the board with the library's mission. It is more than suggestive that, in a 1926 brochure about the board, the only illustration other than a picture of the library building was a drawing of the exhibit case housing the Declaration of Independence and the Constitution. When the state department transferred the documents to the library in 1921, Congress had approved Putnam's request for funds for a protective case, and the librarian had made the 1924 installation ceremony, attended by the president, the secretary of state, and a representative group of congressmen, an occasion of profound reverence. Any picture of "the Shrine," as it was called, could be counted on to evoke patriotic sentiment, and its image in the trust fund booklet securely consolidated private largesse with American democracy.[31]

The librarian also addressed carefully the issue of the performance of modern compositions. While Sonneck and Engel prided themselves on the music division's reputation for acquiring the works of new and controversial composers, Putnam muted that emphasis. Perhaps thinking that modern music might not be congenial to at least some congressmen, he admitted that such works might be "tentative and ephemeral," but insisted that "some will prove of permanent beauty and value." The audiences, he stated, would be small but they would include "persons of the requisite understanding, seriousness of purpose, and influence in the musical world," which would make the influence of the concerts "far reaching." Finally, he declared that the endowment was "absolutely consistent" with the library's policy of "doing for American scholarship and cultivation what is not likely to be done by other agencies."[32]

Under the chairmanship of Secretary of the Treasury Andrew Mellon, who bore the responsibility of ensuring "a responsible and conservative policy," the trust fund board combined official functions with the flexibility of a private corporation.[33] Long-term gifts would be accepted by the board and the Joint Committee on the Library, without further oversight or reports to congress. The board therefore assured privacy to donors who might dislike having their names featured in the *Congressional Record* or newspaper accounts, and the reduction in congressional scrutiny must likewise have been congenial to Putnam, since it enabled him to work discreetly with a much smaller oversight group.

Just five months after the passage of the trust fund act, a flow of gifts began,[34] and Putnam stated that the Coolidge gift and the establishment of the board had initiated a "new era" for the library, for Congress had in effect endorsed his far-reaching plans for its future. Private funding would enable the library to command the collections to rival and perhaps even surpass European national libraries. It also permitted Putnam to develop a long-time pet scheme of assembling a corps of experts to build the collections and "interpret" them to students, investigators, and the public at large—"the cultivation of the exceptional, for the stimulus and benefit of the superior understanding."[35] Even better, the gifts had the effect of a snowball en route downhill during the expansive, apparently prosperous days of the late 1920s; they rolled up generous appropriations in the process. In 1926 congress approved $345,000 for the construction of a new stack and a rare book room; in 1928, it approved up to $600,000 to purchase land for a new building plus a large budget increase; and in 1930 it appropriated $1.5 million for the purchase of the Vollbehr Collection of incunabula and up to $6 million to construct both an addition to the library and a new building.

This important change in the Library of Congress's resource base marked another departure from the nineteenth-century concept of the library as a democratic lending institution supported by funds from the public coffers. It highlighted instead a different tradition—that of the nineteenth-century philanthropists such as James Lenox, John Carter Brown, John Crerar, Henry E. Huntington, J. Pierpont Morgan, and William L. Clements whose gifts produced a set of institutions affluent enough to acquire important research collections. These "reference libraries" fit the model of cultural institution formation that Paul DiMaggio has described as the high culture model: the organization of museums and symphony orchestras by the wealthy elite as private nonprofit institutions with boards of trustees. Insulated from the general public, the trustees defined canons of art and music as central to the institutional mission, in effect sealing them off from the public at large and from lower cultural forms, yet allowing entry to those desiring to be educated to the cultural forms the elite deemed most desirable. Given its history of congressional control, relatively late admission of the public, and restrictions on public borrowing, the Library of Congress was arguably as much a product of elitism as it was a public institution. But joining the tradition of the publicly supported library with that of the privately endowed reference library enabled the Library of Congress to surmount the potential weakness of each type: the sometimes shifting levels of government support for public libraries, and public disinclination to come to the assistance of privately funded institutions.[36] Public funding had enabled Putnam to achieve his objectives of making the Library of Congress a national organizer of scholarly resources and the leader among American libraries. Private support would enable him not only to build comprehensive collections but also to achieve broader authority for the library as a cultural institution.[37]

Folk Culture in the National Collections

At about the same time the trust fund board was established, Carl Engel was learning about Robert Winslow Gordon's efforts to amass a collection of American folk songs. Gordon developed an interest in folk song at Harvard, where he studied with Barrett Wendell and George Lyman Kittredge, and when he left Harvard in 1918 to become an assistant professor of English at the University of California, Berkeley, he had begun to collect and record folk songs systematically. Before the 1920s, there was scholarly interest in Native American music among anthropologists and members of the American Folklore Society (established 1888), but Gordon's Harvard mentors were primarily interested in traditional English ballad survivals. Gordon's ideas were more eclectic, and he began lugging an old-fashioned Edison phonograph to the San Francisco and Oakland waterfronts, where he asked workmen and sailors to sing into the machine—

a significant departure from the academic tradition of collecting song texts.[38]

Gordon was also unorthodox about publication of his material; he chose the popular men's pulp magazine *Adventure* rather than a scholarly journal. From July 1923 to September 1927 he edited a column titled "Old Songs that Men Have Sung," which included unpublished sea-chanties, lumber camp songs, songs of the Great Lakes and the canals, of pioneers and the west, of mountain folk, spirituals, and plantation songs. Asking readers to send him their versions of folk songs, Gordon began a collection that he hoped would encompass the entire body of American folk music. In four years he received more than 10,000 song texts and answered over 4,000 letters.[39]

Some of Gordon's Berkeley colleagues were unsympathetic to his unorthodox methods. Moreover, the subject of folk survivals was not particularly important in literary studies, and publication in a pulp magazine was not the sort of credential that led to tenure.[40] Thus the English department let Gordon go, with the cushion of a sabbatical year, and he returned to Harvard, planning to complete his Ph.D. Instead, however, he decided on a year-long collecting journey that would take him from Appalachia to the deep South, to the Great Lakes and the maritime provinces of Canada.[41] Since most collectors restricted their activities to a single area or region, Gordon's ambitious plan marked him as one of the first collectors whose scope was continental.[42]

Gordon never completed his route; he stopped in Darien, Georgia, his wife's former home, where he was assured of acceptance in the African American community, and settled down to collecting. He had used the Library of Congress during his research on song origins and relationships, and while writing the *Adventure* column, he appealed to the music division staff for assistance in answering readers' inquiries. Hoping to find financial support, he described his vision of a national collection to Carl Engel and asked for advice about funding.[43] Describing folk songs as reflecting the values of an earlier America—a simpler society, and a more honest, genuine populace—he pointed out that such music would appeal to a public that worried about the effects of speakeasies and jazz on the American character as well as to those who sought to preserve the remains of early Anglo-America.

> Eventually I think the study and preservation of American materials is quite as important as the collection and preservation of our Indian materials. And they are passing just as rapidly now. I'll bet a cookie that a hundred years from now the backers of such a national project would be better remembered by this nation than the man who offered 10,000 or 15,000 or 20,000 for a new stunt aeroplane flight. That's what I'm going to fight hard for later. Whenever I get the chance. I could organize right now a group of real workers, trained collectors, a national bureau if the funds were available.[44]

Unlike the Coolidge concerts, there was a precedent for federal involvement in field collecting; the Bureau of American Ethnology had workers in the field recording Native American languages, music, and traditions as early as 1879. Moreover, collections of ethnographic materials had been established, for example, at the Bishop Museum in Honolulu (1889), the Peabody Museum of Archaeology and Ethnology at Harvard (1866), the Southwest Museum in Los Angeles (1907), and the Phoebe Apperson Hearst Museum of Anthropology at Berkeley (1901). But these collections largely focused on native groups. The interest in American folk song, on the other hand, spanned a variety of efforts, as the academicians tracing bygone English ballads were joined by local collectors fanning out to capture the Appalachian mountaineer and western cowboy traditions. In 1910, John Lomax published his *Cowboy Songs and Other Frontier Ballads*, and Hubert G. Shearing and Josiah H. Combs' *A Syllabus of Kentucky Folk-Songs* appeared the following year. Several more collections, featuring ballad survivals among mountain white people but also including some authentic American ballads, had appeared by 1920.[45]

Engel considered folk music important to national musical development, and he was extremely interested in advancing music research, which he thought had received very little encouragement in the United States.[46] He hoped that the library might become the headquarters for a postdoctoral department of musicology that would engage scholars in primary research, and to that end, he was pursuing a relationship with the Curtis Institute of Music in Philadelphia. Gordon, whose comprehensive approach and commitment to historical, philological, and musicological analysis he admired, would be valuable to this project. Accordingly he sought support for an endowment for a "Chair" of American Folk Music at the library. And Gordon, for his part, wrote optimistically of the prospects for "a real clean up" of available material within two years, thus making the task of establishing a collection seem one that could readily be accomplished.[47]

Engel and Putnam enlisted a group of donors for their folk song initiative that was arguably less interested in altering attitudes toward American culture than in supporting the Library of Congress. Two members of the trust fund board provided gifts: $100 from Treasury Secretary Andrew Mellon and $1,000 from John Barton Payne, who was the director of the American Red Cross, but perhaps more important, hailed from West Virginia.[48] Other portions of the initial five-year funding came from Mrs. Annie Bloodgood Parker of Strafford, Pennsylvania ($1,000 per year over five years), a devotee of early American music and a long-time benefactor of the music division,[49] and from Mrs. Mary Sprague Miller ($250 with the promise of further gifts).[50] Finally, a late appeal to Putnam's old friend, Frederick Keppel of the Carnegie Corporation, brought the largest gift of $2,500.[51]

Two broad cultural themes supported the folk song initiative: musical heterogeneity and nostalgia. Just as European composers and critics had made vernacular music more acceptable to American critics, Americans interested in new musical forms were recognizing that jazz, popular songs, and folk music would become part of the American music heritage. Others adopted an any-thing-is-better-than-popular-music stance. Still others continued to worry that an American national music would never emerge.[52] Meanwhile, the public was listening to the ethnic programs featured by small, local radio stations, and commercial recording companies were producing blues and hillbilly music for African American and southern audiences, while ethnic record companies re-corded the music of immigrants' homelands.[53] Significantly, Gordon had em-phasized both disappearing tunes and the importance of folk music as an alter-native to popular forms in his appeal to Engel. The fear of losing contact with a simpler past—more authentic, more tradition laden, more patriotic, more truly American—gave rise to a desire to make American heritage and traditions more concrete, more knowable, more immediate. For example, the American Wing of the Metropolitan Museum of Art opened in 1923, featuring authentic period rooms and furniture. That same year, the Thomas Jefferson Memorial Founda-tion purchased Jefferson's home at Monticello, and in 1926 John D. Rockefeller committed himself to the rescue of colonial Williamsburg while Henry Ford established the Ford Museum and Greenfield Village.[54] Such efforts perhaps moved others to re-evaluate historical materials. By the late-1920s, for instance, rare book room curator, V. Valta Parma, had begun to rescue dime novels from copyright storage. And by 1929, the Coolidge Foundation had interrupted its usual classical focus to devote the annual festival to American folk music.[55]

Eager to profit by Gordon's summer fieldwork and by his "his wide-spread influence with collectors of such material, who through his influence may be induced to deposit it here,"[56] Putnam and Engel moved ahead rapidly. On April 20, 1928, Engel announced that the library planned a national collection of folk songs, to be directed by Gordon, to ensure their preservation and to recognize the value of the folk heritage. "There is a pressing need for the formation of a great national collection of American folk-songs," he stated. "The logical place for such a collection is the national library of the United States, the Library of Congress in Washington. This collection should embody the soul of our people;" Engel responded, "it should comprise all the poems and melodies that have sprung from our soil and have been handed down, often with manifold changes, from generation to generation as a precious possession of our folk. . . . It is richer than that of any other country." Engel emphasized that "The time has come when the preservation of this valuable old material is threatened by the spread of the popular music of the hour;" he specified the need for "a scientific and critical approach," and cited Gordon's qualifications as an authority on American folk song.[57]

In May, Gordon gave a lecture at the library that raised significant interest in his work, and on July 1 he joined the staff, at a monthly salary of $300.[58] He then returned to his collecting. He contacted other fieldworkers, but mostly amateurs and regional collectors rather than scholarly societies, since he had decided to build a network of local organizations to support a national center at the Library of Congress. Busy with these efforts, he made no changes in his method of operation. Putnam and Engel, however, had assumed that he would move to Washington, and Engel prompted him repeatedly for news. By November, Putnam was exasperated enough to telegraph his wife to ask his whereabouts.[59] Gordon then sent a project report that discussed the production of publications and the formation of a Washington research center as future activities; he responded to Engel's protest that more accountability was required, by declaring that his work lay "largely beyond the frontier of knowledge" and had to be conducted by trial and error. Usatisfactory, sporadic communications continued through much of 1929. But when Gordon failed to submit a description of his work for the Librarian's *Annual Report* for 1929, Engel threatened to withdraw support unless Gordon exhibited "methodical handling of affairs and a substantial progress."[60]

The threat had the intended effect, and Gordon moved to Washington. But his relations with Engel and Putnam failed to improve since he demanded control over his material, remained uneager to open it to others, and jealously guarded the rights in material others deposited. His close connections with the commercial field led to a report in the trade journal, *The Talking Machine and Radio Journal*, that praised the Library of Congress and the government for recognizing hillbilly and African American music as "the basis of American folk-song and music."[61] But Putnam did not want the library identified with popular music. He was probably also unenthusiastic about Gordon's long involvement (on his own time) with the Victor Company's lawsuit over the ownership of the hillbilly song "The Wreck of Old 97." Eager to return to fieldwork, in 1930 Gordon obtained a $1,300 grant from the American Council of Learned Societies to improve recordings. But he was dissatisfied with the machines, and instead of leaving Washington he spent his time testing wire, cylinder, and disc recorders.[62]

Funding for the folk song project was exhausted at the end of 1931, but the Carnegie Corporation provided assistance to continue work until June 10, 1932. In March, Putnam and Engel notified Gordon that the library would not retain his services after the end of the fiscal year (later modified to the end of 1932), and they refused his offer to serve as voluntary director. His final report noted that he had collected approximately 8,000 texts with music for some 700 titles, including 4,000 from his own collection. The archive also contained 900 songsters, more than 1,500 volumes of pulp magazines including folk song columns, and loaned materials from several collectors. Theses, books, journals, and copies of material in other collections had been acquired plus 350 records from the Victor Company in addition to Gordon's 1,000 or more wax cylinder recordings.[63]

As Gordon left the library, scholarly interest in folk culture had begun to multiply. During the late-1920s, several collections of African American folkore appeared, and Benjamin Botkin founded the journal *Folk-say* in 1929. Two years later, Constance Rourke published *American Humor*, the first of a series of books on folk culture that declared the interest of American intellectuals in the American heritage, to the grudging acceptance of such notable critics as Van Wyck Brooks. During the early-1930s scholarly organizations such as the Modern Language Association and the American Council of Learned Societies began to organize folklore sections and fund surveys of the field.[64] In 1933, the library obtained funding from the council for the fieldwork of John Lomax, who became an honorary consultant and curator of the archive. The Rockefeller Foundation and the Carnegie Corporation subsequently funded Lomax's collecting, but appropriated funds were not available until July 1937 when Congress finally provided support.

Critics might have noted that the Archive of American Folksong was established on speculation—or at least on an assumption that folk music would become part of American musicology. The archive was a pioneer in the field, predating the academic establishment of folk song, folklore, and American studies. Moreover the initiative did not come from groups of scholars or field collectors but from the library and the funding through Engel's and Putnam's personal appeals. Their project was atypical in a library profession that deferred to established cultural authorities and in general privileged print over other cultural forms. The active acquisition of folk music was unusual in an institution in which the administrators collected high culture but systematically culled lesser materials. It was highly innovative, but an unlikely candidate for a national library or for appropriated funds.

The introduction of this particular cultural form to the library occurred, nevertheless, at a time when the study of folk song began drawing support from American musicologists and from supporters of high musical culture who became interested in reclaiming the folk heritage. Thus the archive's establishment reflected increasing interest by experts, but the collection became possible only because the formation of the trust fund board enabled long-term private funding. The small budget necessarily shaped the archive's collecting ability, it limited the attempt to establish a national center, and staffing and funding problems became more acute as the economy descended into depression. Thus the intellectual claim remained small in a sense; the archive did not define a canon of American folksong, nor did it claim either systematic documentation or a comprehensive collection.[65] Progress toward such goals could only be gradual.

On another level, however, its impact was highly significant. First, the claim of cultural significance was largely accepted—by congress, by librarians, by musicologists, and by collectors. It was a large claim; to support the acceptance of American folk song as a field of study was also to assume a role in shaping the American music establishment—and also the developing folklore and American studies fields. It also took part in a more general ongoing reconstruction of American culture achieved through evoking the past and preserving its memories as part of the composition of American national memory. Every step that Putnam, Sonneck, and Engel had taken to build the music division collection, to assert its authority, to organize a continuing concert series, and finally, to reach toward a research center with a faculty, revealed the ambition to exert national influence on the music establishment. Such a role was entirely congenial to Putnam's efforts to enforce the library's national hegemony and to foster its progress in the 1920s toward what he considered its "appropriate destiny as not merely a collection of material for purposes merely utilitarian, but an embodiment so far as may now be possible, of influences for the promotion of culture."[66] By expanding the definition of institutional collections to include the oral tradition, by defining the American musical heritage to include the rural poor, the uneducated, and the disadvantaged, and by proclaiming a center for the support and study of a tradition far closer to the popular than the classic, the Library of Congress extended its national authority to a celebration of American memories that would find even more sincere appreciation during the Great Depression.

Notes

1. John Y. Cole, "Storehouses and Workshops: American Libraries and the Uses of Knowledge," in *The Organization of Knowledge in Modern America, 1860-1920*, eds. Alexandra Oleson and John Voss, (Baltimore, 1979), 364-85.

2. Neil Harris, "Cultural Institutions and American Modernization," *Journal of Library History* 16 (Winter 1981): 42; on the blurring of the traditional distinction between high and low culture see also Michael Kammen, *American Culture, American Tastes: Social Change and the 20th Century* (New York, 1999), 9-13.

3. Jane Aikin Rosenberg, *The Nation's Great Library: Herbert Putnam and the Library of Congress, 1899-1939* (Urbana, 1993), 36-41; John Y. Cole, "The Library of Congress and American Scholarship," in *Libraries and Scholarly Communication in the United States: The Historical Dimension*, eds. Phyllis Dain and John Y. Cole, (New York, 1990), 45-61.

4. This case has an affinity with Gramsci's consensual cultural hegemony. T. Jackson Lears has suggested the application of the concept to "hegemonic values in the complex organizations that have shaped modern culture." In the particular case of the Library of Congress, efforts to establish hegemony were directed to institutions or specialized groups (other libraries, Congress, librarians, scholars), and had to be pursued both upward within the government and downward to civil society, rather than the usual Gramscian focus on a dominant group transmitting its culture to the rest of society via coercion or consensus. See T. J. Jackson Lears, "The Concept of Cultural Hegemony: Problems and Possibilities," *American Historical Review*, 90 (June 1985): 587-88; Paul Ransome, *Antonio Gramsci: A New Introduction* (Westport, Conn., 1992), 132-52.

5. Wayne A. Wiegand, "Tunnel Vision and Blind Spots: What the Past Tells Us About the Present; Reflections on the Twentieth-Century History of American Librarianship," *Library Quarterly*, 69 (January 1999): 3-4; Wayne A. Wiegand, *The Politics of an Emerging Profession: The American Library Association, 1876-1917* (New York, 1986), 231.

6. William Warner Bishop, "The Library of Congress, 1907-1915: Fragments of Autobiography," *Library Quarterly*, 18 (January 1948): 3.

7. *Annual Report of the Librarian of Congress* (hereafter abbreviated ARLC) 1909 (Washington, D.C., 1909), 149-82. Sections 59-60 addressed retention of copyright deposits. After the passage of the 1909 act, the library was no longer a library of record, but all copyrighted material was listed in the *Catalogue of Copyright Entries*. In fiscal 1909-10, 27 percent of the book and pamphlet material was deemed appropriate, but by 1924-25 only 17 percent was selected. Copyright deposits of books and pamphlets increased 46 percent between 1909-10 and 1924-25, from 49,000 to over 106,000. During the same period, selected items ranged from 13,000 to 18,000. Figures are calculated from *ARLC*.

8. Bishop, "Library of Congress," 3; Thorvald Solberg to Librarian of Congress, 21 November 1910; Superintendent of Reading Room to Librarian of Congress, 18 June 1909; Chief, Music Division to Chairman, Copyright Commission, 4 August 1909; Appleton Prentice Clarke Griffin to Herbert Putnam, 25 June, 9 July, 5 August 1909; Chairman, Copyright Commission, to

Register of Copyrights, 6 October 1909, all in Box 135, Central File, Library of Congress Archives, Manuscript Division, Library of Congress (hereafter cited CF-LCA). Most of the library's collections were in print format during the early-twentieth century. Copyright deposits of motion pictures began in 1893, but by 1913 they had been discarded because of the highly flammable film stock and lack of fireproof storage. The systematic acquisition of recordings did not begin until 1925 when classical recordings from the Victor Company entered the collections. Sound recordings were not received on copyright deposit until 1972.

9. Kammen, *American Culture*, 62-5; Henry F. May, *The End of American Innocence: A Study of the First Years of Our Own Time, 1912-1917* (Chicago, 1959), 30; Jack Sullivan, *New World Symphonies: How American Culture Changed European Music* (New Haven, 1999), 1-40.

10. Quoted in Carol June Bradley, "Oscar G. T. Sonneck: Architect of the 'National Music Collection,'" *Journal of Library History*, 16 (Spring 1981): 296.

11. *ARLC* 1902, 27; see also Herbert Putnam, "O. G. Sonneck: Remarks at the Funeral Service, November 1st, 1928," *Musical Quarterly*, 15 (1929): 1-2. Putnam may have remembered his decision as somewhat more emphatic than the report indicated, but his insistence that the library would be able to foster study and research in music as no other institution could is entirely characteristic.

12. Herbert Putnam to Richard Aldrich, 7 October 1908, Box 156, CF-LCA.

13. "Music: The Collections" undated typescript, Box 156, CF-LCA.

14. On the influence of science, see Frederick Lewis Allen, *Only Yesterday* (New York, 1931), 141.

15. Herbert Putnam to Charlotte Munroe Putnam, "Sunday, 6 p.m." 1908, Box 8, Herbert Putnam Papers, Manuscript Division, Library of Congress; "Music: The Collections," LCA.

16. Carl Engel, "Views and Reviews," *The Musical Quarterly*, 14 (April 1928): 299; *ARLC* 1917, 66-68 includes Sonneck's last report, which nevertheless featured a long list of needs.

17. Putnam held the position open in case Sonneck decided to return. See Cyrilla Barr, *Elizabeth Sprague Coolidge: American Patron of Music* (New York, 1998), 156.

18. *ARLC* 1922, 73; Carl Engel to Putnam, 7 October 1922; Putnam to Engel, 10 October 1922, Box 156, CF-LCA. Efforts to have the music division examine copyright receipts sent to the library between 1870 and 1909 resulted in only a 2 percent selection rate, mostly second copies; see Thorvald Solberg to Librarian of Congress, 28 August 1917, Box 135, CF-LCA; Carol June Bradley, *American Music Librarianship: A Biographical and Historical Survey* (New York, 1990): 26; *ARLC* 1911, 103-04. Sonneck excluded eight classes of material, including arrangements, minstrel music, vaudeville songs "of a low order," and adaptations; see Chief, Music Division to Chairman, Copyright Commission, 4 August 1909, Box 135, CF-LCA.

19. Barr, *Elizabeth Sprague Coolidge,* 156-58. Sonneck had already alerted Putnam to her hopes for perpetuating the festivals; see Cyrilla Barr, "The 'Faerie Queene' and the 'Archangel:' the Correspondence of Elizabeth Sprague Coolidge and Carl Engel," *American Music*, 15 (Summer 1997): 162-63.

20. Bauer, "Carl Engel, July 21, 1883-May 6, 1944," *The Musical Quarterly*, 30 (July 1944): 251; Barr, "Faerie Queene,'" 163-64; Carl Engel to Elizabeth Sprague Coolidge, 7, 13 November 1923, Box 54, Coolidge Foundation Collection, Music and Performing Arts Division, Library of Congress (hereafter Coolidge Collection). Putnam defined the Music Division as devoted to music literature rather than music as an art. See "Library Affairs in Congress," 60-2, Folder A, 1 December 1908, CF-LCA.

21. Mary Howe, *Jottings* (Washington, D.C. 1959), 109-110. Howe was a leader of Washington musical activities, a founder of the National Symphony Orchestra, and a frequent accompanist for the gifted amateur violinist and later Speaker of the House Nicholas Longworth; see Clara L. Chambrun, *The Making of Nicholas Longworth: Annals of an American Family* (orig. 1933; reprint Freeport, N.Y., 1971), 211-24.

22. The Commissioners, appointed by the President, were responsible for advising on the location of statues, fountains, and monuments in the District of Columbia and on the selection of models and artists. Putnam did not have far to go to find the chairman, who at that time was Charles Moore, the acting chief of the Library's Manuscript Division since 1918. See "Moore, Charles," Box 187, CF-LCA.

23. Engel to Coolidge, [November or December], 1923, Box 54, Coolidge Collection.

24. Howe, *Jottings*, 110; "The Audiences," Box 156, CF-LCA. Mary Howe states that she composed the list, but Putnam undoubtedly refined it. One list of invitees is in his handwriting.

25. Engel to Oscar Sonneck, "received 2/16/24," Carl Engel Correspondence, Music and Performing Arts Division, Library of Congress, hereafter Engel Correspondence; *ARLC* 1924, 4-5; *Washington Post*, February 10, 1924; *Evening Star* (Washington, D.C.), February 10, 1924, pt. 1; "The Audiences," CF-LCA.

26. Putnam to Coolidge, 25 October, 8 November 1924, Box 53, Coolidge Collection; Rosenberg, *Nation's Great Library*, 94-101.

27. Putnam to the Honorable The Speaker of the House of Representatives, 4 December 1924, Box 167, CF-LCA. Nicholas Longworth was elected speaker on December 7, replacing

Frederick Huntington Gillett. Gillett was also a member of the Committee on the Library. In Putnam to Coolidge, 15 December 1924, Box 53, Coolidge Collection, Putnam intimates that he sent the offer letter so that a specific individual would get it—presumably Gillett.

28. U.S. Congress, House of Representatives, 68th Congress, 2d Session, *House Report 1063*, December 20, 1924, Box 135, CF-LCA.

29. Putnam to Coolidge, 13, 15 December 1924, Box 53, Coolidge Collection.

30. Quoted in Michael E. Parrish, *Anxious Decades: America in Prosperity and Depression, 1920-1941* (New York, 1992), 52.

31. *The Library of Congress Trust Fund Board* (Washington, D.C., 1926), Box 167, CF-LCA; Herbert Putnam, "Our National Library," *Review of Reviews*, 79 (February 1929): 60. Putnam later noted that in dealing with Congress, "though their reason had to be satisfied, the surest appeal was to their emotions;" see Herbert Putnam, "The University and the Library," *Library Journal*, 56 (1931): 348.

32. *ARLC* 1925, 4-5.

33. *Library of Congress Trust Fund Board*, CF-LCA.

34. James B. Wilbur, a Board member, on August 10, 1925, offered 1,000 shares of 7 percent preferred stock of the Public Service Company of Northern Illinois, at about $100 per share to enable the library to acquire photocopies of manuscripts in European archives that related to the history of the United States. On January 2, 1926, New York publisher Richard R. Bowker established an endowment of $10,000 for bibliographical services, and the noted collector Joseph Pennell, who died on April 23, willed his estate to the Division of Prints. The bequest of Mrs. John Boyd Thacher who died February 18, 1926, was her husband's collection of incunabula, early printing, and manuscripts. In April, Putnam announced that William Evarts Benjamin had provided an endowment for a chair of American History and the Carnegie Corporation funded a chair in the fine arts. In 1927 Archer M. Huntington endowed the purchase of materials relating to Spain, Portugal, and South America, and in 1928 funded a chair of Spanish and Portuguese literature, while John D. Rockefeller's gift of $700,000 contributed to the manuscript copying project and to the development of the bibliographical apparatus. Later developments included the organization of "The Friends of Music in the Library of Congress," led by Speaker Nicholas Longworth, establishment of the Beethoven Association's Sonneck Memorial Fund "for the aid and advancement of musical research," and the Daniel Guggenheim Fund for the Promotion of Aeronautics, Inc.'s endowment for a chair of aeronautics and the purchase of material. Finally, it was especially gratifying to Putnam's ambitions for the Library that Henry C. Folger selected a neighboring site to construct a library to house his Shakespeariana collection. All gifts were reported in *ARLC*.

35. *Library of Congress Trust Fund Board*, CF-LCA; *ARLC* 1925, 4-5.

36. With the founding of the James J. Hill Library in St. Paul (1921) and the Eastman Memorial Foundation in Laurel, Mississippi (1923), the reference library tradition seemed to be reviving in the 1920s. See Robert J. Usher, "The Place of the Endowed Reference Library in the Community," in *Essays Offered to Herbert Putnam*, eds. William Warner Bishop and Andrew Keogh, (orig. 1929; reprint Freeport, N. Y., 1967), 467-73; Paul DiMaggio, "Cultural Entrepreneurship in Nineteenth-Century Boston: The Creation of an Organizational Base for High Culture in America," in *Rethinking Popular Culture: Contemporary Perspectives in Cultural Studies*, eds. Michael Schudson and Chandra Mukerji, (Berkeley and Los Angeles, 1991), 374-97; Paul DiMaggio, "Cultural Boundaries and Structural Change: The Extension of the High Culture Model to Theater, Opera, and the Dance, 1900-1940," in *Cultivating Differences: Symbolic Boundaries and the Making of Inequality*, eds. Michele Lamont and Marcel Fournier, (Chicago, 1992), 21-57.

37. The American Library Association heartily approved the library's initiative. See Rosenberg, *Nation's Great Library*, 104.

38. Donald K. Wilgus, *Anglo-American Folksong Scholarship Since 1898* (New Brunswick, N.J., 1959), 143-44, 153-54; Debora Kodish, *Good Friends and Bad Enemies: Robert Winslow Gordon and the Study of American Folksong* (Urbana, 1986), 19-21; 44-48. See also Peter T. Bartis, "A History of the Archive of Folk Song at the Library of Congress: The First Fifty Years" (Unpublished Ph.D. diss., University of Pennsylvania, 1982).

39. "Memorandum {Biographical}", undated, Miscellaneous Box, R. W. Gordon Collection, Archive of Folk Culture, Library of Congress (hereafter Gordon Collection).

40. Kodish, *Good Friends,* 48-49.

41. "The Trip {Biographical}," undated; Miscellaneous Box, Gordon Collection. Gordon financed his travel with a contract with the *New York Times Magazine* for a series of folk song articles, a $1,200 Sheldon Traveling Fellowship from Harvard, and donations and discounts from the Ford, Eastman, and Edison companies; see Kodish, *Good Friends,* 56-59.

42. Wilgus, *Anglo-American Folksong Scholarship,* 179-80.

43. Kodish, *Good Friends,* 119-20, 152-55.

44. R. W. Gordon to Engel, 14 January 1927, Correspondence and Reports, Gordon Collection.

45. Peter T. Bartis and Hillary Glatt, *Folklife Sourcebook: A Director of Folklife Resources in the United States,* 2d rev. and expanded edition (Washington, D.C., 1986); Wilgus, *Anglo-American*

Folksong Scholarship, 147-48, 157-59, 167-71, 175-77; Benjamin Filene, *Romancing the Folk: Public Memory and American Roots Music* (Chapel Hill, 2000), 16-20.

46. Engel, "Views and Reviews," 298. The American Council of Learned Societies created a Committee on Musicology in 1929, and he became its first chair. The American Musicological Society was not founded until 1934, see Bradley, *American Music Librarianship*, 29.

47. Oscar Sonneck to Engel, 23 May 1928, Engel Correspondence; Engel to Gordon, Jan. 28, 1927, 16 September 1927, Gordon Collection; Engel, "Views and Reviews," 300; Gordon to Engel, 25 January 1927; 2 March 1928, Gordon Collection.

48. Putnam to John Barton Payne, 26 May 1928, Librarian's Letterbooks, No. 646, LCA.

49. *ARLC* 1931, 199-200; Putnam to Mrs. Parker, 26 May 1928, Librarian's Letterbooks, No. 646, LCA. Mrs. Parker headed the committee that prepared *Church Music and Musical Life in Pennsylvania in the Eighteenth Century* (Philadelphia, 1926-27).

50. Adolph C. Miller, an economist, was a member of the Federal Reserve Board. For the pledges, see pp. 43, 44, 50, and 66, Librarian's Letterbooks No. 650, LCA.

51. Nolan Porterfield, *Last Cavalier: The Life and Times of John A. Lomax, 1867-1948* (Urbana, 1996), 521; *ARLC* 1928, 144; Putnam to Frederick Keppel, 26 May 1928, Librarian's Letterbooks No. 646, LCA.

52. See, for examples, John Tasker Howard, Jr., "Our Folk-Music and Its Probable Impress on American Music of the Future," *Musical Quarterly*, 7 (April 1921): 167-71; Arthur de Guichard, "Need for American Folk Song as Basis for Musical Education," *Musical America*, 17 (November 30, 1912), 22; H. F. Martin, "Where is Our National Music?" *Musical Digest*, 10 (May 4, 1926): 3.

53. Filene, *Romancing the Folk*, 34-39.

54. Allen, *Only Yesterday*, 170-72; Lynn Dumenil, *The Modern Temper: American Culture and Society in the 1920s* (New York, 1995), 82-83; Paul A. Carter, *The Twenties in America* (London, 1969), 24; Lawrence W. Levine, "Progress and Nostalgia: The Self Image of the Nineteen Twenties," in *The Unpredictable Past: Explorations in American Cultural History* (New York, 1993), 204; Charles B. Hosmer, Jr., *Presence of the Past: A History of the Preservation Movement in the United States Before Williamsburg*, (New York, 1965).

55. Clark Evans, "Librarian in Disguise: V. Valta Parma and the Development of Popular Culture Collections at the Library of Congress," in *Pioneers, Passionate Ladies, and Private Eyes: Dime Novels, Series Books, and Paperbacks*, eds. Larry E. Sullivan and Lydia Cushman Schurman, (New York, 1996), 24-26; Barr, *Elizabeth Sprague Coolidge*, 181, 245.

56. Putnam to Payne, 26 May 1928, LCA.

57. *ARLC* 1928, 143-44. Neither the announcement nor Gordon's lecture would have taken place without consultation with the Congressional Joint Committee.

58. *Evening Star* (Washington, D.C.), May 24, 1928; Kodish, *Good Friends*, 160.

59. Kodish, *Good Friends*, 161, 165, 168.

60. Gordon to Engel, 14 November 1928; Engel to Gordon, 1 September 1929, Correspondence and Reports, Gordon Collection.

61. Quoted in Kodish, *Good Friends*, 178.

62. George Herzog, *Research in Primitive and Folk Music in the United States*, American Council of Learned Societies, *Bulletin* no. 24, (Washington, D.C., 1936), 47; Kodish, *Good Friends*, 176-88; Porterfield, *Last Cavalier*, 292. These were the first experiments with such equipment, and Gordon also employed motion picture film to record and store material—a step toward the use of microfilm.

63. Kodish, *Good Friends*, 189-92; Porterfield, *Last Cavalier*, 292. Gordon salvaged some of the material from copyright rejects; see *ARLC* 1932, 321.

64. Herzog, *Research in Primitive and Folk Music*; "Report of the Committee on Folksong of the Popular Literature Section of the Modern Language Association," *Southern Folklore Quarterly*, 1 (June 1937): 1-73; Lewis Perry, *Intellectual Life in America: A History* (Chicago, 1989), 338-40.

65. Filene, *Romancing the Folk*, 46.

66. Herbert Putnam, "The Treasures in the National Library," *Current History*, 34 (1931): 238-52.

Home Libraries and the Institutionalization of Everyday Practices Among Antebellum New Englanders

Ronald J. Zboray and Mary Saracino Zboray

On 11 January 1845, John Park, a sixty-eight-year-old retired academy teacher, finished reading in his Worcester boardinghouse James Russell Lowell's *Conversations on Some of the Old Poets*. A recent birthday gift from his neighbor, "Colonel" George W. Richardson, the finely bound book was a handsome addition to the 3,000 volumes Park had collected during his long life. Owing to his cramped quarters, he had stored more than 2,000 of these away in a nearby office space he affectionately called "my 'Library.'" As he retired after reading, little did he think that his precious books were in imminent danger or that he would soon be roused with alarm. "At our front door," Park later confided to his diary, "I heard Col Richardson Exclaiming 'Dr Park's Library is on fire!'"[1]

Park, Richardson, and a band of local residents raced over to save the library. They found an inferno "like the mouth of an oven, under and behind one of my bookcases—the contents of which, mostly folios and quartos, were in full blaze." The few buckets of water the group splashed did little to stop the conflagration, which was "spreading along the wall and behind other bookcases." Fire engines were all too slow in arriving; so, with almost superhuman strength driven by desperation, the neighbors moved most of the collection out of harm's way. "[A] number of my friends now seized such of my bookcases as were nearest the fire," Park recorded, "and heavy as they were, with an effort which astonished me, they took five cases, books and all into Mr. Thomas's Office, a few

0026-3079/2001/4203-063$2.50/0   American Studies, 42:3 (Fall 2001): 63-86

Dr. John Park -- 1775--1852

Figure 1: This portrait of John Park with his treasured library is still affixed inside one of his diaries. The John Park Diaries (Ms. q Am. 1352). *Boston Public Library/Rare Books Department. Courtesy of the Trustees.*

doors distant in the same entry." When firemen finally came, they indiscriminately hosed down the walls, ceilings, remaining bookcases, and everyone present. "[We] were as wet as though we had fallen into a river," Park noted. The flames were at last extinguished, leaving all but fifteen or so "valuable folios and quartos" and some "small books" among many charred or water damaged volumes. "At sun rise . . . visiters began to come" to the site as if to pay respect to the books consumed or injured.[2]

What was it that moved these Worcester residents to rise before dawn, shiver in a deluge of water, summon up herculean courage, and, in short, risk their lives to save a personal library? Surely, some of their heroism was commanded by regard for Park himself. Some no doubt sprang from an esteem for literary property; his library, after all, was worth a fortune and rivaled in size and scope many institutional collections. A greater portion of this neighborly valor, however, was likely a reflection of the tremendous value these people placed upon personal libraries as agents of culture in the local community. At that time, when the tax-supported public library was nearly nonexistent, social and circulating libraries relatively rare, and Sunday school libraries exceedingly limited, book borrowers had to depend upon holdings of family members, friends, and neighbors as much if not more than those of institutions. Park's library was at his friends' disposal when they drew from it titles ranging from sensationalistic novels such as Eugene Sue's *Mysteries of Paris* to ponderous theological works like George Campbell's *The Four Gospels*. Nearly 100 individuals—a patronage surpassed by few social libraries—used his collection between 1839 and 1850. It is not just size that lends the comparison, for his library was a social library of sorts, too. His diary gives ample evidence of friends calling to admire his new editions or sitting and chatting with him over texts. Writing to his daughter about the fire, he reflected upon these library chats: "circumstances often lead me into conversations with my more serious friends . . . on theological subjects, and occasion[al] references to authors in print —sometimes to sustain *my* views— sometimes to gratify my friends." In this way, libraries like Park's were instrumental to the everyday production of social and cultural meaning.[3]

The relationship between library history and cultural history has long interested scholars. In assessing the state of the field in his 1952 essay, "The Study of American Library History," Jesse H. Shera asked scholars to search for the deeper social and cultural contexts in which libraries grew, flourished, and changed over time. The library, he reminded his colleagues, "is an agency of the entirety of the culture." He explained that it "is one portion of the system of graphic communication through which . . . culture operates, and its historic origins are to be sought in an understanding of the production, flow, and consumption of graphic communication through all parts of the social pattern." Library historians have since answered his call, but with reluctance to step figuratively outside institutional walls. Most have followed the development of institutions and their relationship to society and culture from, as Wayne Wiegand points out, "the inside out." According to Wiegand, most library scholarship "focuses too much on the institution, the people who practice librarianship within that institution, and the expertise used by the people within the institution itself."[4]

This essay attempts to study library history "from the outside in" by peering into private lives as lived rather than assessing particular institutional constructions. In order to follow the "production, flow, and consumption" of reading materials through "all parts of the social pattern," we place the institutional library in its closest extrinsic context—namely, the analogous everyday literary practices of ordinary people, and the cultural values implied in those practices.[5] These practices encompassed a wide range of activities similar to those of institutions, from book collecting and cataloging, to dissemination through borrowing and lending, to conversing about and evaluating libraries and texts. Some book owners self-consciously acted as "librarians," that is, as custodians of their own circulating collections; others commented upon their relationship to the emerging public institution. And, as was the case with library-sponsoring associations, users of personal libraries wove social networks over their literary exchanges.[6]

This account of everyday practices argues for a cultural history of the library not as a thing but as a process consisting of a cluster of discrete-though-related activities requiring neither institutional support nor even specialized rooms serving the information needs of community members or strangers. The institutional history of libraries thus becomes a subset of society-wide practices of collection (and preservation), arrangement, cataloging, retrieval, and circulation of cultural artifacts, while the institution itself becomes a technology offering to enhance what people are already doing.[7] Assessing the effectiveness and plumbing the nature of the nascent public library, in short, depends on gaining an accurate picture of the common practices it aimed to augment, remedy, or replace.

That antebellum New England not only pioneered the tax-based public library, but also had such a rich literary culture makes it an ideal site for studying the relationship between everyday practice and institutionalization.[8] Elite, middle, and working classes alike, albeit to varying degrees, participated in local literary life. The region, after all, had the nation's highest literacy rates by 1850 for both black and white adults—93 and 98 percent, respectively—and the quality of that literacy was high enough to support a broad-based reading public and popular literary associations like the village lyceum.[9] These highly literate New Englanders were also "very social"—so much so that books and reading became instrumental to forging and maintaining social ties; literariness infused everyday social encounters and literature was given meaning through social expression.[10]

The very "everydayness" of what we call "socio-literary experience" suggests its relative independence from top-down influences through public institutions like libraries. Indeed, institutional leverage upon the practices of most

ordinary people was probably weak, for few relied primarily upon formal libraries for reading materials.[11] Yet, even if they did, they found that in many regards
these institutions held more in common with their home counterparts than not.
Both were often simply collections in locked shelves set in a corner of a multi-
functional room. "Our Library occupies a conspicuous place under the portrait
of Bishop Fenwick in the study-room," James Healy, an Irish-African American
seminarian at the College of the Holy Cross testified in 1849.[12] Nor were institutional libraries much better organized than home ones, for the
professionalization of librarianship, with its systematic methods of acquiring,
storing, sheltering, and cataloging holdings, awaited the future.[13]

Because home and institutional libraries coexisted throughout the period,
however, it would be misleading to cast the institution as merely a distillation of
everyday practice. There were key differences between the two: one was a corporate, sometimes entrepreneurial, entity dependent upon membership, fees,
shares, dues, or tax support, while the other was a personal and nonprofit collection of reading materials. As such non-owners used them according to unwritten
rather than codified rules. Being unwritten, they depended upon the mutual trust
of owner and user, rather than adherence to impartial regulations. While it is true
that home libraries, being so pervasive, probably more informed institutional
development than vice versa, the influence was not exclusively unidirectional.
Rather, the two existed symbiotically, for they shared many of the same practices and stemmed from a common "habitus," (i.e., a pool of dispositions shaped
by prior action and commitments). To add to the complexity, everyday practices
were institutionalized in that they were enacted within the same socio-cultural
field in which institutions necessarily thrived and operated, and hence could
even mirror the activities of those institutions.[14]

To understand the institutionalization of everyday literary practices, we draw
upon testimony found in nearly 4,000 manuscript diaries and letters authored by
a diverse set of New Englanders between the years 1830 and 1861. These informants often eloquently described their socio-literary experiences as home "librarians" and the role they and their collections played as agents of literary culture within their social networks. We begin with their productive practices of
creating and organizing libraries: acquisitions, arrangement, and cataloging. From
there we follow the flow of books to other people, especially out and back into
the home through lending. Finally, we explore the common reception of home
libraries as highly valued expressions of social relations.[15]

Production

The library that John Park's community saved from fire was unusually immense and broad, but having a good collection was an ideal toward which even
the lowliest New England reader strived. "Oh! this is one of the deprivations of
poverty, not being able to buy books," boot-and-bonnet maker Martha Osborne
Barrett, a prodigious reader, complained in 1854 after seeing "an advertisement

of a new edition of Wordsworths poems complete." She had earlier that day withdrawn Wordsworth's *Memoirs* from a local library and no doubt would have liked to own it, for she extracted it profusely for future reference. Books and some magazines were relatively expensive items, indeed, luxuries to people for whom even a cheap pamphlet novel represented hours of labor. Strained finances severely limited the extent of libraries, but, still, poor families managed to pull together small collections from gifts, ephemera, and a few purchases. Vermont farm laborer Charles Cobb had only few—twelve music books and ledgers worth thirteen dollars, several odd books valued at "a ninepence apiece," and bound numbers of the *Saturday Evening Post*—but he treasured these volumes as much as Park did his; he frequently tallied up their value, lent them, or "swapped music books for a spell."[16]

The dimension of home libraries was clearly unstable, however. They expanded with wealth and contracted with hard times, not unlike institutional holdings, but book owners aligned the fluctuation with that of their personal fortunes. Upwardly mobile bibliophiles like Cambridge lawyer Mellen Chamberlain, who started out as a poor New Hampshire farmer's son, marked his achievements in the numbers of volumes he acquired. "My library has increased by more than one hundred valuable books," he assessed a landmark career year in 1859. Income was not the only inflationary factor. Inheritances or long-term loans could suddenly expand a paltry collection in much the same way that institutions could swell with a generous bequest or donation. "Uncle Waldo made me a splendid donation of Hume, Smollett, Bisset, Lardners [*sic*], Burke, 16 vols for my library," one grateful college student exclaimed. Conversely, losses through fire or theft, or financial downturns might strangle both the home or public library's growth. John Park, for one, was forced to sell his cherished run of *Edinburgh Review* in 1842; "I feel very unwilling to part with it," he sighed with remorse, "but my dividends have been so much curtailed by the mismanagement of Banks, that I must raise the wind, somehow." And he was not alone in seeing literary wealth go up in smoke; one Vermont lawyer rebuilt his law library practically from scratch at Boston bookstores after an 1846 fire "made him a beggar almost."[17]

Size, however, was secondary to selectivity among home library builders. To be sure, selectivity reflected limited funds, but it also denoted a utilitarian mind-set that purchased according to need or special interest. For example, between January 1856 and April 1858, Saco millworker J. Edwin Harris, who made about seventeen dollars a month, purchased fourteen identifiable books for his library, most of them relevant to his special reading interests and goal of becoming a fiction writer or poet: ten volumes of English, American, and Scottish poems, a few novels, miscellaneous titles, and two different story papers that he had bound by the volume. Middling folk also built modest, well chosen collections but tried to cover a few areas instead. "Most of our library is composed of Books of a Moral character of which kind we have a great number," one newlywed accountant averred in 1838; "We now need to make a good selection [of] some good histories & Scientific works—However the world was not built in a day, neither can we expect to obtain, with our present means, a complete library in a day." As the aim of having a home library was to read and even study all of one's books, limitations were often self-imposed. Indiscriminate buying suggested desultory reading habits. "[E]very book assists and does its respective part in the formation of a library," an engineer opined at the beginning of his career; "and I trust that ere I am many years older I shall . . . have a respectable looking if not a select library, and trust that many of their contents may be transferred to my vacant mind." Selectivity sometimes guided donors as well. Travelers might return home bearing locally rare books with a recipient's taste in mind. A Bangor woman while abroad bought "all [Jean Paul] Richter's works in 4 large volumes" for her neighbors who could read the tomes' German prose. In this tendency to build with purpose, home librarians shared a sense of "mission" with institutions that controlled their acquisitions.[18]

Shelves were often lined with stray books of no seeming purpose that, however, spoke more eloquently than the rarest text. These were often books imbued with personal meaning—out-of-date almanacs inscribed by deceased relatives, gift volumes presented during courtship, personal journals filled with memories, or old textbooks worn and torn by years of schooling—that often held the greatest and deepest value for home librarians. The absence or loss of such books was sometimes felt more deeply than their presence. "How I should have valued them!!" Mary Poor complained four years after her father died in 1849; "I have not one single book that was my father's, with his name written in it in his own hand, but a hymn book & that I value above price." Of course, these intimate meanings would little interest librarians judging a book's value by its suitability to a collection. The user's relationship to an institution's books was one of detachment, as well. "Changed some old books away for new ones," one Providence housewife succinctly wrote, as did many other users. Institutional borrowers seldom invested meaning in a book (though not a text) that all too quickly went back to its place on the library's shelves.[19]

With both selectivity and intimate meaning guiding library building, it follows that home librarians classified and arranged their books according to some personally relevant method. The lack of a set standard for organizing collections led to improvisation among even institutional librarians, who might variably shelve according size, format, alphabet, subject areas, or some mixture of any or all; once shelving was determined, it was up to successors to "understand the arrangement of the books." Very few diarists and correspondents described their own taxonomies, but they nonetheless left evidence of definite schemes. "[H]e has arranged his books to his own mind," a Bostonian declared in 1841 after her husband settled into a new library room. People necessarily fashioned mental compartments for their literary objects before carving out space on a shelf. Harriet Low, a wealthy Salemite with many books, was so fastidious that she would not allow her domestics to assist her in arranging books in her cases. "The servants know nothing about books," she griped, assuming they would create a haphazard mess. In this sense, arranging books was both an exercise in the organization of knowledge and the classification of memories, not merely an expedient way to store items.[20]

Although most were silent about their particular shelving schemes, a few informants left traces of them in manuscript library catalogs. For the compiler, these were probably not mnemonic aids; institutional and home librarians alike knew well their usually modest collection and its place upon shelves. While institutional catalogs helped borrowers select items from large collections that they usually could not browse, ordinary people's catalogs were not so functional. Borrowers, as we will see, often perused personal collections during social calls. Besides, most home collections were too small to warrant a catalog. Insofar as they mimicked printed forms that advertised an institution's significance, catalogs signified their owners' regard for their collections' public value and social worth.[21] Above all, these taxonomies give insight into compilers' minds and their relations to their books.

One farmer and schoolteacher from Wilton, New Hampshire, Levi Abbott, is a good case in point. Sometime around 1855, he arranged in his diary his fifty-some-odd books into the following categories: lexicons, Greek books, French books, English schoolbooks, poetical, miscellaneous books, law books, and musical items. His system suggests that he considered language groupings and fields of practical application as categories more important than genre. Yet not all of his Greek books were in that language nor were they limited to Greek history; for example, he placed "Virgil [in] German" into this group; Alexander Adam's *Roman Antiquities* was also located in this set—a catchall of his books on classical literature and history. An even closer look at his list evinces the pride this upwardly mobile farmer, who acquired an education against the wishes of his father, took in his various gentlemanly occupations: the lexicons, his academy and college years while mastering classical languages; the textbooks, his time spent as a teacher; the law books, his legal training and practice; and his choral music books, his vocal attainments. The miscellaneous category tellingly included books not obviously marking career milestones: a bible, album, biography, moral tract aimed at youth, and lecture on the lungs—a testament to his ill health.[22]

Enoch Hale, a Newburyport printer, sometime editor, and fishyard laborer, conceived a more elaborate classification system for his sixty or so books, thirteen sets of periodicals, and hundreds of pamphlets. His catalog listed his collection alphabetically by subject and format. In contrast to Abbott, Hale lumped together foreign language lexicons within a diverse set of textbooks under "Sciences &c"; these books culled from his years at grammar school he filed neatly into one compartment, reflecting what he felt was a singular "period of about 12 years." Despite the many topical categories, this printer was ultimately more concerned with format (bound books versus pamphlets and documents) than genre or subject headings. He consigned most of his political works, for example, to the group "Documents, Pamphlets, &c" instead of "Political," which was reserved for books only. His political awareness led him to distinguish among national, state, and local items; he hoped to acquire more of these, for that "would give the collection most value, both as regards my own use, and its worth, intrinsically, in any other respect." He would refer to it as he would try time and again to succeed as a journalist. If his collection was a form of intellectual capital upon which he could draw as he made his way in life, then his catalog was like an account book.[23]

Dissemination

Books flowed from personal libraries into other people's hands and back through myriad acts of lending and borrowing. Literary circulation played into rhythms of everyday life—from visiting to enlivening working hours—just about everywhere people congregated. Some people even circulated material from afar by sending literary loans back and forth by express, mail, or courier.[24] Personal collections thus were ever on the move as they traversed land and sea and passed through many hands. Beyond being a way to have more reading matter than one could afford to purchase, nearly every act of circulation ultimately expressed personal relationships. Through it, literature bound lender and borrower together. One young Beverly woman was moved to write after an 1852 call, "Miss W. loaned me a book. I like her *much*."[25] Even in this typically terse diary entry, sociability and book lending are clearly linked.

Most lenders were also borrowers. This was true even for those with large libraries like John Park; while incapacitated with a sore foot in 1849, his doctor carried over *Researches into the Physical History of Mankind*. Two or more people sometimes generated a constant interflow of books, described by one female seminary student in 1836 as "the mutual accommodation system . . . [of] lend[ing] each other books to save buying so many." The well-read millworker, J. Edwin Harris, also struck up similar relationships with other operatives who exchanged with him at the workplace or boardinghouse. "Evening—Read Whittiher's [*sic*] Poems which I have borrowed of Miss Tibbitts," he recorded in 1858, "I have lent her Longfellows." When the back-and-forth flow was equal, both parties could at least double books at their disposal—the very logic behind membership libraries.[26]

Borrowing and lending, though related, were distinct. Borrowing was as practical as it was sociable; it was the obvious solution for a limited budget or for those who wanted to widen the array of books at hand. Those who had only meager formal libraries nearby—or none at all—had to depend on private collections. Most of the titles that Charles Cobb read in his tiny Vermont village, which had only a Sunday School library that he avoided, were borrowed from neighbors and local kin; because of their generosity, he dipped into *Don Quixote*,

"The Rangers," "old posts," and a *Classical Dictionary*. Institutional libraries, even if nearby, could not always supply specialized needs, such as those of lawyers who interdependently circulated law books among themselves. And even coveted titles might be tantalizingly out of reach. "[D]o you own Goethe['[s Faust and will you lend it to [my son]?" a Bostonian in 1837 asked her brother, and explained, "there is such a rage for German now prevailing that it is next to impossible to get such a thing from a public library." A surge in popularity created a long-term vacancy on the shelves. One need only follow the peripatetic life of the Mexican War narrative, *Chile con Carne*, at the Taunton Social Library. It spent no more than 30 of its first 200 days upon the shelves, as it circulated to about a tenth of the society's 280 members. Libraries could not always sate users' appetites.[27]

Instead of seeking specific titles, most borrowers were opportunists hungering for a varied diet of good reading materials. Often they simply wanted something—anything different from the usual fare—to read, taking advantage of whatever was at their disposal. "H. O. S. called in a few minutes, she said she wanted ~~some~~ a book to Read," one Beverly shoebinder confided to her diary, "so she [k]new where to come[,] for [my brother] J has so many books."[28] If some borrowers availed herself of friends' well-stocked library, others looked to on-the-job literary perks. "Mr Mann has a good library of useful books which I can obtain," a factory accountant explained of his boss in 1836; "I think now I shall not be in a great hurry to leave him."[29] Such was the power of lending.

From lenders' perspective, this power could be used either to personal advantage or for a social end——the good of employees, kinfolk, neighbors, and friends. Antebellum institutions, though tending toward social control, were still relatively disinterested lenders; influence was implied in the very selectivity of acquisitions.[30] While institutional librarians probably suggested books to patrons at times, the choice was ultimately that of users from limited options. Private lenders through social pressure wielded more power. They could deprive borrowers of any volition, pressing books into hand with orders to read them. Zealots who proselytized ideas in this way usually irked those coerced to borrow. "A particular friend of yours Mr— was in the store to see me," a Universalist clerk from Andover complained to his millworker fiancée in 1835; "he lent me some newspapers . . . (you probably know what kind) so that I might get right on my religious views."[31] Because not all ideologically motivated lenders were so adamant, most borrowers could decline loans. Still, pressure to conform, especially within small communities, was strong.

More often, however, lenders manifested a socially genial rather than self-interested spirit. They anticipated borrowers' needs—"carrying" literary loans to folks poorer than themselves, those bedridden, or in need of amusement. "This afternoon I took Henry & went up to Mrs Lunt's to carry some books for her husband & children," a Gardiner, Maine, widow recorded in her 1845 diary. "Her husband has broken one of the bones in his wrist," she explained. If some callers had missions, others simply wanted to share the bounty with friends who had similar reading tastes. "Call[e]d to see Mrs Lassell and carried her, 'Light and shadows of Scottish Life,'" a Providence stablekeeper's wife recorded in 1851; "It is a great favorite with me and I hope she will like it." It did not always take an interested party to come calling with a loan. Guests often went home from social visits with an unexpected literary prize tucked underarm and promises to return it, perhaps in exchange for another—and thus the relationship could be continued.[32]

Institutional lenders fulfilled similar social purposes as well, but indirectly, through borrowers' activities. People "tended out" to libraries as favors. Overworked milliner Martha Barrett recounted a busy 1855 day: "have been to the *Library* . . . Took *'Belford Regis'* . . . for myself and *'Farmingdale'* for Julia B. Have scarcely had time to think." Library goers also made the trip a social event, as did Lynn schoolteacher Mary Mudge, who in August 1854 "took a walk down to the Library" because a relative "wanted to get 'Drew's Travels'"; on the journey home the two "called at Mrs Arbers" where they were rewarded for singing with "some Pumpkin pie." Informants like Mudge seldom described sociabilities within libraries; like shoppers in bookstores, library patrons evidently transacted business quickly and quietly, unless librarians were willing to chat. Ancillary activities, such as the lyceum or membership meetings, evoked more descriptive journal entries. Nonetheless, the very term "social library," implied conviviality—membership within a group of people sharing a love of books. The pride that members had in belonging might be conveyed in recording an initial visit. "I made the following selection of books for my own perusal: Bryant's & Holmes' Poems," one young downeaster proclaimed. "These are the first books I have ever taken from the Hallowell Social Library." Though he did not mention circulation terms or whether or not he paid a fee or bought a share, many users did.[33]

As interpersonal lending depended upon custom or individual negotiation, rules regarding it, though seldom spelled out, were strongly implied, else the system would have easily broken down. Not surprisingly, these unwritten rules resembled those of institutions. One of the most important and obvious was returning materials in good condition and in due time. While institutions tracked their numerous transactions through dated charge records, personal lenders with few books and a limited circle of borrowers hardly needed to keep accounts. Instead, they expected borrowers would bring a book "back home" in good condition, in less than a year if no time limit was imposed, but they could tolerate lapses of up to two or three years.[34]

Lenders were less certain that their borrowers would remember what they took from whom. Aids to the memory, such as book labels with owners' names or inscriptions nudged the forgetful. Some more careful lenders and borrowers recorded transactions in diaries. While some borrowers kept lists, most simply scribbled a terse line amid records of other daily events. Lenders, by contrast, tended to be more systematic. Mary Poor devoted a page of her pocket memo-

ENCOURAGEMENT TO BOOK-LENDERS.

"IF YOU PLEASE, SIR, MASTER'S SENT BACK THE FIRST VOLUME, AND HE SAYS, WILL YOU BE SO GOOD AS TO LET HIM 'AVE THE SECOND?"

Figure 2: This cartoon lampoons unwary home librarians and book borrowers who dared to break the most important of unwritten rules: returning materials in good condition. "Encouragement to Book-Lenders," in *Harper's New Monthly Magazine* 2 (May 1851): 859. *Courtesy of American Antiquarian Society.*

randa to "Books lent"—a list of titles and names she crossed out as items came back:

> ~~Mrs Hewson~~
> ~~1 vol of Scotts~~' works.
>
> Mrs Haley—New wine
> in old bottles.
> ~~Mrs Box - Festus~~
>
> Mrs Barnard.
> True Christian Religion—
>
> ~~Mrs Winchester~~
> ~~David Copperfield~~

More elaborately, John Park dated his charges, frequently inventoried outstanding ones, and noted returns with an "X."[35]

Fearing unbearable shame, most people returned borrowed books. Charlotte Forten, an African American schoolteacher from Salem, declared in 1857 that she "should not have been able to meet" one lender "could I not have replaced" a lost title borrowed of her. Such diligence was instilled in childhood. A downeaster boasted that her six-year-old "feels an amusing responsibility when she has borrow'd books—to keep them nice & return them soon." These attitudes evidently carried over to some institutional borrowing. Of 14,560 individual charges made at the Taunton Social Library between 7 May 1856 and 3 March 1859 only two books were lost, and one of them, *Billets & Bivouacs*, was "Paid for" by the guilty party, a forty-three-year-old laborer. Over the years at venerable institutions like the Boston Athenaeum the number of lost books inevitably accrued, as examiners witnessed. Elliot Cabot found there in 1860 that "Those missing are chiefly among the books used by school boys & *clergymen*," of which his wife mused, "how satisfactory!" Paying institutional fines could signal negligent attitudes toward everyday informal borrowing. When in 1835 a Dartmouth College student was fined for a keeping a book "several days too many," he chided himself: "This is my luck,—no, it is my fault—it is a bad habit. I am always dilatory in returning books, even when borrowed of friends."[36]

Much delinquency was due to secondary lending—passing a borrowed book on to another person. Because the practice was so prevalent, institutions often forbade it and with good reason: borrowed books lent out again could easily vanish into the maze of social networks. One businessman who lent an expensive borrowed playbook frantically searched for it when the lender finally called it in. He entreated his sister to

go down . . . & ask Miss Sarah Woodbridge if she can find
Sheridans Plays which I lent to her sister Julia some two or
three years ago & if she can if she will give it to you. I borrowed the book & have been asked to return it. I have been to
every book store in New York & am informed that the edition
is out of print. If you get it please to send it to me straight.[37]

Fruitlessly scouring bookshops was penalty enough for lost books.

The risks of sending books out into the world could be reduced simply by
inviting users into the home library to read or look over the collection. Sometimes owners, if absent, gave keys to bookcases or library rooms to neighbors,
but, if present, more often let informal callers make themselves at home with
their books. "This afternoon visited Br. Ray at Br. Otis' and had the privilege of
reading some of the Books of Elder Otis' library," one pious Methodist reported
to his diary in 1830. Outsiders thus had open access to home libraries because
reading itself was a social activity—one associated with family life, visiting,
and entertaining guests—rather than a recluse's pastime. Indeed, through listening to books read aloud guests momentarily "borrowed" a text. "Miss Shepard
showed us some of her beautiful books, and read one or two exquisite pieces of
poetry," Charlotte Forten recorded after visiting her teacher with a classmate.[38]
Reading a selection aloud could lead to lending the book itself to the enthused
listener.

Reception

Reception of libraries differs from that of texts, which as been the area of so
much recent scholarly effort.[39] Texts are not all that are involved in library reception, for much of it concerns physically responding to a collection's "needs"
through storing and maintaining books, but also evaluating one's own or others'
holdings. Yet another type of response emerges from people's assessment of a
collection's ability to fulfill their needs, ranging from reference questions to
encouraging sociability.[40] Because evidence of library reception is often indirect, these categories are far from distinct. For example, much time expended in
preserving one's books suggests high regard for the collection. Stating that a
collection is valuable can be based on an unspoken judgment that it can solve
one's reference queries, but so might dedicating a room or shelving to volumes
to make finding answers that much easier. Then, too, esteem for one's books
might be expressed though proudly noting their display. And the success of a
library in advancing sociability can be discerned in descriptions of social activities taking place in proximity to it and involving it.

Whether home libraries contained lavish English editions or local newspapers, owners demonstrated their regard by lovingly tending to their collections
in much the same way that institutional librarians periodically "examined" books
and were otherwise charged "to take good care of all the books and other prop-

erty belonging to the Library."[41] The confluence of duties between the amateur and "professional" reflected, of course, practical and customary ways to safeguard books. That home librarians, however, voluntarily assumed these duties showed a deep valuation of their reading materials.

Covering books or sets of periodicals was probably the most basic form of preservation. Although wealthier folks (and even some workers) took their materials to binders or printers, many people were able—indeed, obliged—to do the job themselves. "Cover all your books," a Salem housewife enjoined her teenaged daughter away at school. Similar injunctions resounded throughout the region, and it was one commandment children and adults alike heeded. While none but skilled artisans could bind in leather, amateurs honed and passed down homespun methods. A needle, thread, and strong paper or fabric was all that was necessary. "This morning my little Henry Clay came into the office with his new Spelling book, and asked to have it covered," a physician in Chester, Massachusetts, wrote of his son; "I put on a strong paper cover, and fastened it with a needle and thread." Some binders swore by bonnet paper, others by wallpaper or brown wrapping paper. A Glastonbury farmwoman employed cloth she starched. These makeshift binders were used by schools and Sunday schools, and, frequently, several people combined efforts in book covering and labeling sessions that could take place in sociable settings in school, church, or home.[42]

Book owners jotted down other miscellaneous preservation techniques similar to any librarian's. Proper handling was the first line of defense: one bibliophile upbraided a college student for "not us[ing] with sufficient care" a book he was reading. Shelving or storage came next. Shelves and bookcases could be expensive; one Worcester resident commissioned a case for twenty-five dollars only to see it destroyed in a fire before it was completed. Some industrious home carpenters made their own simple shelves and racks or repaired broken ones, but many people simply set aside a table top, trunk, box, or closet for books. No matter how safe the haven or careful the user, well-used items were destined to wither. Charles Cobb was convinced that having his father stitch several dog-eared music books together with a leather needle would "save them from coming to pieces." Beyond that some people spoke of "overhauling"—a general inspection resulting in repair work and re-covering.[43]

More tedious and annoying than shelf inspections were cleansing overhauls of entire library rooms. "I never was more tired out," one Vermont woman protested after tackling the chore. Readers were temporarily displaced. The "ever dreaded anniversary has come!" John Park moaned when his wife tore up the parlor yet once again in 1847; "Take books and pictures down—up comes carpet—wash—scrub—I take refuge in a neighboring room." Because, as he explained, the job involved evacuating and rearranging books on shelves, it exhausted the laborer, usually a woman. "I was working hard all the morning, cannot ever remember when I have perspired so much," Salemite Harriet Low complained to her diary in 1831 when she "put all the books in order into the

bookcase" by "having to stoop to the floor to pick them all up." Her professional counterpart, Harvard Law Librarian Mellen Chamberlain, similarly felt
exhausted: "Tired & dusty from handling books all day, shall be pleased when
this work is over." Although the two, institutional and home librarians, inhabited different spaces—one public, one private—they did not live in worlds apart.
It was no coincidence that institutional librarianship, work akin to routine household chores, was often as undervalued and ill compensated as women's domestic labor.[44]

Fastidiously kept home libraries with well-lit fireplaces, sumptuous car-
pets, gas fixtures, and comfortable furnishings saw much domestic and social
activity not necessarily related to reading, but which fused library reception with
routines of everyday life. One housewife sewed in her library, sometimes spending the evening there with her husband. Other folks received guests, smoked,
conversed with friends, or even napped in theirs. Thus, libraries housed not only
books, but cherished memories. "I love to sit here in this cozy little library," a
young Connecticut woman explained, "it has very many pleasant associations
connected with it."

A good reception of home libraries, of course, might stem from time spent
alone with books. One engineer considered his library a "sanctum" for "conversing with authors long since dead." However, valuation was most often socially conceived—evident when social callers remarked upon the "very fine" or
"splendid" quality, or breadth of their host's collections. Charlotte Forten "wanted
to spend weeks" in Theodore Parker's vast "principal library" when she visited
his home in 1857. Her thrall mirrored that of visitors overwhelmed by "number-
less" books housed at great institutions, from Oxford's Bodleian to New York's
Astor. Home libraries in this sense conveyed cosmopolitanism as well as social
standing. Persis Andrews, living in Dixfield, Maine, assayed a provincial
neighbor's "style of living" thus: "Library &c compare," she emphasized, "with
those of good society in Town or City."[45]

Most New Englanders could not devote a room to their library even if they
had a surfeit of books. They nonetheless found an appropriate spot wherever
they could. Some hid old books in attics or trunks to preserve them from mold
and mildew, but they usually strategically positioned them to share living space
with users. One schoolteacher on a modest salary kept her small collection in a
bookshelf near a table by her stove; here she entertained her guests by reading
aloud. A traveling fiddler propped his music books atop a seldom used melodean
in the entry that served as both clothes closet and buttery. John Park's boardinghouse library spilled into his parlor and bedroom, in much the same way that
books worked their way into every nook and cranny of his life. "Some intruder
was in possession of our bedroom," he recorded the night a new tenant was
mistakenly shown his room. "The poor stranger said he . . . he seemed to have
got into a College!—alluding to my bookcases." The placement of books within
enclaves of domestic activity such as hallways was not only practical, it demon-

REVERIES OF THE CIGAR.

Figure 3: Sumptuously furnished home libraries such as the one this young man occupies were also the site of everyday activities, including resting, writing, smoking, taking tea, and daydreaming. "Reveries of the Cigar" in *Harper's New Monthly Magazine* 11 (June 1855): 6. *Courtesy of Hillman Library, University of Pittsburgh.*

strated that reading, rather than being distanced from everyday life practices, merged with them.[46] Sequestered books were often little used ones.

Perhaps because only the wealthy carved out a library chamber for reading, most people probably expected little more from their institutions, which were usually collections rather than discrete buildings with public reading rooms. Except for periodical reading rooms and the relatively few libraries that provided adequate provisions for study, repositories were generally places for storing and exchanging books, not for lingering or leisurely reading. While some partisans used reading rooms for political rallying, few library patrons remarked upon social interactions, and even less on interior spaces.[47] Uninviting library environments may account for this, but other factors were at work. For one, everyday reading was associated with quotidian spaces—the kitchen, nursery, garden, parlor, under a tree, on a rock by the seaside, or even in noisy public settings. "Went up to the railroad this morn," J. Edwin Harris wrote on 20 June 1858; "sat down and looked over Massey's Poems."[48] In addition, women secluded in the home necessarily combined domestic work and reading such that the phrase "sewed & read" appears frequently in their diaries. Most importantly, reading was a social activity often performed aloud, as much as half the time, to listeners.[49] Cloistered reading in libraries, even when feasible, could seem expendable, even undesirable.

Though institutions discouraged sustained reading, they might seem better able to afford answers to reference questions, but in reality they lacked services for doing so. Most people therefore relied on noninstitutional resources as a first resort. They enlisted knowledgeable acquaintances, as in the case of one Cambridge housewife referring to a neighbor as "our Reference Man" who "cannot be replaced like a Reference Book." Other querents went to private collections. "[S]topping in Charlotte's a few minutes . . . [,] looking in her dream-book to find the interpretation of a dream which I dreamt about her last night," a Normal School student recounted in 1850. And one could always consult one's own holdings. For example, in 1837 John Park noted a question that had arisen from a church group discussion: one participant "expressed a wish to know by what authority sacrifices and some other parts of the Mosaic ritual seemed to have been set aside before the time of our savior." The question stumped Park, but rather than go for answers to the nearby American Antiquarian Society, of which he was a member, he turned to his library: "after examining many of my theological books, I found it in Shuttleworth's 'Consistency of Revelation,' the second volume of Harper's 'Theological Library,' Chaper XVII.[th] and elsewhere." Park was not alone; in fact, in over 50,000 literary encounters our informants report, none other than those recorded by college students clearly show going to an institutional library with a specific reference question—not surprising in a time when most shelves or stacks were closed.[50]

Conclusion

By the mid-nineteenth century, the idea of the public, tax-supported library took hold as a way of providing all citizens with free reading materials. Although the concept was in theory a beneficent one, it both signaled and perhaps exacerbated the erosion of social practices that maintained the vibrancy of everyday literary experience among antebellum New Englanders. Although these practices intersected with institutional processes, they were not self-consciously "institutionalized," arising as they did from custom and quotidian realities. Most important, everyday practices were enacted by individuals tied by social relations, rather than by institutional bonds. Once the responsibility of enriching and maintaining literary experience for citizens fell primarily upon the state, the public institution was expected to appropriate the role once assumed by the individual book owner immersed within a dense social network. Public institutions as indiscriminate servants of the people may have been more impartial and effective in outreach than individuals, to be sure. But in the transfer of responsibility, reading lost some of its social meaning, for the locus of book exchange—an institution rather than a neighbor—became abstract.

At the same time, the public library would serve emerging needs that the formerly dominant informal social circulation may not have been able to address as easily. The century's socio-economic transformation toward industrialism and corporate agricultural distribution and processing had already severely strained social relations well before the public library became a reality. For people cut adrift by the changes from social networks of literary exchange, the public library promised access to reading material otherwise unavailable. Increasingly, too, new career paths were being forged that required a wide array of specialized information: public libraries could better offer this, too. Knowledge, in general, was expanding, fragmenting, and becoming ever more technical, while reference questions were becoming more vexing yet crucial to industrial and business enterprise.[51] Little wonder that collections mounted, reference services were extended, silent study and reading became the norm, or that library reading rooms proliferated.

Not only did public libraries come to serve the new order, they also helped to legitimize it, for they often stood as symbolic statements of a community's public commitment to "knowledge," especially in their encouragement of an associational form of sociability, in a way that private libraries could not. Thus, institutional libraries for a time ironically symbolized the very socio-literary relations they would eventually reconfigure and, in some instances, replace. Hence, incidents in which fires devastated or destroyed institutional libraries often elicited such extensive notice to suggest a personal sense of connection.[52]

Of the many conflagrations, none seemed as devastating as the one at the Library of Congress in 1851. Having watched his own library go up in flames, the tragedy weighed upon John Park perhaps more heavily than other observers. Beginning his lengthy account "Fire in Washington," he mourned the "60,000 volumes . . . destroyed," and concluded by noting that "Among the few articles saved is the original Declaration of Independence. Many of the books were rare works, and can never be replaced."[53] The sense of cultural loss was similar to that which motivated Park's own neighbors to jeopardize their own lives on that cold night in January 1845. As everyday literary practice became increasingly institutionalized, institutions became invested, for a time, with not a little of the social feeling surrounding those practices.

Notes

Research for this essay was undertaken with funding from a National Endowment for the Humanities Fellowship for University Teachers (1998-1999) and dual Honorary Visiting Fellowships at the Schlesinger Library at Harvard University's Radcliffe Institute (1998-1999).

1. John Park, "Fire at Brinley Block," undated description between 11 and 12 Jan. 1845, Journal, vol. 3, by courtesy of the Trustees of the Boston Public Library (hereafter, "BPL"). On the gift, see 7 Jan. 1845; on storage in the warehouse, 7 Sept. and 9 Oct. 1843. James Russell Lowell, *Conversations on Some of the Old Poets* (Cambridge, Mass., 1845).
2. Park, "Fire at Brinley Block"; see also entry for 12 and 13 Jan. 1845 in the same journal.
3. Michael Harris, introduction to Jesse H. Shera, "The Expansion of the Social Library," reprinted in *Reader in American Library History*, ed. Michael Harris (Washington, D.C., 1971), 45. Eugene Sue, *The Mysteries of Paris, A Novel*, trans. Charles H. Town (New York, 1844); George Campbell, *The Four Gospels: Translated from the Greek, With Preliminary Dissertations, and Notes Critical and Explanatory*, 2 vols. (Andover, Mass., 1837). John Park to Louisa Park Hall, 5 Feb. 1845, in John Park, Journal, vol 3., BPL, pp. 626-27.
4. Shera, "On the Value of Library History," 12; Wayne A. Wiegand, "American Library History Literature, 1947-1997," in *Library History Research in America: Essays Commemorating the Fiftieth Anniversary of the Library History Round Table*, ed. Andrew B. Wertheimer and Donald G. Davis, Jr. (Washington, D.C., 2000): 4-34, quote on 21.
5. Scholarship on "everydayness" ranges from Henri Lefebvre's *Critique de la vie quotidienne* (Paris, 1947), to, on the one hand, Pierre Bourdieu's *Outline of a Theory of Practice*, trans. Richard Nice (1977; Cambridge, 1993), and, on the other, to the *Alltagsgeschichten* school, whose work is introduced in Alf Lüdtke, ed., *The History of Everyday Life: Reconstructing Historical Experiences and Ways of Life* (Princeton, N.J., 1995). Cf. Michel de Certeau's *The Practice of Everyday Life*, trans. Steven Rendall (Berkeley, 1984).
6. D.W. Davies, *Public Libraries as Culture and Social Centers: The Origin of the Concept* (Metuchen, N.J., 1974), 14, ch. 2; Joseph F. Kett, *The Pursuit of Knowledge Under Difficulties: From Self-Improvement to Adult Education in America, 1750-1990* (Stanford, Calif., 1994), 40-47; Thomas Augst, "The Business of Reading in Nineteenth-Century America: The New York Mercantile Library," *American Quarterly* 50 (1998), 290-91.
7. John Y. Cole, "Storehouses and Workshops: American Libraries and the Uses of Knowledge," in *The Organization of Knowledge in Modern America, 1860-1920*, ed. Alexandra Oleson and John Voss (Baltimore, 1979), 364-84; Jacob Schmookler, *Invention and Economic Growth* (Cambridge, Mass., 1966), 196-215.
8. Sidney Ditzion, *Arsenals of a Democratic Culture: A Social History of the American Public Library Movement in New England and the Middle States From 1850-1900* (Chicago, 1947) and Jesse H. Shera, *Foundations of the Public Library: The Origins of the Public Library Movement in New England 1629-1855* (Chicago, 1949). On institutionalization, see: Ferdinand Tönnies' *Gemeinschaft und Gesellschaft: Abhandlung des Communismus und des Socialismus als empirischer Culturformen* (Leipzig, 1887); Stephen H. Riggins, ed., *Beyond Goffman, Studies on Communication, Institution, and Social Interaction* (Berlin, 1990); Jeffrey C. Alexander, *Real Civil Societies: Dilemmas of Institutionalization* (Thousand Oaks, Calif., 1998); and Michael Walzer, "The Civil Society Argument," in *Dimensions of Radical Democracy: Pluralism and Citizenship*, ed. Chantal Mouffe (London, 1992), 89-107.
9. Comparative data from the Federal Census of 1850 via the Inter-university Consortium for Political and Social Research, *Historical, Demographic, Economic, and Social Data: The United States, 1790-1970* [Computer file] (Ann Arbor, Mich., c. 1970s). William J. Gilmore, *Read-

ing Becomes a Necessity of Life: Material and Cultural Life in Rural New England, 1780-1835 (Knoxville, Tenn., 1989); David Jaffee, "The Village Enlightenment in New England, 1760-1820," *William and Mary Quarterly*, 3d. ser. 47 (July 1990): 327-46; Mary Kupiec Cayton, "The Making of an American Prophet: Emerson, His Audiences, and the Rise of a Culture Industry in Nine-teenth-Century America," *American Historical Review* 92 (1987): 597-620; Mary Kelley, "Read-ing Women/Women Reading: The Making of Learned Women in Antebellum America," *Journal of America History* 83 (1996): 401-24. Kelley hints at how the institutional histories of readers shaped the habitus of their everyday practice, as does Richard D. Brown in *Knowledge Is Power: The Diffusion of Information in America, 1700-1865* (New York, 1989), chs. 6-9.

10. Karen V. Hansen, *A Very Social Time: Crafting Community in Antebellum New England* (Berkeley, 1994); Ronald J. Zboray and Mary Saracino Zboray, "Books, Reading, and the World of Goods in Antebellum New England," *American Quarterly* 48 (1996): 587-622.

11. On the period's weak institutions, see John Higham, *From Boundlessness to Consolida-tion: The Transformation of American Culture, 1848-1860* (Ann Arbor, Mich., 1969).

12. James A. Healy, 6 Feb. 1849, Diary, Holy Cross College Archives and Rare Books (here-after, "CHC"). F. Allen Briggs, "The Sunday School Library," reprinted in Harris, *Reader in Ameri-can Library History*, 65-66; Shera, *Foundations of the Public Library*, 165; David Kaser, *The Evolution of the American Academic Library Building* (Lanham, Md., 1997), 7-8.

13. Carl M. White, *A Historical Introduction to Library Education: Problems and Progress to 1951* (Metuchen, N.J., 1976), 1-19; David Kaser and Ruth Jackson, "A Century of Personnel Concerns in Libraries," in *A Century of Service: Librarianship in the United States and Canada*, ed. Sidney L. Jackson, Eleanor B. Herling, and E.J. Josey (Chicago, 1976), 129-133; Arthur T. Hamlin, *The University Library in the United States: Its Origins and Development* (Philadelphia, 1981), 33.

14. Pierre Bourdieu defines habitus in his *Esquisse d'une Théorie de la Pratique précédé de Trois Études D'Ethnologie Kabyle* (Geneva, 1972), 31.

15. The three-part division of production, dissemination, and reception appears in Ronald J. Zboray and Mary Saracino Zboray, *A Handbook for the Study of Book History in the United States* (Washington, D.C., 2000) and in idem, "Transcendentalism in Print: Production, Dissemination, and Common Reception," in *Transient and Permanent: The Transcendentalist Movement and Its Contexts*, ed. Charles Capper and Conrad Edick Wright (Boston, 1999), 310-81. This essay draws from our recently completed book manuscript, "Everyday Ideas: Socio-Literary Experience Among Antebellum New Englanders." The material we used and our methods are described in our "Tran-scendentalism in Print"; we have since refined the data and added more. We have consulted 930 informants who wrote 2,816 letters, 798 diaries, and 185 miscellaneous documents, for a total of 3,799 items, with an additional 400 from the Civil War era, for comparison. Only six of the docu-ments consulted were in printed form and 110 were archival transcripts——all of the rest were in manuscript.

16. Martha Osborne Barrett, 22 Dec. 1854, Diary, Phillips Library, Peabody Essex Museum (hereafter, "PEM"); William Wordsworth, *Poems of Williams Wordsworth* (New York, 1855); Chris-topher Wordsworth, *Memoirs of William Wordsworth*, 2 vols. (Boston, 1851). On costs of books, see Ronald J. Zboray, *A Fictive People: Antebellum Economic Development and the American Reading Public* (New York, 1993), 11-12. Charles M. Cobb, 21 Sept. 1851, 20 Apr. 1851, 8 Apr. 1852, "The Recorder No. 21. Extra October 7, 1849," 19 Apr. 1850, 4 Mar. 1851, 27 and 31 Oct. 1847, 26 and 29 June 1851, 17 Sept. 1851, Journals, transcription, Vermont Historical Society (hereafter, "VHS").

17. Mellen Chamberlain, 1 Feb. 1860, Diary, BPL; Stephen Salisbury III, 9 and 10 Apr. 1854, Diary, Salisbury Family Papers, courtesy American Antiquarian Society (hereafter "AAS"); Park, 3 and 6 Jan. 1842, Journal, vol. 3, BPL; Susan D. Tucker, 20 Jan. and 11 Feb. Journal, VHS.

18. Joshua Edwin Harris, Journals, 1 Jan. 1856-13 Sept. 1856, 14 Sept. 1856-30 June 1858, 1860-1861, Joshua Edwin Harris Papers, Maine Historical Society (hereafter "MeHS"); I. Reynolds Hixon, 20 Dec. 1838, Diary, Old Colony Historical Society (hereafter, "OCHS"); James Barnard Blake, 15 Feb. 1851, Diary, AAS. Lucy (Pierce) Hedge to Mary Pierce Poor, 22 Sept. 1839, Poor Family Papers, Schlesinger Library, Radcliffe Institute, Harvard University (hereafter, "SL"). Jean Paul [Richter], *Jean Paul's Sammtliche Werke*, 4 vols. (Paris, 1836-1838).

19. Zboray and Zboray, "Books, Reading, and the World of Goods in Antebellum New En-gland"; Mary Pierce Poor to Lucy Pierce Hedge, 18 Apr. 1853, Poor Family Papers, SL; Aurilla Ann Moffitt, 13 July 1847, Personal Journal, OCHS.

20. Mellen Chamberlain, 6 Jan. 1847, Journal, BPL; Lucretia Anne [Peabody] Everett to Sarah P.E. Hale, Boston, 4 Oct. 1841, Hale Papers, Sophia Smith Collection, Smith College (here-after, "SSC"); Harriet Low, 22 Apr. 1831, Journal, transcript [original in the Low-Mills Family Papers, Library of Congress], PEM. Zboray, *A Fictive People*, Appendix 2, 196-210; Henry Petroski, *The Book on the Bookshelf* (New York, 1999), 12.

21. Jim Ranz, *The Printed Book Catalog in American Libraries, 1723-1900* (Chicago, 1964), 7-9.

22. Levi Abbott, Journal, 1841-1863, p. 200-201, New Hampshire Historical Society (hereafter, "NHHS").

23. Enoch Hale, undated December entry and 20 Dec. 1849, Diary, PEM. Cf. Pierre Bourdieu's use of "cultural capital" in his *Distinction: A Social Critique of the Judgment of Taste*, trans. Richard Nice (Cambridge, 1977), but also Stephen Greenblatt's metaphorical use of "circulation" in *Shakespearean Negotiations: The Circulation of Social Energy in Renaissance England* (Berkeley, 1986).

24. Elizabeth Edwards to Rebekah S. Salisbury, 11 July 1840, Salisbury Family Papers, AAS; John Park, 24 Feb. 1846, Journal, vol. 4, BPL; Anthony D. Currier to Mary Ann Loring [Currier], 7 May 1835, Mary Ann Loring Currier Letters, Andover Historical Society (hereafter, "AHS"); Mary Pierce Poor to Lucy Pierce Hedge, 28 Feb. 1855, Poor Family Papers, SL; Annie White to Cyrus C. Farnum, 24 Sept. 1843, Hooker Collection, SL.

25. Emmeline Augusta Ober, 2 June 1852, Diary, Beverly Historical Society (hereafter, "BHS").

26. Park, 18 Mar. 1849, Journal, vol. 3, BPL; James Cowles Prichard, *Researches into the Physical History of Mankind* (London, 1836); Mary Pierce to John Pierce and Lucy (Tappan) Pierce, 10 Dec. 1836, Poor Family Papers, SL; Joshua Edwin Harris, 12 Feb. 1858, Journal, Joshua Edwin Harris Papers, MeHS.

27. Charles M. Cobb, 3 May 1851, 30 Aug. 1851, 1-5 May 1850, and 16 Mar. 1851, Journal, VHS; Daniel P. Thompson, *The Rangers; or, The Tory's Daughter: A Tale, Illustrative of the Revolutionary History of Vermont, and the Northern Campaign of 1777* (Boston, 1851); John Lemprière, *Classical Dictionary, for Schools and Academies* (Claremont, N.H., 1838); Augustus Rogers, 31 Aug. 1847, 29 July 1851, 2 Apr. 1852, and 15 June 1853, Diaries, Rogers Family Papers, PEM; Sarah P.E. Hale to Edward Everett, 16 Feb. 1837 [?], Hale Papers, SSC; Benjamin R. Dean, Librarian, Taunton Social Library, Record of Books Circulated, 7 May 1856-3 Mar. 1859, OCHS. S. Compton Smith, *Chile con Carne; or, The Camp and the Field* (New York and Milwaukee, 1857).

28. Sarah E. Trask, 18 Feb. 1849, Diary, BHS.

29. I. Reynolds Hixon, 2 Mar. 1836, "Retrospective," Diary, OCHS.

30. On social control, see Dee Garrison, *Apostles of Culture: The Public Librarian and American Society, 1876-1920* (New York, 1979). Selectivity biases can be glimpsed in Briggs, "The Sunday School Library," 69-70; Hamlin, *The University Library in the United States*, 37; and Robert A. Gross, "Much Instruction from Little Reading: Books and Libraries in Thoreau's Concord," *Proceedings of the American Antiquarian Society* 97 (1987), 162-75.

31. Anthony D. Currier to Mary Ann Loring [Currier], 16 May 1835, Mary Ann Loring Currier Letters, AHS.

32. Olive Gay Worcester, 26 Oct. 1845, Journal, transcript, Swanton Family Papers, SL; Aurilla Ann Moffitt, 11 Aug. 1851, Personal Journal, OCHS. John Wilson, *Lights and Shadows of Scottish Life* (New York, 1851). Visiting in the region is treated in Karen V. Hansen, "Rediscovering the Social: Visiting Practices in Antebellum New England and the Limits of the Public/Private Dichotomy," in *Public and Private in Thought and Practice: Perspectives on a Grand Dichotomy*, ed. Krishan Kumar and Jeff Weintraub (Chicago, 1997), 268-302.

33. Martha Osborne Barrett, 6 Jan. 1855, Diary, PEM; Mary Russell Mitford, *Belford Regis; or, Sketches of a Country Town* (Philadelphia, 1835); Julia Caroline Ripley Dorr, *Farmingdale* (New York, 1854); Mary Mudge, 18 Aug. 1854, Diary, SL; William Allen Drew, *Glimpses and Gatherings During a Voyage and Visit to London and the Great Exhibition in the Summer of 1851* (Augusta, Me., 1852). Zboray and Zboray, "Transcendentalism in Print," 351-2; "X," Miseries of a Librarian," *New England Galaxy* 7:362 (17 Sept. 1824): 1; Carroll Norcross, 15 May 1852, Diary, Cargill-Knight-Norcross Families Papers, MeHS; William Cullen Bryant, *Poems* (Philadelphia, 1851); Oliver Wendell Holmes, *Poems* (Boston, 1851). George H. Clark, 17 Oct. 1846, Diary and memorandum book, Henry B. Dexter Papers, Rhode Island Historical Society (hereafter, "RIHS"); Ezra Warren Mudge, 5 Mar. 1833, Miscellaneous accounts, 1832-1833, and 17 Nov. 1834, Diary, Lynn Historical Society (hereafter, "LHS"); Levi Call, 19 Jan. 1861, Diary and accounts, NHHS; Christopher Keith, 25 Feb., 14 Apr., and 19 May 1858, Diary, Miscellaneous Manuscripts Collection, RIHS; Joseph Lye, 6 Oct. 1828, "A Diary of my daily occupations," [transcript], LHS; and Julius Catlin, 18 Mar. 1844, Diary, Connecticut Historical Society (hereafter, "CHS").

34. Several informants speak in terms of bringing the book to its home: Charles M. Cobb, 6 June 1852, Journal, VHS; Seth Shaler Arnold, 20 July 1849, Journal, VHS; Hannah Hicock Smith, 21 May 1845 and 15 Jan. 1849, Diary, State Archives, Connecticut State Library (hereafter, "CSL"); Harriet Low, 22 Sept. 1831, Journal, PEM. Lenders of newspapers seldom expected them back, for the custom of mailing them in lieu of letters made them the property of addressees.

35. Samuel May, Jr., to Richard D. Webb, 15 Apr. 1860, BPL; and miscellaneous book inscriptions, 1820s-1840s, throughout A.S.W. Rosenbach Collection of Early American Judaica, American Jewish Historical Society, Waltham, Mass.; Cindy Dickinson, "Creating a World of

Books, Friends, and Flowers: Giftbooks and Inscriptions, 1825-1850," *Winterthur Portfolio* 31 (1996): 53-66. Exceptional borrowers who kept accounts include Brookline minister John Pierce, "Book Lists," 1814-1849, Poor Family Papers, SL; and Emma Gammell, 12 Apr. 1851, Pocket Memorandum, 1851, NHHS. Mary Pierce Poor, list of books at back of pocket memorandum, 1850, vol. 19, Poor Family Papers, SL. Walter Scott, *The Poetical Works of Sir Walter Scott*, 6 vols. (New York, 1849); August K. Gardner, *Old Wine in New Bottles; or, Spare Hours of a Student in Paris* (New York and Boston, 1848); Philip James Bailey, *Festus, A Poem* (Boston, 1849); Emanuel Swedenborg, *The True Christian Religion: Containing the Universal Theology of the New Church* (Boston, 1833); Charles Dickens, *David Copperfield* (New York, 1849-1850). John Park, Journal, vol. 3, concluding pages, BPL; on periodicals lent by him extracted from these pages, see Zboray and Zboray, "Transcendentalism in Print," 351, Table 6.

36. Charlotte Forten, 5 Mar. 1857, *The Journals of Charlotte Forten Grimké*, ed. Brenda Stevenson (New York, 1988), 199; Persis Sibley Andrews Black, 12 Aug. 1849, Diary, MeHS. Benjamin R. Dean, Record of Books Circulated, 7 May 1856-3 Mar. 1859, OCHS; *Billets and Bivouacs; or, Military Adventures* (London, 1858); Elizabeth Dwight Cabot to Ellen Twisleton, 19 May 1860, Cabot Family Papers, SL; Cyrus Parker Bradley, 18 Sept. 1835, Diary, NHHS.

37. Brown University, "Powers and Duties of The Library Committee and Regulations of the Library," in Michael H. Harris, ed., *The Age of Jewett: Charles Coffin Jewett and American Librarianship, 1841-1868* (Littleton, Colo., 1975), 64; Shera, *Foundations of the Public Library*, 128-29. William Watson to Sarah Watson Dana, 23 Feb. 1838, Dana Family Papers, SL.

38. On invitations, see Frederick Lathrop Gleason, 1 Jan. 1861, Journal, CHS; Augustus Dodge Rogers, 12 Apr. 1847, Rogers Family Papers, PEM; Mellen Chamberlain, Diary and Commonplace Book, 5 June 1843, BPL; Park, 24 Jan. 1839, Journal, vol. 3, BPL; Annie B. Lawrence, 1 Apr. 1839, Diary, Lamb Family Papers, Massachusetts Historical Society (hereafter, "MHS"). On keys given, see: John Park, 1 Aug. 1844, Journal, vol. 3, BPL; Elizabeth Dwight Cabot to Ellen Twisleton, 22 Oct. 1854, Cabot Family Paper, SL. Osmon Oleander Baker, 9 Jan. 1830, Diary, NHHS; Forten, 27 May 1854, *Journals*, 62.

39. We summarize some of this scholarship, and add to it, in Ronald J. Zboray and Mary Saracino Zboray, "'Have You Read . . . ?': Real Readers and Their Responses in Antebellum New England," *Nineteenth-Century Literature* 52 (Sept. 1997): 139-70.

40. Persis Sibley Andrews Black, 21 Jan. 1843, Diary, MeHS; Mellen Chamberlain, 9 Oct. 1846, Journal, BPL; John Park, 10 June 1848, Journal, vol. 4, BPL; Ellen Wright Garrison to Eliza Wright, 19 Dec. 1860, Garrison Papers, SSC; Charlotte Adams to Asher Adams, 25 Feb. 1852, Chamberlain Adams Family Papers, SL; Cyrus Parker Bradley, 3 Mar. 1835, School Journal, and 3 Sept. 1835, Diary, NHHS.

41. Charles Coffin Jewett, "The Preface to the Brown University Library Catalog of 1843," reprinted in Harris, *The Age of Jewett*, 63.

42. Joshua Edwin Harris, 9 and 23 Dec. 1856, and 18 May 1857, Journal, Joshua Edwin Harris Papers, MeHS; Francis Bennett, 4 Feb. 1854, Diary, AAS; Cobb, 19 Apr. 1850, Journal, VHS; Sarah Smith (Cox) Browne to Sarah Ellen Browne, 25 Sept. 1856, Sarah Ellen Browne Papers, SL; Thaddeus Kingsley DeWolf, 10 Dec. 1855, Diary, New England Historic Genealogical Society (hereafter "NEHGS"); Hannah Hicock Smith, 17 Apr. and 4 July 1849, Diary, CSL; Selina Cranch Bond, 22 Mar. 1846, A Daily Journal, MHS; Mary M. Dawley, 1 Sept. 1857, Diary, RIHS; Forten, 14 Feb. 1856, *Journals*, 150; Olive Gay Worcester, 22 Mar. 1834, Journal, Swanton Family Papers, SL; John Park, 11 Feb. 1840, Journal, vol. 3, BPL; Eunice Hale Waite Cobb, 17 Jan. 1839, NEHGS; Sarah L. Edes, Diary, 1 Jan. 1853-31 Dec. 1853, AAS.

43. Mellen Chamberlain, 7 Aug. 1847, Journal, BPL; Stephen Salisbury III, 9 Oct. and 5 Nov. 1853, Diary, Salisbury Family Papers, AAS; Edwin Leigh Furness, 16 Dec. 1848, Journal, MeHS; Elizabeth Edwards to Rebekah S. Salisbury, 19 June 1840, Salisbury Family Papers, AAS; Helen M. Warner, 9 Aug. 1851, School Journal, NEHGS; Cynthia A. Congdon, 30 Dec. 1852, Congdon Family Papers, RIHS; Charles M. Cobb, 22 June 1851, Journal, VHS; Persis Sibley Andrews Black, 27 June 1852, Diary, MeHS; Augustus Dodge Rogers, 25 Aug. 1847, Diary, Rogers Family Papers, PEM; Francis Bennett, 18 June 1854, Diary, AAS.

44. Susan D. Tucker, 2 Nov. 1854 and 23 May 1851, Journal, VHS; John Park, 1 Nov. 1849, Journal, vol. 4, BPL; Harriet Low, 22 Apr. 1831, Journal, PEM; Mellen Chamberlain, 21 and 20 Jan. 1847, Journal, BPL. Shera, *Foundations of the Public Library*, 107; compare with Jeanne Boydston, *Home and Work: Housework, Wages, and the Ideology of Labor in the Early Republic* (New York, 1990), ch. 4.

45. Louise L. Stevenson, *The Victorian Homefront: American Thought and Culture, 1860-1880* (New York, 1991); Jane C. Nylander, *Our Own Snug Fireside: Images of the New England Home, 1760-1860* (New York, 1993), 107, 112, 225; Mary Lynn Stevens Heininger, *At Home With a Book: Reading in America, 1840-1940* (Rochester, N.Y., 1986). Cornelia D. Jocelyn Foster, 6 and 12 Mar. 1861, Diary, Jocelyn Family Papers, CHS; Annie B. Lawrence, 1 Apr. 1839, Diary, Lamb Family Papers, MHS; James Barnard Blake, 6 July 1851, Diary, AAS; Stephen Salisbury III, 11 Apr. 1852, Pocket Diary, Salisbury Family Papers, AAS; Frederick Lathrop Gleason,

11 Apr. 1860, Diary, CHS. Lucy A. Charnley [Bradner], 13 May 1857, Journal, CHS; James Barnard Blake, 25 Feb. 1851, Diary, AAS; John Park, 10 June 1848, Journals, vol. 4, BPL; Forten, 31 Jan. 1857, *Journals*, 187. Olive Gay Worcester, 7 Sept. 1838, Journal, Swanton Family Papers, SL; Frederick Lathrop Gleason, 19 Apr. 1860, Diary, CHS; Persis Sibley Andrews Black, 21 Jan. 1843, Diary, MeHS.

46. Helen M. Warner, 9 Aug. 1851, School Journal, NEHGS; James Amsted Brown, 16 May 1858, Journal, VHS; Sarah P.E. Hale to Edward Everett Hale and children, 28 June 1846, Hale Papers, SSC; Forten, 7 Mar. 1858, *Journals*, 290-91; Charles M. Cobb, 19 Apr. 1850, Journal, VHS; John Park, 8 July 1845, Journal, vol. 3, BPL. Zboray and Zboray, "Books, Reading, and the World of Goods."

47. Alexander Hill Everett, 16 and 30 Jan., 2, 14, and 15 Feb. 1839, Diary, Hale Papers, SSC; Julius Catlin, 2 and 3 Apr. 1840, Diary, CHS; Weeks, Jordan, & Co., to Caleb Cushing, 21 Feb. 1840, Caleb Cushing Papers, Library of Congress.

48. Abigail L. [?] Pierce to Lucy Pierce, 10 July 1841, Poor Family Papers, SL; Caroline Gardner Cary Curtis, 8 May 1859, Diary, 1859, Cary Family Papers III, MHS; Hannah Lowell (Jackson) Cabot, May 1837, Diary, transcript, Almy Family Papers, SL; John S. Gardiner to "Carl Rufus," 18 Nov. 1853, Gardiner Family Papers, SL; Mary Pierce Poor to Lucy Pierce Hedge, 2 Aug. 1859, Poor Family Papers, SL; Forten, 27 Aug. 1857, *Journals*, 253. Joshua Edwin Harris, 20 June 1858, Journal, Joshua Edwin Harris Papers, MeHS.

49. Ronald J. Zboray and Mary Saracino Zboray, "Reading and Everyday Life in Antebellum Boston: The Diary of Daniel F. and Mary D. Child," *Libraries & Culture* 32 (Summer 1997), 291; idem, "Transcendentalism in Print," 341.

50. Louisa Lee Waterhouse, 15 May 1839, Journal, 1839-1841, L.L. Waterhouse Papers, MHS; Helen M. Warner, 14 Dec. 1850, Diary, NEHGS; John Park, 2 and 3 Apr. 1837, Journal, vol. 3., BPL. Philip Nicholas Shuttleworth, *The Consistency of the Whole Scheme of Revelation with Itself and Human Reason* (New York, 1836).

51. On the fragmentation of knowledge, see, for example, the essays in Hamilton Cravens, Alan I. Marcus, and David M. Katzman, eds., *Technical Knowledge in American Culture: Science, Technology, and Medicine since the Early 1800s* (Tuscaloosa, Ala., 1996).

52. James Healy, 6 May 1849, Diary, CHC; Electa Kimberly, 14 Mar. 1857, Diary, CHS; William Willis, 8 Jan. 1854, Diary, microfilm, Portland Public Library, original in MeHS.

53. John Park, 24 Dec. 1851, Journal, vol. 5, BPL. Other reports of the fire include: Willis, 24 Dec. 1851, Diary, MeHS; and Susan D. Tucker, 25 Dec. 1851, Journal, VHS.

Reading *versus* the Red Bull:
Cultural Constructions of Democracy
and the Public Library in
Cold War Wisconsin

Christine Pawley

During the run-up to the November 1952 election, newspaper readers in Luxemburg, a small town in Kewaunee County, Wisconsin, encountered competing appeals for their vote. The Republican Party dramatized the choices facing the electorate. "Joe McCarthy Says: Give Ike a Good Staff to Control the Red Bull!" proclaimed a typical advertisement. "It's time we all saw Red! Vote Solid Republican November 4th." Depicting a pawing and snorting bull as "Communism and Corruption," the ad continued: "In China, Europe and the Middle East, the red bull has enslaved almost three quarter billion humans. . . . In Washington, the headlines tell of corruption and red influence in high places. . . . Contrast all this," it asked "with clean Republican government in Wisconsin. Free of deals and debt . . . free of communism and corruption!"[1]

The lines of the cold war had formed, as Republicans and other critics pointed to the Stalinist domination of Eastern Europe as evidence that although the Democrats had won World War II, they had lost the peace.[2] Fascism may have gone underground, but already some in politics and the media had found a new bogey: communism.[3] By the late 1940s, accusations of disloyalty were multiplying; in February 1950, Joseph R. McCarthy, Republican senator from Appleton, Wisconsin (a few miles from Kewaunee County), loaned his name to a phenomenon that was already under way.[4] Public rhetoric was infused with the vocabulary of patriotism and anti-communism, often presented as synonymous with

0026-3079/2001/4203-087$2.50/0   American Studies, 42:3 (Fall 2001): 87-103

democracy. Media reports helped to sustain a continuous sense of urgency. School textbooks also adopted language that reflected the new cultural climate. Whereas in the mid-1940s educational journals had stressed the need for international government and social-science education, four or five years later, calls for heightened patriotism, loyalty and anti-communism were common.[5] Religious leaders, too, stressed political issues in their sermons. As a young evangelical preacher at Protestant revivals, Billy Graham repeatedly hammered home a message that identified communism with Satan. Speeches by Francis Cardinal Spellman and the pages of the *Brooklyn Tablet* and the Knights of Columbus's monthly magazine *Columbia* reinforced the pro-McCarthy views of Catholic conservatives.[6]

But in the same *Luxemburg News* issues as the strident Republican advertisements, a public library column urged readers to consider all sides of a question before making up their minds in the forthcoming election. "Reading only one newspaper or one news magazine is a sure method of acquiring a closed mind on political issues," earnestly counseled library assistant Helen Arnold. "If we read *Time* and the *U.S. News*, we ought also to read the *New Republic* and the *Nation*. . . . [S]oon we'll find ourselves evaluating material, separating truth from that which is false, or hoping we are."[7] The essence of democracy, this writer implied, lay in the careful, reasoned consideration of alternative views in the light of printed evidence.

These two styles of rhetoric, each making use of a distinct cultural construction of the meaning of democratic participation, aimed for specific, practical outcomes. While McCarthyite advertisements urged voters to elect a Republican president and Congress, the library-inspired articles appealed for support on a different, but not unrelated, issue. In 1950, Kewaunee County and its neighbor, Door County, joined in a state-sponsored experiment to introduce library service to a rural area. Funded jointly by the state of Wisconsin and the two counties, the Door-Kewaunee Regional Library Demonstration established rural bookmobile service, expanded small-town library collections, and organized cooperative cataloguing and book selection. From early in 1950 to the end of 1952, county residents enjoyed access to not only a vastly improved book collection, but also films, pamphlets, a business information service, book talks, and children's story hours.

But now, in the fall of 1952, the demonstration faced a referendum. A "Yes" vote would ensure continued county funding. A "No" vote would dissolve the regional library and sell the bookmobiles. While official Republican campaign literature did not explicitly call for the end of the library project, its rhetoric was far from encouraging. "GREATEST DISAPPEARING ACT ON EARTH" screamed an advertisement in which a cartoon donkey waved a banner of WASTE over a sack of YOUR HARD-EARNED TAX MONEY. "NOW YOU SEE IT AND NOW YOU DON'T!"[8] By linking appeals to patriotism and fiscal conservatism, Republicans sent a message that did not bode well for the survival of the regional library.

On the other side of the political and cultural divide, library supporters argued that voting for the library made fiscal sense. With laborious—almost painful—logic, the library column spelled out the calculations:

> An 80 acre farm valued at $8,625 . . . paid $3.66 in taxes. With
> five individuals in the average family it meant a charge of 73¢
> per individual. Considering that a school age child used 27
> books and each adult used 2 books, that would mean that 58
> books were used per family. Dividing $3.66 by 58 meant that
> each book cost the family about 6.3 cents. The total value of
> the books used was $20.00.[9]

Less ponderously, 58 local teachers signed a plea; "We, the Rural Teachers of Kewaunee County wish to thank you . . . and sincerely hope you continue such a fine program at the Referendum vote in November."[10]

The Demonstration Area

When Wisconsin Free Library Commission (WFLC) officials were searching for an area for the proposed demonstration, Door and Kewaunee Counties seemed a perfect choice. Occupying the Door Peninsula (an area of outstanding beauty on Lake Michigan), the counties had an appropriate demographic profile—neither too rich, nor too poor. More important, local librarians and citizens had to be enthusiastic, and the municipalities willing to take part.[11] The chosen area had a total population just over 38,000, two-thirds of whom lived in rural areas. The median income for the two counties was also similar: $2,438 for families in Door County, $2,323 for families in Kewaunee County.[12] Local industry included ship-building in Sturgeon Bay and Kewaunee. World War II had brought boom-town conditions, as shipyards expanded their industrial output, but much of the region was still heavily rural, and even remote.[13] Off the northern tip of Door County lies Washington Island; there, and in other coastal villages, local inhabitants were engaged in fishing waters that could be turbulent and treacherous. The strait between Washington Island and the mainland—Porte des Morts (Death's Door)—was the site of many wrecks. But fishing communities were not the only inhabitants of northern Door County. For decades prosperous Chicago and Milwaukee families sailed up Lake Michigan to picturesque villages like Ephraim for the summer months. With these affluent visitors came cultural practices virtually unknown elsewhere on the peninsula: an art association, regatta, botany classes and concerts.[14] By 1950, northern Door County had an established tourist industry that attracted not only the wealthy but also campers and resort visitors.

But in the peninsula as a whole, the most common occupation was agriculture.[15] In the late 1940s, agricultural workers still dwelt in enclaves of the ethnic groups who had migrated there in the nineteenth century. In the south of

Kewaunee County, Czechs had settled in Tisch Mills and near Pilsen was a community of Poles. Centered on the Door County town of Brussels were Belgians (many of whom still spoke Walloon), while further north were groups of Norwegians, and Icelanders on Washington Island. German communities, too, were common in Kewaunee County and southern Door County. Often including several generations, families were tightly knit. Women shared farm labor, as did children.

The WFLC most wanted to reach these rural farm families. Cultural authorities defined the rural population's lifestyle—especially literacy levels—as a problem. "More than half the counties of the United States, all of them rural, are being depopulated," wrote Baker Brownell, professor at Northwestern University, in support of the WFLC's proposal.[16] Since the late 1890s the WFLC had sponsored traveling libraries that brought reading materials to some of Wisconsin's most remote areas.[17] But by the late-1940s, 23 percent of Wisconsin's population still lacked free library access, and rural literacy rates were also low. Most adults in the two counties had no more than an eighth-grade education, and often less. Among farm men and women in Door County, barely one-quarter had more than an eighth-grade education, while in Kewaunee County, this was true of only 18 percent.[18] Most of the area's farm children attended their local one- or two-room school for all eight grades. And rural children's school performance persistently failed to match that of their urban counterparts. The nearer a child came to living in an urban environment, concluded Eugene Rector, University of Wisconsin graduate student in rural sociology, the better his or her chance of successfully concluding the eighth grade.[19] But local people did not necessarily share this gloomy view. Some ethnic groups especially valued their freedom from government "interference" in America, on the grounds that their forebears had often fled oppressive economic and political regimes in their native lands.[20] They felt that their children were doing fine with a grade-school education in one-room schools that their local communities controlled. "One old German farmer used to sit right in the front row of the county board," recalled former regional library director Jane Livingston. "He had learned in school all right, and if it was good enough for him, it was good enough for his kids."[21]

Despite a local culture which tended not to value formal education, the Kewaunee County Board voted to fund the Demonstration. And the Door County Board, priding itself on being more "progressive" than its southern neighbor, felt it had no choice but to follow suit.[22] But not everyone rejoiced over this result. "It surely is a fine muddle when something like this can be put over without the taxpayer knowing until it has cost twelve to fifteen dollars a year in additional taxes," fumed a Luxemburg newspaper reader. "About the only thing we may be able to learn about this demonstration set up is that it will be very expensive reading."[23] And while library supporters strove to win over the local county boards, the WFLC waged a major funding campaign in the state legislature. Margie Sorenson Malmberg, librarian and Wisconsin Library Association activist, took a leave of absence from the Appleton Public Library to steer the legislation through both houses.[24] In September 1949, library officials and supporters were rewarded in their efforts, when, over Republican Governor Oscar Rennebohm's veto, the Wisconsin Legislature passed a law that allowed the WFLC to "establish a single demonstration . . . in a limited, predominantly rural area . . . now lacking an efficient coverage by existing library systems."[25] Thus for the first time, the State of Wisconsin agreed to provide funds in direct support of community library service. These state funds were to be matched by the communities involved. Otherwise, the law only set out general guidelines for the project. The details were left to the WFLC to work out in conjunction with the areas to be selected.

For Culture and Democracy: the Public Library

During the Progressive era, reformist librarians like John Cotton Dana had rejected an elitist, high-culture model of the public library as "storehouse of treasures." Instead, they advocated that public libraries play a role in promoting a more democratic and egalitarian society. However, during the 1920s, Progressive ideals declined as faith in government waned and business-oriented values reasserted themselves.[26]

The revival of "big" government during the New Deal and World War II gave fresh impetus to the cultural democrats. During the 1940s, cultural authorities continued to ponder the library's role in the light of the growth and influence of the mass media. At the center of the debate were faculty and researchers at the University of Chicago's Graduate Library School (GLS). A highly productive GLS professor was Douglas Waples, author of several influential studies of reading.[27] In 1942, Waples edited a collection of papers that assessed ways in which mass communication could help "preserve the democratic way of life."[28] Contributors included Bernard Berelson, former Waples student, and now working for the Federal Communications Commission.[29] Berelson pointed to print's effectiveness in "shaping" public opinion: "It is important that [print's] effects serve the public interest within the democratic framework. The public interest is best served when the people have a clear comprehension of the relevant alternatives in public policy."[30] Another contributor, Ralph Beals of the Washington, D.C. Public Library, argued that this clear comprehension could be achieved through public library use.[31]

Thus, library leaders like Waples, Berelson, and Beals looked to cultural institutions to revive the republican value of an informed citizenry and to restore democratic participation by all on an equal basis. In particular, they recommended that public libraries enhance their role as "Arsenals of a Democratic Culture" and providers of adult education.[32] But in a study of the 1940 presidential campaign, Berelson had argued that local "opinion leaders" exercised much more influence on public opinion than the mass media.[33] Opinion leaders were the politically alert; they read and listened to campaign material much more than "followers." To the friends, family, and neighbors who relied on them for advice, opinion leaders were a far more trustworthy source of information than the "more remote newspaper and radio."[34] Three years later, Berelson again made use of the concept of "opinion leader," this time linked with the public library. In 1949, Robert D. Leigh, University of Chicago political scientist, headed a team of social scientists that published the *Public Library Inquiry* (PLI), a study of American public librarianship, commissioned by the American Library Association (ALA) and funded by the Carnegie Corporation.[35] The PLI attempted to justify librarians' belief that the public library helped create and maintain democratic society.[36] It published its findings in seven volumes that focused on different areas and included Berelson's study of public library users, titled *The Library's Public*. Berelson argued that since the principal users of the public library were middle-class and well-educated opinion leaders, libraries should focus resources on serving this influential segment of the public.[37] However, many practicing librarians reacted with outrage. Berelson's phrase "opinion leaders" became a code for what some librarians argued was an elitist approach to library service. An unsigned 1951 *Wisconsin Library Bulletin* article sharply commented that the new Door-Kewaunee bookmobile service "supplies good evidence that those who may not be the 'opinion leaders' in the community enjoy the atmosphere of the public library that is transported in the bookmobile to the smallest village or community center."[38]

Faced with controversy over their role in the community, librarians struggled to realize the ideal of the public library as an influential, but local and non-elite, cultural institution. In an open letter to the Wisconsin library community written in 1947, John Chancellor, a recently-appointed WFLC member, wrote a strong condemnation of two adverse social trends that he felt constituted the main threat to democracy.[39] First was the tendency towards centralized organizations and the domination of economic life by large-scale monopolies. Second was the growth of commercially-motivated popular media industries, "powerful communication industries . . . dominated, for the most part, not by motives of enlightenment or social service but by a profit motive." Moreover, Chancellor complained, these operated "on the principle that more attention—hence more patronage—is gained if the appeal is to emotions, to selfish instincts, to the sensual and intellectually lazy sides of people tired from monotonous and uncreative work." Thus he intertwined the two elements of his critique. The mechanization and monopolization of advanced industrialization forced people into alienating and dehumanizing work, while popular commercial media responded to their desire for distraction from unsatisfying work offering commodified, prepackaged entertainment that filled their non-working hours. In seeking a remedy for these "dangerous tendencies," Chancellor called upon a reinvigorated public library—a "virile library system"—which might permeate "the everyday lives of the people in every city ward and every rural village with personnel and materials—printed, audio and visual—focused on making daily living more intelligent, creative, healthy and hence enjoyable." What is more, by providing an "entering wedge for other agencies to join in the same kind of effort and, by raising the tastes and hence demands of the people," such a library system might "eventually influence the great commercial communication systems in the right direction."[40]

The following year, the WFLC published a 64-page booklet that set out its vision for the future of public libraries in Wisconsin, and that echoed many of Chancellor's concerns.[41] For more than 50 years the Madison-based WFLC had consulted University of Wisconsin-Madison faculty for expert help, particularly in compiling specialized reading lists. This working relationship between the university and the state, characterized as the "Wisconsin Idea," was common in many different fields. Now, in its pamphlet *The Wisconsin-Wide Library Idea*, the WFLC renewed the Wisconsin Idea, stressing the state's and the university's responsibility for involving as partners-in-democracy all of Wisconsin's citizens, including those living in remote rural areas. The vehicle was to be the rural public library—but not the old "small recreational depot" that was "unfortunately the total picture of a library carried in the minds of most people and public officials today." Downplaying the value of reading for pleasure in favor of a more utilitarian approach, the WFLC emphasized the need for an "efficient, flexible institution for informal education, information, inspiration and recreation easily accessible and easily used by all people of all ages everywhere in the State."[42] The Door-Kewaunee Regional Library Demonstration was to spearhead this "democratic" thrust.

The Demonstration in Theory and Practice

The demonstration began in January 1950. The plan provided library services through existing "units" (permanent town or village libraries), plus two new bookmobiles that would make scheduled daytime stops every two or three weeks, with evening stops in larger communities. Bookmobiles would carry a wide selection of books—at least a thousand volumes—and also pamphlets, magazines, booklists, and reading suggestions. Commission officials envisaged two informal standards for the project's success. First was the type of reading materials that patrons would choose. Drawing a clear distinction between fiction and nonfiction, and echoing professional librarians' age-old concerns about the value of fiction, the WFLC intended the demonstration to emphasize nonfiction. Despite evidence—confirmed again and again in the 1930s by Waples and other GLS researchers—that public library users overwhelmingly preferred novels, the WFLC felt no qualms about imposing an "expert" view about what library patrons ought to be reading.[43] A focus on local democratic participation in the library as a cultural institution, did not, it seems, preclude steering readers towards what library authorities had already decided was good for them. Indeed, past failures at attracting readers to non-fiction would be overcome by "an able librarian . . . on hand to fit [the collection] to the serious interests of people."

After all, the WFLC argued, "Experience has shown that a community will use two or three times as much non-fiction as fiction if served by a bookmobile rather than a station." All in all, the WFLC felt that "the whole regional project may stand or fall on the quality of the bookmobile service."[44]

In fact, as Commission staff understood, the key to success lay in their own efforts at winning over the voting population of the two counties. County funding depended on the November 1952 referendum, and from the beginning, officials worried about a potential lack of adult use. In December 1950, WFLC Secretary Walter Botsford wrote to library consultant Gretchen Knief, "The thing that has bothered us for some time is what you warned us about and what we tried to prevent—that is, too much of the budget and the expenditure of time goes to the children."[45] The WFLC had identified adults as their main target for reasons of principle: after all, it was adults who would spearhead the renewal of democracy. Their ability to win adult users became their second yardstick as the WFLC anxiously monitored the project's progress.

However, not all project staff shared these two goals. While in their public rhetoric and private correspondence the Madison-based Botsford and Chancellor might emphasize non-fiction to adults, in the two counties themselves librarians had no qualms about focusing on children or supplying readers with the fiction that they preferred. Project director Jane Livingston as well as other library staff remembered growing up in rural Wisconsin and identified with the Door and Kewaunee children, many of whom, they said, were "starved" for books. "I was delighted with the job because the first thing that Jane said was, well you're going to be working with rural children who had never had library service," recalled a former bookmobile librarian, "and I grew up going to a one-room school, so I thought, oh what a great opportunity! It was the best job I ever had." Local librarians also recognized that vital voting support for the library came from *parents*—adults who wanted the service primarily for their children rather than for themselves.[46] Neither did local staff necessarily defer to the cultural authority of experts when it came to book selection. Although Commission fieldworkers made recommendations, local project employees and volunteers who might—or more likely, might not—have professional qualifications in librarianship decided what to buy for the collection. The fieldworkers were careful to advise, but not to impose: "We had great supervision and advice from the Madison people," a librarian commented. "They never interfered, but they offered to help."[47] As a source of cultural authority, then, the librarians hardly spoke with a single voice.

At first it seemed that WFLC concerns about who was using the library, and for what, were unwarranted. Overall circulation statistics indicated that the project was a staggering success. Between 1942 and 1948, circulation ranged from a low of 71,140 in 1946 and a high of 77,682 in 1944. But once the project got under way, these figures soared. In 1950, circulation showed an 83 percent increase over 1949. Two years later, it had risen again, to 222,141—an increase of 160 percent over 1949.[48] But these gross circulation figures failed to provide the sort of detail that the WFLC needed to gauge the likelihood of their political success. Were adults using the library to the extent that the library staff hoped? Moreover, what sort of reading was taking place? Were users checking out the "right" materials—those informational pamphlets, journals and nonfiction books that would justify Commission leaders' faith in libraries as vehicles for democracy?

Two sample surveys administered in late spring of 1951 and 1952 showed that WFLC fears that children's use would dominate were entirely justified. According to these more detailed studies, combining unit and bookmobile use, adults accounted for only about thirty percent of circulation, and once the figures were split between units and bookmobiles, the picture worsened. In the units, circulation divided evenly between adults and children. But in the bookmobiles (representing half of the total circulation) children constituted 88 percent of the total in 1951, and 91 percent in 1952.

Gender was yet another issue. In the early 1950s, existing research indicated that women and girls tended to use public libraries more than men and boys.[49] Was this pattern also true of the Demonstration's bookmobile users? After all, children could not vote, and the WFLC was certainly not interested in raising democratic participation only by women. Yet here too, the Demonstration's experience confirmed previous studies: 94 percent of the bookmobiles' adult users were women, who accounted for 95 percent of adult book charges. Adult men made only two percent of male books charges. So not only were adult users in a distinct minority, but adult males counted for only a tiny fraction.[50]

What these figures cannot tell us, of course, is why this is the case. A likely factor was that while the WFLC organized some evening stops, most took place during the day at times and places that were not convenient for men of working age—which included most males over the age of fourteen. Another possibility is that women took it upon themselves to pick out reading matter for their husbands.[51] Or perhaps the time periods of the samples made a difference; in the spring and summer, male farm workers would have little time for recreational or even informational reading. But maybe it was simply that these rural men did not buy into the library's rhetoric of civic engagement through reading, and neither did they develop strategies of library use. Like the German farmer who felt his own education set an adequate standard for his children, they perhaps saw no need, and had no desire, for the cultural goods that the bookmobiles contained.

Adult Reading Choices[52]

Whatever the underlying reasons, the WFLC had evidently been correct in their fear of low adult use. And among the 600 charges made by married women patrons whose records have survived, reading choices also failed to fulfil the WFLC's hopes. The presence of an expert librarian on the bookmobile, the experts believed, would channel adult readers towards educative pamphlets and serious non-fiction. But conforming to previously-revealed patterns, Door-Kewaunee women patrons overwhelmingly checked out fiction. A favorite author was Kathleen Thompson Norris, a prolific novelist of Irish Catholic descent who wrote stories that idealized family life and the role of women as mothers of many children.[53] Close behind Norris were other best-selling women novelists— Faith Baldwin, Frances Parkinson Keyes, Mazo de la Roche and Daphne Du Maurier—all of whom set their stories against a backdrop of romanticized middle- and upper-class family life, sometimes in the historical past.

The nonfiction that the women patrons borrowed ignored current political issues; rather, they echoed the domestic themes that dominated their favorite fiction. By far the most popular genre of nonfiction consisted of home-centered craft books with titles like *Painting Patterns For Home Decorations*, *How To Beautify And Improve Your Home* and *Use and Care of Furniture*. Cookbooks and manuals of food preparation, too, were popular, including *Betty Crocker's Picture Cookbook* (one of the best-selling cookbooks of all time) and *Home Freezing For Everyone*.[54] Women patrons also checked out sewing and knitting titles, like *The Complete Book of Knitting* and *Sewing For The Home*, in addition to books about gardening, like *Garden Flowers In Color* and *Grow Your Own Vegetables*. Among periodicals, the most popular was *Good Housekeeping*, followed by *House and Garden* and the *Ladies Home Journal*.

Cultural historians continue to debate the nature and meaning of the 1950s preoccupation with hearth and home, especially for women. This period is often depicted as a era when Rosie the Riveter was steered back towards containment in a domestic cage (though perhaps not very successfully, and not for long).[55] Preoccupation with domesticity was also reflected by the spread of suburbia: newly-built single-family homes on the outskirts of cities, equipped with up-to-date household appliances and furnishings. Popular magazines, television shows, and advertisements portrayed the model family as focused on the home, raising children, and spending time together around the TV or the backyard barbecue. The middle-class domestic idyll depended on a home-based wife and mother whose role was to control the family's operations from the kitchen—now relocated from the back of the house to a central and commanding position.[56] This tranquil vision would seem to be at odds with the political "reality" of the atomic age and the Cold War. But historians have pointed to the phenomenon of domestic containment as forming an "ideological duality" with the anti-communist hysteria of the late-1940s and early-1950s. "McCarthyism," comments Elaine Tyler May, "was fueled, in large measure, by suspicion of the new secularism, materialism, bureaucratic collectivism, and consumerism that epitomized not only the achievement but the potential 'decadence' of the New Deal liberalism."[57]

Despite the apparent ubiquity of the suburban ideal, Door Peninsula women must have struggled to relate such popular images to their own lived reality.

Local newspapers carried some advertising of consumer products for the home, but for many rural residents, these must have seemed hopelessly out of reach, with the price of even a "low" end bedroom suite at about half the average monthly wage. Most Door Peninsula families lived in traditional homes unlike the ranch-style houses that dominated the new housing developments springing up around the nation's large cities. While most had electricity, many still lacked indoor plumbing. And few rural women had escaped from the endless kitchen and farm chores even during the war years.

Yet, despite their focus on domestic concerns, far from reinforcing traditional gender roles, the women's library choices had the potential to open up new worlds, just as cultural authorities believed, though not in the way that they intended. Instead of choosing to educate themselves as citizens, the women borrowers opted for fiction, instruction manuals, and popular magazines that connected them to the middle-class domestic consumerism preoccupying suburbanites. But rather than induce a mindless conformity to corporate-generated values, these women's reading experiences may have represented multiple small acts of resistance. First, like Janice A. Radway's romance readers, the Door-Kewaunee women, carving out part of the day for the personal pleasure of reading a novel, departed from the domestic ideal.[58] In the traditional, patriarchal families that in the prewar years constituted the norm on the rural Door Peninsula, finding time for emotional "replenishment" must have been a rarity. Second, as Jessamyn Neuhaus points out, paradoxically, the very act of reading domestic instruction manuals prompts a reappraisal of traditional gender roles. By "stating assumptions about women's lives," cookbooks, gardening and sewing books "left room for those 'assumptions' to be questioned."[59] The manuals and magazines introduced women to new ways of homemaking, ways that differed from the practices of their mothers and grandmothers, and opened up space for the exercise of individual taste and difference.

Democracy in Action: the Referendum

On November 4, 1952, the nation went to the polls to elect a new president. At the same time, citizens of Door and Kewaunee Counties voted on funding for the Regional Library Demonstration, the final test of the WFLC's democratic partnership principle. The referendum asked simply, "Shall Kewaunee [or Door] county continue to participate in the Door-Kewaunee Regional library or some similar library?"[60] Although the results would be non-binding, county supervisors were widely expected to base their decision about the library's future on the referendum as a statement of the people's will.

From the beginning, the WFLC had made strenuous efforts to "market" the project to voters, legislators, and other professionals. Promotional pamphlets, spots on local radio stations, and articles in newspapers and the state library literature contributed to the publicity campaign. Satisfied bookmobile users added their two cents' worth. Wrote Mrs. John Marnard of Luxemburg in March 1951:

> Where else can one obtain so much for so little? Children's books—so many, so interesting—adult books—romance, adventure, mystery,—fiction of all kinds; cook books, books of manual arts, science, biography—name it and you can have it. ... Perhaps one reason I am so enthusiastic over the Bookmobile service is because books are so expensive. Very few of us can buy all the books we want to read, and there are so very many books to which one only wants to refer.[61]

The WFLC also sent out an evaluative questionnaire to gauge the reactions of local library boards. Here, too, replies seemed positive. A trustee wrote from Washington Island, "I am 100 percent in favor of the regional plan. Prior to it, the library service was extremely limited. We were only able to have our library open one day a week, and during January-February found it necessary to close completely." However, under the Regional system, the library could be open three afternoons and evenings the year around.[62]

Local newspapers loaned their support. *Algoma Record-Herald* editors appealed to their readers' civic duty, as well as to their sense of good financial management: "Each of us as intelligent, progressive citizens should look at the proposal from the standpoint of costs . . . and also on the other side of the ledger—just what is the Regional library giving us in return for our hard-earned tax dollars—it's as simple a business proposition as that." On the other hand, some things were beyond price; "Consider what good your children of school age, to say nothing of adults, are getting from the bookmobile service. Can it be measured entirely in cold dollars?," the editors wrote. ". . . We think that you should vote 'yes' on this question . . . and we make no bones about it." The Algoma Woman's Club also voiced its approval of the Demonstration, claiming that the Algoma library under the regional plan had "gained everything and lost nothing."[63]

Yet in most people's minds, the regional library was not the election's main focus. The big question was, who would be the new president: Republican Dwight D. Eisenhower or Democrat Adlai Stevenson? The residents of Door and Kewaunee County can have had little doubt over the issue. The area was traditionally Republican, and Joe McCarthy was virtually their next-door neighbor. Indeed, in a record turnout, 81 percent of Door County and 77 percent of Kewaunee County electors voted for Eisenhower.[64] And although in Wisconsin as a whole, McCarthy was the least successful of the Republican candidates, he was re-elected by 80 percent in Door County, and by 77 percent in Kewaunee County. "A whopping all-time record-breaking vote was recorded Tuesday as Kewaunee county joined the Republican parade . . . . The county voted Republican right down the line," proclaimed the *Algoma Record-Herald*.[65]

Despite the Republican clean sweep, at a first sight the referendum result looked like good news for the library supporters, receiving as it did an overall favorable majority of 910. To succeed, however, it needed a majority in both counties. "Only three Kewaunee county units favored the library—Algoma, Casco village and Luxemburg village," reported the *Algoma Record-Herald*. "Each of the ten towns gave it a resounding slap in the face and Kewaunee City rejected it 652 to 653—just one vote difference."[66] Despite devoting a disproportionate amount of resources to adult services, despite extensive lobbying, and the creative use of publicity, including radio spots, the WFLC had failed to carry Kewaunee County.

The library had faced formidable opposition as traditional parsimony and dislike of government intervention combined with Red Scare rhetoric. "One of the main reasons our Grand Parents came to a 'Land of the Free' is to get away from Gravey Taxes," wrote Clarence Antholt and Gordon Mallien of Brussels in a paid newspaper advertisement. "A 'yes' vote on the Bookmobile issue means favoring the hardships they left."[67] A Kewaunee resident wrote an open letter to a county supervisor that was published in the *Algoma Record-Herald*; "I heartily agree with the stand you have taken in voting negatively on the Door-Kewaunee Regional Library. Why? Because the cost of it was born by so many people and the benefits realized by so few." In this voter's view, the problem was a matter of competing demands on the public purse. Moreover, the prime threat to democracy came not from the lack of citizen participation identified by the WLFC and other cultural authorities, but from international factors beyond American borders highlighted by the cold warriors. "[T]he past decade did not . . . in view of the present and future world conditions, warrant such an enormous cash outlay. . . . Due to the instability of international relationships we may be called upon to defend our freedoms more vigorously than ever before, against an indomitable foe." The Door-Kewaunee Regional Library Demonstration was in direct competition with military spending, and there was no doubt as to which should have priority:

> If we fail, all our Bookmobiles and our entire educational system may be of little consequence. If God will that we survive this crisis . . . then, and only then we shall return to Traveling Libraries and improvements in our educational program. If we are called upon to reimburse a military commensurate with an all out war effort, the tax burden will be great enough without also having to pay for a bookmobile service.[68]

The Long Run

Bitterly disappointed, the WFLC tried to put a brave face on their defeat. Comforting themselves with the truly remarkable circulation increases, they argued that the Demonstration was indeed a success. Others, too, were disappointed. While the Door County supervisors, following their referendum mandate, quickly appropriated $30,000 to establish a Door County regional library, efforts to persuade the Kewaunee supervisors to follow suit came to no avail. The *Algoma Record Herald*, in an implied criticism of the voters' short-sightedness, reported on low educational attainment in Kewaunee County; "We blush as we write this. Kewaunee county residents over 25 years of age have the lowest education median in the state with half having completed 8.4 years."[69] Later in December a delegation of teachers argued for two hours in favor of some kind of rural library service in Kewaunee County, but despite their best efforts, the bookmobile service was dead.[70]

Yet as the library records show, those whom both sides—cold warriors and cultural authorities—were trying to win over, that is, the residents of the two counties, were convinced by the rhetoric of neither. Overall circulation figures proved that, contrary to conservative contentions, the library did reach large numbers of people. The bookmobile service played a considerable part in the lives of rural children as well as their teachers and mothers. But the benefit they derived from the library services was not what cultural authorities had hoped. Rather than supporting the cultural democracy role of the library, patrons valued the library for something less elevated: its supply of popular fiction and consumer-oriented magazines.

On the Door Peninsula the public library continued to grow in the local community. In the decades following the referendum, Door County continued to fund its bookmobile, helping to raise, as Jane Livingston has commented, a "generation of readers."[71] Permanent community libraries continued to expand in Door County, resulting in the present system headquartered in Sturgeon Bay, with its eight branches in smaller towns and villages. In 1971 the Sturgeon Bay Library moved out of its 1908 Carnegie building and into new quarters, built with the aid of a successful local fund-raising drive.

In Kewaunee County, despite the disappearance of the bookmobile after 1952, the two existing permanent libraries in Algoma and Kewaunee have prospered, and some villages are now considering establishing their own library buildings and collections. Other opportunities for Peninsula inhabitants to participate in print culture have also increased. Several communities boast bookstores. The one-room schools have disappeared, replaced by large consolidated systems to which the rural children travel daily by bus. These schools have their own library-media centers, staffed by professionals and accessible to students and teachers on a daily basis.

It is in public libraries' fundamental nature that they should struggle to balance contradictory demands, continuously faced as they are with redefining their role and justifying their expenditure of local resources. The ideologies that underlie their claim to cultural authority and that focus on civic participation perpetually vie with a populist imperative that requires them to identify and respond to consumer demand. In their professional rhetoric, public library experts continue to appeal to the same cultural democratic principles articulated since the Progressive Era. But in their everyday use, libraries are still dominated by women and children who prefer popular materials above anything else that they have to offer. In recent decades, Door Peninsula elected officials have recognized the cultural and monetary value of recreation through provision of an infrastructure that supports a seasonal flood of visitors through the southern peninsula to northern tourist destinations. But local tax support of the recreational reading choices of the whole region's year-round inhabitants can also represent a democracy of cultural value, a reality well understood by local librarians. At the turn of the twenty-first century, in many parts of the United States, when federal, state, and local tax measures (often initiated through local referenda) have resulted in public institutions like schools and libraries finding themselves in severe financial straits, the prevailing political climate appears to favor individual consumer expenditure over the collective provision of public goods. An expert, professional rhetoric that continues to privilege utilitarian, informational genres at the expense of voters' preference for recreational reading at the public library is unlikely to reverse this trend.

Notes

1. *Luxemburg News*, 30 October 1952.

2. David Halberstam, *The Fifties* (New York, 1993), 9.

3. Since the Soviet nuclear capability provided the Eastern Bloc countries with virtual immunity from actual attack, their most strident American critics found a surrogate in those fellow-Americans who most sympathized with communism. See Stephen J. Whitfield, *The Culture of the Cold War* (Baltimore, 1991), 9.

4. Halberstam, *The Fifties*, 49.

5. Paul Boyer, *By the Bomb's Early Light: American Thought and Culture at the Dawn of the Atomic Age* (Chapel Hill, 1994), 322-27.

6. Whitfield, *Culture of the Cold War*, See especially ch. 4, "Praying: God Bless America," 77-100.

7. *Luxemburg News*, 23 October 1952.

8. *Luxemburg News*, 16 October 1952.

9. *Luxemburg News*, 30 October 1952.

10. *Luxemburg News*, 18 September 1952.

11. Anne Farrington. "Wisconsin's First Regional Library," *Minnesota Libraries* 16, no. 7 (1950): 201.

12. U.S., Department of the Interior, Bureau of the Census, *Census of Population: 1950*, Volume II "Characteristics of the Population, Part 49: Wisconsin" (Washington, D.C., 1952), 49-13; 49-112.

13. William F. Thompson, *Continuity and Change, 1940-1965*, vol. VI, *The History of Wisconsin* (Madison, Wis., 1988), 96.

14. U.S., W.P.A., Federal Writers' Program, *Wisconsin: A Guide to the Badger State* (New York, 1941), 317.

15. *Census of Population: 1950*, Volume II, 49-96.

16. Baker Brownell, "Foreword," in *The Idea in Action: A Report on the Door-Kewaunee Regional Library Demonstration, 1950-1952* (Madison, Wis., 1953), 5.

17. Some traveling libraries were also sponsored, especially in the early days, by private individuals or organizations such as women's clubs. See Christine Pawley, "Advocate for Access: Lutie Stearns and the Traveling Libraries of the Wisconsin Free Library Commission, 1895-1914," *Libraries and Culture* 35, no. 3 (2000), 434-458.

18. *Census of Population: 1950*, Volume II, 49-122.

19. Franklin Eugene Rector, "Social Correlates of Eighth Grade Attainment in Two Wisconsin Counties" (Unpublished dissertation, University of Wisconsin, Madison, 1954), 21-22; 107.

20. Robert C. Nesbit, *Urbanization and Industrialization, 1873-1893*, vol. III *The History of Wisconsin* (Madison, Wis., 1985), 45; 52.

21. Interview, 23 October 2000.

22. *Ibid.*

23. Alvin M. Cherney to the editor, *Kewaunee Enterprise*, 13 June 1950.

24. John Chancellor, "The Local Solution" in *The Idea in Action: a Report on the Door-Kewaunee Regional Library Demonstration, 1950-1952* (Madison, Wis., 1953), 7.

25. *Wisconsin Library Bulletin* 47, no. 2 (1951): 39.

26. The Progressive era is usually defined as lasting from about 1890 to 1920. See Kevin Mattson, "The Librarian as Secular Minister to Democracy: The Life and Ideas of John Cotton Dana," *Libraries and Culture* 35, no. 4, (2000): 514-534, especially 520-21.

27. John V. Richardson Jr., "Douglas Waples (1893-1978)," *Journal of Library History* 15, no. 1 (1980): 76-83. Books by Waples include *People and Print: Social Aspects of Reading in the Depression* (1937), and *Libraries and Readers in the State of New York* (1939).

28. Douglas Waples, (ed.), *Print, Radio and Film in a Democracy* (Chicago, 1942), v. Two experts in the emerging field of communications, political scientist Harold D. Lasswell and sociologist Paul F. Lazarsfeld, contributed essays to this collection. Lasswell was head of war communications research at the Library of Congress from 1939 to 1945, while Lazarsfeld directed the Bureau of Applied Social Research at Columbia University from 1940 to 1950.

29. Berelson had worked as a librarian before he entered the GLS in 1938. After working for the FCC, he joined the Bureau of Applied Social Research at Columbia University in 1944, and in 1946 joined the faculty of the GLS, eventually becoming its dean.

30. Bernard Berelson, "The Effects of Print Upon Public Opinion" in *Print, Radio and Film in a Democracy*, ed. Waples, 63.

31. Ralph A. Beals. "Implications for Communications Research for the Public Library," in *Print, Radio and Film in a Democracy*, ed. Waples, 160; 173

32. The title of a well-known history of public libraries written in the 1940s: Sidney Ditzion, *Arsenals of a Democratic Culture: A Social History of the American Public Library Movement in New England and the Middle States from 1850 to 1900* (Chicago, 1947).

33. Paul F. Lazarsfeld, Bernard Berelson, and Hazel Gaudet, *The People's Choice: How the Voter Makes Up His Mind in a Presidential Campaign* (New York, 1968).

34. *Ibid*, 51, 155.

35. The seven volumes included *The Library's Public* by Bernard Berelson; *The Public Librarian*, by Alice Bryan; *The Public Library in the Political Process*, by Oliver Garceau, studies on government publications, the book industry, and the information film, and *The Public Library in the United States*, by Robert D. Leigh.

36. The PLI identified what they called the "Library Faith" in the following terms: "Reading books in order to learn is good and useful; the public library contributes to democracy because it facilitates reading books by providing free access; it is a source of knowledge for an informed citizenry, on which the continuation of democracy depends." See Douglas Raber, *Librarianship and Legitimacy: The Ideology of the Public Library Inquiry* (Westport, Conn., 1997), 39, 67.

37. Bernard Berelson, *The Library's Public* (New York, 1949), 127, 130.

38. *Wisconsin Library Bulletin* 47, no. 2 (1951): 40.

39. Although the Wisconsin Free Library Commission had a salaried staff headed by the Commission Secretary, overall authority rested with a volunteer board. In 1949, this included three *ex officio* members and four citizens appointed by the Governor. The *ex officio* members were: John Callahan (State Superintendent); Edwin B. Fred (President, University of Wisconsin) and Clifford L. Lord (Director, State Historical Society). Citizen members were: Ella Veslak, librarian of Shawano, Wisconsin; William J. Deegan Jr, City Manager of Superior, Wisconsin; John P. Barton, University of Wisconsin-Madison Professor of Rural Sociology; and John Chancellor. Chancellor had been a public librarian in New York and New Haven before moving to Wisconsin and taking up farming.

40. John Chancellor, "An Open Letter from a New Commission Member," *Wisconsin Library Bulletin* 43, no. 9 (1947): 143-144.

41. Drawing on its historical antecedents, the Commission titled the pamphlet, *The Wisconsin-Wide Library Idea for Voluntary Education through Reading: A detailed but tentative statement from the Wisconsin Free Library Commission.*

42. *Wisconsin-Wide Library Idea*, 3

43. In *What People Want to Read About: A Study of Group Interests and a Survey of Problems in Adult Reading* (published by a conjunction of cultural authorities—the American Library Association with the University of Chicago Press, in 1931), Douglas Waples and co-author Ralph W. Tyler established a hierarchy of reading priorities among adults, and claimed that "More people read to forget than to learn." But, they went on, "[T]he problem of making recreatory reading more valuable is essentially the same as the problem of making informational reading more attractive." In other words, "information reading" was intrinsically more valuable than "recreatory reading," but if it could only be made as attractive as fiction, adults would readily turn to this worthier genre.

44. *Wisconsin-Wide Library Idea*, 17-20.

45. Walter S. Botsford to Gretchen Schenk, December 22, 1950. Archives, State Historical Society of Wisconsin, Series 1967, Box 110.

46. Interviews, 22 October 2001, 14 March 2001.

47. *Ibid*.

48. *The Idea in Action*, 31.

49. For a comparison of studies on library users' demographic characteristics, see Berelson, *The Library's Public*, 19-50.

50. Bookmobile patrons recorded their own circulation information on yellow slips of paper, on which were preprinted spaces for author, title, patron name and address, date and so on. The great majority of these slips were probably destroyed at the time the Demonstration ended, or even before. But some have survived. Packed away in the Commission archives can be found about 6,000 circulation slips—representing only a small fraction of those filled out—but providing the basis of a database containing 5,819 usable records. About one-third (1,935) of the records are undated. The dates of the remaining two-thirds (3,885) cluster into two groups. The smaller group (1,694 or 44 percent) represents materials borrowed from the bookmobile around the end of October, and the beginning of November 1950. The larger cluster (2,191 or 56 percent) represents books borrowed in July 1951. A database of these records contains a single file consisting mainly of fields of data taken directly from the yellow slips themselves: patron name, book title, date, and so on. The total number of individual users was 1,816. But because it was not possible to determine from all these individuals whether they were male or female, young or old, the total number of usable names was reduced to 1,770, or 97 percent. The judgment of age is based on several factors. First, these early 1950s adults signed themselves Mr., Mrs., or Miss. This is the most important criterion. It is validated by the criterion of handwriting (patrons filled out the slips themselves). If small children's slips were filled out by their mothers (in days before daycare), the mothers often also charged out books of their own. A third and related factor is that patrons from the same family seemed to visit the bookmobile together, so that several siblings might charge out books at the same time. I feel confident of the general age groupings that result; what I am less sure of is the exact boundary of the "child" category. Older teenagers might well be counted in the "child" category. Lastly, the overall findings support the project's own findings with respect to age.

51. This supposition is supported by an editorial in the *Algoma Record-Herald*. After recommending that (the implicitly male) readers borrow a particular title available in the public library, the editorial concluded, "Perhaps you can get your wife to bring it home for you, too!" (*Algoma Record-Herald*, 4 September 1952).

52. Closer analysis of the content of specific library charges—what patrons actually chose to read—is the focus of a forthcoming paper. The aim here is to make a broad comparison between patrons' actual selections and library experts' intentions.

53. For a discussion of Norris's opposition to birth control and her advocacy of large families, see Anne G. Balay, "'Hands Full of Living': Birth Control, Nostalgia and Kathleen Norris." *American Literary History* 8, no.3 (1996): 471-95.

54. Karal Ann Marling, "Betty Crocker's Picture Cook Book: The Aesthetics of American Food in the 1950s," in *Prospects: An Annual of American Cultural Studies* 17 (1992), 79.

55. Eugenia Kaledin, *Mothers and More: American Women in the 1950s* (Boston, 1984), 61.

56. Clifford E. Clark Jr., "Ranch-House Suburbia: Ideals and Realities," in *Recasting America: Culture and Politics in the Age of Cold War*, ed. Lary May (Chicago, 1989), 171-91.

57. Elaine Tyler May, *Homeward Bound: American Families in the Cold War* (New York, 1988), 10-11.

58. Janice A. Radway, *Reading the Romance: Women, Patriarchy, and Popular Literature* (Chapel Hill, 1991).

59. Jessamyn Neuhaus, "The Way to a Man's Heart: Gender Roles, Domestic Ideology, and Cookbooks in the 1950s, *Journal of Social History* 32, no. 3 (1999): 547.

60. *Algoma Record-Herald*, 30 October 1952.

61. Mrs. John Marnard, "From a Bookmobile Patron," *Wisconsin Library Bulletin* 47, no. 2 (1951): 45.

62. *The Idea in Action*, 19-20.

63. *Algoma Record-Herald*, 9 October 1952.

64. In Door County, McCarthy received 7,513 votes as opposed to 1,902 votes received by his opponent, Democrat Thomas R. Fairchild. In Kewaunee, the vote was 6,412 to 1,941. See James R. Donoghue. *How Wisconsin Voted, 1848-1960* (Madison,Wisc., 1962) 97, 57. See also Michael Paul Rogin, *The Intellectuals and McCarthy: The Radical Specter* (Cambridge, Mass., 1967), especially chapter 3.

65. *Algoma Record-Herald*, 6 November 1952

66. *Ibid.*

67. *Sturgeon Bay Advocate,* 30 October 1952.

68. Open letter dated March 19, 1953, to Mr. Ray P. Fulwiler, Supervisor, Fourth Ward, Algoma, Wis. from Frank Wessely, *Algoma Record-Herald*, 30 March 1953.

69. *Algoma Record-Herald*, 4 December 1952.

70. *Algoma Record-Herald*, 18 December 1952.

71. Interview, 23 October 2000.

The Celebration of Health in the Celebration Library

Juris Dilevko and Lisa Gottlieb

Introduction

"Certainly Celebration, though still irredeemably optimistic in names and objectives," wrote architectural historian Vincent Scully (1996) of the Florida town developed by the Walt Disney Company, ". . . may suggest a reasonable shape of reality at last." The reality, however, is shaped by a number of factors extending beyond the town's New Urbanist façade. As displayed in the Preview Center, the five cornerstones of the town of Celebration are education, wellness, technology, place, and community. Although Disney selected these concepts to attract potential residents, Frantz and Collins (1999) point out that "[t]he cornerstones represent a new way of living as much as a new development" (115). In other words, the cornerstones serve as guideposts for the conceptualization of this new town as both a public venture of the Disney corporation—one referred to by a Disney executive as both "our fourth [theme] park" and as "a living laboratory for the American Town" (47)—and as the actual community this venture engenders.

Of the five cornerstones, community is perhaps the most fundamental and the most difficult to define. On the one hand all New Urbanist developments focus on community. On the other hand, a multitude of characteristics work together to create the "social infrastructure" of a particular community (Frantz and Collins 1999, 116). For example, the formation of a community can flow from the other cornerstones of Celebration. The role of education and health care, and the sense of place as expressed through a town's physical environment,

0026-3079/2001/4203-105$2.50/0   American Studies, 42:3 (Fall 2001): 105-133

all contribute to the identity of a community, both in terms of how the community views itself and how others perceive it.

As Lewis (1979) remarks, even seemingly inconsequential aspects of the human landscape are a significant part of "our unwitting autobiography, reflecting our tastes, our values, our aspirations, and even our fears, in tangible, visible form" (12). Beginning with the premise that a library is an ideological formation, or what Meinig (1979) refers to as a "symbol of the values, the governing ideas, the underlying philosophies of a culture" (42-43), we examine the Celebration public library within the context of this nascent community. The choices, whether conscious or subconscious, made in the creation of this environment make a statement about its intended inhabitants, its community members. As first time visitors in someone's house, we scan this manufactured environment for clues about its inhabitants. Invariably, such factors as the arrangement of rooms and the (often ostentatious) display of certain items and the concealment of others reflect more than just decorative taste. Indeed, such factors reveal something fundamental about the people who dwell there. In the same way, we gravitate to bookshelves because we are convinced that the books—their topics, authors, genres—provide insight into the personality of the individual. In a very concrete sense, we read and interpret the character of this person through his or her intellectual surroundings. This can also be done on a larger scale.

Starting from the premise that public libraries reflect the intellectual landscapes of their respective communities, we compare the nonfiction print collection of the Celebration, Florida, library with another branch library—Buenaventura Lakes—in the same Osceola county system and with a standard collection development tool—the *Public Library Catalog*—used as a benchmark by many public libraries. We argue that the Celebration library contributes to what George Ritzer calls "the new means of consumption." The nonfiction collection of Celebration contains health and fitness books to an extent not found in Buenaventura Lakes or in the *Public Library Catalog*, thus reflecting the philosophical emphasis of Celebration as a whole. Our analysis of the Celebration library is part of a larger goal to explore the collection development practices of public libraries in small towns of the United States and to interpret their collection choices and emphases as an integral part of the socio-cultural history of each community.

Cyzyk (1993) and Quinn (1995) have argued that the act of collection development is an inherently political gesture that has real consequences for how a community understands and filters the world. Library collection development, therefore, not only shapes a library, but also is a means of expression of what Pitts (1996) refers to as "community topography" (49). Wiegand (1999) suggests that much of the historical scholarship on library and information science is concentrated on "biography, library expertise, and big library institutions, and its focus largely devoid of analysis of the impact collections and services have had on library users . . ." (23). He approvingly quotes Zweizig, who believed that library scholars should examine carefully "the library in the life of the user" rather than the "user in the life of the library" (Wiegand 1999, 24). We attempt to fill in some of the gaps identified by Wiegand by examining the role of small libraries in the life of a community. In addition, we follow the tradition of Harris (1973) and Garrison (1979), who argue that American libraries in the late-nineteenth century functioned as loci of control—"stabilizing agents"—through an emphasis on proper behavior and the provision of "approved" books. We ask whether small public libraries at the turn of the twenty-first century are also functioning, through their collections, as homogenizing centers where power, in the Foucauldian sense, is exercised through the promotion and valorization of a particular viewpoint.

Welcome to Celebration

Encompassing 4,900 acres, the town of Celebration is a 30-minute drive south from downtown Orlando. Originally part of a 10,000-acre parcel of Disney-owned land that bridged both Orange (home to Walt Disney World) and Osceola (home to Celebration) counties; Disney got the 1965 Florida State Legislature to make the area an autonomous district outside the jurisdiction of either county. Named the Reedy Creek Improvement District (RCID), it was granted "the autonomy and centralized control of a private government" (Frantz and Collins 1999, 69). The Disney company was freed from county controls. Although both "Orange and Osceola County officials felt slighted . . . when Disney revealed its plan to bypass the counties entirely as administrative districts" (Fjellman 1992, 119), these feelings were ameliorated because "Disney would clearly bring a great deal of money into the area if it were allowed to do what it wanted" (120).

The relationship between Disney and Osceola County became further complicated during the planning of Celebration. Disney needed to de-annex from RCID the 4,900 acres designated to become Celebration and re-incorporate them with the county. While this shift from autonomy to county authority might seem out of character for Disney, the underlying reason for this de-annexing was quite clear. If Celebration were to remain part of RCID, which contains the four Disney theme parks, then its residents would by law be able to vote on matters pertaining to the district as a whole. Since the area had no residents, the Disney Company alone held voting rights. As an Osceola County official explained, Disney "didn't want eight thousand dwelling units full of people voting on how to paint the Magic Kingdom" (Frantz and Collins 1999, 70). Thus while Disney retained ownership of the Celebration land, the developmental guidelines for the town—from zoning regulations to housing prices—were established through lengthy negotiations with Osceola County.

The county played a key role in establishing housing prices in Celebration. The neighborhoods or villages that comprise the town were developed in phases. In the first phase, Disney built 350 houses and 150 apartments in Celebration Village. Twelve hundred prospective buyers and renters entered a lottery to win occupancy of one of these 500 residences. The second phase added 230 apartments and 95 houses in the West Village and 300 houses in the North Village. Although housing prices ranged widely, they differed significantly from Osceola County as a whole. When Celebration Village opened in 1997, the cost of townhouses—the most affordable purchasing option—began at $120,000. This was followed by cottage homes priced at $220,000 and village homes at $300,000. At the other end of the spectrum, the price of estate homes began at $600,000. In comparison, United States census data shows that in 1990, before Celebration entered the picture, only 15.2 percent of "owner-occupied housing units" in Osceola County were valued between $100,000 and $149,999—the starting range for houses in Celebration. Rather, 64 percent of houses in Osceola County were valued between $50,000 and $99,999, with 13.6 percent valued at less than $50,000. Furthermore, only 7.5 percent of Osceola County homes were valued at more than $150,000. In January 1999, Celebration promotional literature listed house prices starting at $160,000—double the average price for the county (Ross 1999, 285). Interestingly, the county itself wanted higher priced housing in Celebration. Florida officials wanted Disney to provide non-rental housing options below $100,000, which would have been consistent with Disney's intent "to foster a community that is diverse in age and income" (Rymer 1996, 69). In contrast, county officials wanted Disney to build predominantly extensive, upscale houses that would generate significantly more property-tax revenue, which, in turn, would cover Celebration infrastructure costs (Frantz and Collins 1999, 74).

Yet, as Rymer (1996) points out, "diversity doesn't mean license" when it comes to the physical appearance of Celebration (69). All homeowners must conform to the standards set forth in the Celebration Pattern Book, from which residents select their preferred style of house. These guidelines not only proscribe the structural details of the various options but also regulate these elements within the town. For example, while homebuyers may choose from an approved list of house paint colors, the color selected must not already be present on the same side of the street within a three-house radius unless the color is white. Similarly, a particular style of house cannot be repeated within a two-lot space. Guidelines restrict landscaping options as well. For instance, the Pattern Book stipulates that "no more than two different species of canopy tree, two different species of ornamental tree, five different species of shrub or hedge, and four different species of ground cover" can adorn a house (Ross 1999, 88). The result is a rather homogenous environment—one that feels "packaged, . . . somewhat more like a theme park than a town" (Pollan 1997, 57). Disney, however, argues that such homogeneity is necessary for fostering a sense of community. Joe Barnes, the author/architect of the Celebration Pattern Book, explains that "[i]f you're building a house at Celebration, you're building more than just an individual house on an individual lot; you're creating community" (Rymer 1996, 69).

Notably, the homogeneity that characterizes Celebration's physical appearance also characterizes the town's demographics. According to United States census data for 2000, the total population of Celebration is 2,736. Of this population, 93.6 percent of residents indicated their race as White only, compared to 1.7 percent as African American only and 2.4 percent as Asian only. Furthermore, 7.6 percent of the total population identified themselves as Hispanic or Latino (of any race). Blair (2001) reports that "only 12 of Celebration's 1,093 houses and apartments are owned by blacks" (A21). By contrast, the population of Osceola County is 7.4 percent African American, 2.2 percent Asian, and 29.4 percent Hispanic or Latino (of any race). In addition, according to an AT&T phone survey of 145 families who moved to Celebration during phase one, 98 percent "had some college education" while 38 percent "had graduate, medical, or law degrees" (Ross 1999, 327).

The nonfiction print collection

Celebration can be examined as a community through its "community topography" (Pitts 1996, 49) that is expressed through its library collection. Indeed, the emphasis placed on conformity in Celebration raises the question of whether the library contributes to a subconscious promulgation of value judgements based on a ready acceptance of existing societal standards and opinions, what Gramsci (1971) in *The Prison Notebooks* identifies as the acceptance of the commonsensical, the status-quo or "the spontaneous philosophy which is proper to everybody" (323). In order to address this issue, we analyze what the residents of Celebration have available to read in the permanent collection of their branch library through an identification of predominant topics present in the nonfiction section according to their classification within the Dewey Decimal Classification system (DDC). We use the twenty-first edition of DDC, published in 1996.

Interestingly, the original plan for Celebration did not include a stand-alone public library. Instead, a group of residents, all retirees, persuaded the Osceola County library board to open a branch within the Celebration School in 1998— a process that appears to have bypassed Disney altogether. Considering that education is one of the town's cornerstones, the exclusion of a library would seem to be an oversight. Instead, the education cornerstone included a K-12 grade school and a Disney Institute, envisioned as a type of modern-day athenaeum that would offer social and intellectual programs, including seminars taught by prominent academics. Ultimately, Disney chose to build the Institute in Orlando, closer to the theme parks as "something that would appeal to middle-class Americans and keep adults coming to Disney after their children had grown too old for Disney World" (Frantz and Collins 1999, 48).

Although the community of Celebration lost The Disney Institute, it did, ultimately, gain a library branch, and, therefore, a library collection. A detailed examination of collection choices in a library has the potential to reveal much about the way a community sees itself in relation to contemporary social and economic currents. To be sure, budgetary and space constraints have a large impact on collection development, but they only provide a framework within which individual choices are then made. In the same way, while some public libraries make use of approval plans—the contracting out of collection development functions to external vendors or wholesalers—the creation of "purchasing profiles" (a detailed compilation of categories and types of books to be bought or not, by the vendor on behalf of the library) still remains the responsibility of library staff.[1] Thus, whether or not libraries use approval plans, decisions about what to include in their collections are based on choices made by library staff operating within the prevailing intellectual, psychological, and emotional fabric of their individual communities.

Method

We asked the library system of Osceola County, Florida, to generate a computerized shelf list for the Celebration branch. This shelf list contained the Dewey Decimal call numbers, titles, and author names of all fiction and nonfiction material held by the Celebration branch library as of October 2000. In order to examine whether or not the Celebration library's collection reflects the town's profile, we compared the data collected from the content analysis of nonfiction titles in Celebration with that of the Buenaventura Lakes library, another branch of the Osceola system.[2] This comparison is used to further substantiate observations made based on the distribution of titles across the DDC classes. In other words, we examine whether the representation of certain DDC classes is a Celebration phenomenon or is characteristic of more than one branch in the Osceola county system. In addition to its flagship location in Kissimmee, the Osceola system has seven branches. For comparison we chose at random the Buenaventura Lakes library which is just outside the city limits of Kissimmee, but for all intents and purposes is an extension of Kissimmee.

According to United States census data, the population of Kissimmee in 2000 was 47,814—far greater than Celebration's population of 2,736. Kissimmee's population is more diverse than that of Celebration. While 67.2 percent of the city's residents identified themselves as White only, 10 percent listed their race as African American only and 3.4 percent cited Asian only. These percentages are more reflective of Osceola County as whole than are those of Celebration. An even more pronounced disparity is the 41.7 percent of Kissimmee residents who identified themselves as Hispanic or Latino (of any race), compared with 7.6 percent for Celebration.[3] According to the City of Kissimmee Community Development Department, the median household income for the city was $27,591 in 1989.[4] By contrast, the AT&T phone survey of 145 families that moved to Celebration during the first phase (1997) indicates that 54 percent of households had incomes under $75,000, 31 percent fell between the $75,000 to $150,000 range, and 10 percent of households had incomes above $150,000 (Ross 1999, 327).

While the Buenaventura Lakes shelf list provides one comparison with the Celebration library collection, another method is to use an established collection development tool. Therefore, we also examine the Celebration shelf list in relation to the titles listed in the *Public Library Catalog* (PLC). Now in its eleventh edition, PLC consists of a base volume, with four annual supplements. The latest edition of this base volume was published in June 1999, with annual supplements for 1999, 2000, 2001, and 2002.[5] PLC is an annotated list of reference and nonfiction books for adults, classified by subject, that are "recommended" for inclusion in a public library's collection. As stated in its introduction, "the retention of titles from the previous edition enables the librarian to make informed decisions about weeding a collection . . . and the newer titles help in identifying areas that need to be updated or strengthened" (vii). Because they are arranged according to DDC class, the books recommended by PLC can be examined in terms of both specific titles and percentage representation of topic areas. That is to say, PLC can be used as a rough guide as to the recommended percentage distribution of books by broad Dewey classes.[6] Insofar as PLC serves as a standard collection development model recommended for any public library, the comparison of the Celebration shelf list with PLC, together with the comparison of the Celebration branch with the Buenaventura Lakes branch, addresses the issue of the Celebration collection and community profile both within and beyond the borders of Osceola County. In other words, these two comparisons allow us to gauge the uniqueness of the Celebration nonfiction collection.

Categories of nonfiction

We examined the nonfiction materials, excluding biographies, in terms of their categorization within the Dewey Decimal Classification system (DDC).[7] There were 1,081 nonfiction titles in the Celebration collection and 20,661 nonfiction titles in the Buenaventura Lakes collection. First, we calculated the number of titles within each of the ten main classes of the DDC, known collectively as the First Summary. The results for Celebration showed that the five most represented classes (those with the highest percentage of the library's nonfiction collection) are by percent: Technology (Applied Sciences) (28); The Arts (14.3); Geography & History (13.8); Natural Sciences & Mathematics (11.6); and Literature & Rhetoric (11.2). A complete list appears in Column 3 of Table 1. The most numerous class—600—contained almost twice as many titles as the next most represented class within the collection. These rankings are very nearly replicated in the Buenaventura Lakes nonfiction collection (Column 4 of Table 1). A notable exception is Class 300: Social Sciences, which at 18.4 percent is the second most represented class at Buenaventura Lakes, but is not among the five most represented classes at the Celebration library.

The classes themselves, however, are very general at the First Summary level. For example, Technology (Applied Sciences) covers such disparate topics as Home Economics & Family Living as well as Chemical Engineering. Our next step, then, was to see how the collection was distributed among these top

**Table 1: Holdings Comparison at Dewey 10s Level
between Celebration and Buenaventura Lakes**

Dewey Class	Dewey Topic Description	Celebration* (Percentage)	Buenaventura Lakes* (Percentage)
000	Generalities	1.5	2.8
100	Philosophy & Psychology	4.5	4.1
200	Religion	1.9	3.5
300	Social Sciences	11.1	18.4
400	Language	2.2	2.1
500	Natural Sciences & Mathematics	11.6	4.3
600	Technology (Applied sciences)	28	20.1
700	The Arts (Fine and Decorative Arts)	14.3	12
800	Literature & Rhetoric	11.2	13.2
900	Geography & History	13.8	19.7

*Percentages do not add to 100 percent because of rounding.

five classes within the hundreds level of the DDC, using the topics list from the DDC's Second Schedule. Again, we identified the five most populated classes at this more specific level for Celebration by percent: Medical Sciences (13.7); Recreational & Performing Arts (8.5); Home Economics & Family Living (7.8); American Literature in English (5.9); Animals (4.4); and General History of North America (4.4). This list appears in Column 3 of Table 2. As was the case with the First Summary results, the top five classes identified within the Celebration collection at the hundreds level are also the most heavily represented classes at the Buenaventura Lakes branch (Column 7 of Table 2). The exception was Class 590: Animals, which was represented at Celebration only.

Although the nonfiction collections of the two branches share a similar focus, as defined by the concurrence of the five most represented DDC classes, the actual percentage distribution of books within these five classes also needs to be taken into account. The top two classes in the Celebration library—610: Medical Sciences and 790: Recreational & Performing Arts—appear fourth and fifth respectively in the analysis of the Buenaventura Lakes collection. Conversely, the two classes which house the greatest percentage of the Buenaventura Lakes collection—810: American Literature in English and 970: General History of North America—are the fourth and fifth most numerous classes in Celebration's collection. Only Class 640: Home Economics & Family Living did not shift in rank. In addition, the two classes which house the majority of Celebration's nonfiction holdings—610 and 790—do not have the same ranking within the Buenaventura Lakes collection, although the two are ranked within

Table 2: Comparison of Most Popular Dewey Topics between
Celebration and Buenaventura Lakes Branch Libraries

Celebration Rank	Dewey Class	Dewey Topic Description	Number and (Percent) of Books within Collection (n=1,081)	Buena-ventura Lakes Rank	Dewey Class	Dewey Topic Description	Number and (Percent) of Books within Collection (n=20,661)
1	610	Medical Sciences	148 (13.7)	1	810	American Literature in English	1314 (6.4)
2	790	Recreational & Performing Arts	92 (8.5)	2	970	History of North America	1294 (6.3)
3	640	Home Economics & Family Living	84 (7.8)	3	640	Home Economics & Family Living	1149 (5.6)
4	810	American Literature in English	64 (5.9)	4	610	Medical Sciences	1143 (5.5)
5 (tie)	590	Animals	47 (4.4)	5	790	Recreational & Performing Arts	1062 (5.1)
5 (tie)	970	History of North America	47 (4.4)	6	910	Geography & Travel	975 (4.7)

the top five classes. The percentage of books classified within 610 in terms of the library's entire collection is 13.7 for Celebration, but only 5.5 for Buenaventura Lakes. Furthermore, while the percentage difference between the first and fifth most represented classes at Buenaventura Lakes is 1.2, it spans 9.3 within the Celebration collection.

In our final step we examined more closely the breakdown of titles and topics within the three most represented classes identified at the hundreds level, using the third, thousands-level DDC schedule. Over 75 percent of the titles within Class 610: Medical Sciences fall under just two topics: Promotion of Health (40.5 percent) and Diseases (34.5 percent). Likewise, within Class 790: Recreational & Performing Arts, almost half represent just one subclass, in this case 796: Athletic & Outdoor Sports & Games (48.9 percent). By contrast, the second most represented topic—Public Performances—comprised only 11.9 percent of this class. The results of the breakdown of Class 640: Home Economics & Family Living follow a similar pattern to that of Class 610. Again, over 75 percent of the titles in this class are distributed between two topics: 47.6 percent within 641: Food & Drink and 29.8 percent within 649: Child Rearing & Home Care of Persons.

A similar pattern emerges in the comparison at the hundreds and thousands DDC levels between the Celebration library's collection and the distribution of titles recommended by PLC. Focusing again on the five most numerous hundreds level classes in the Celebration library, the number of titles that fell within these classes in PLC was calculated as a percentage of the total number of titles listed in this publication.[8] These percentages were then compared with the percentages for Celebration. As shown in Column 5 of Table 3, PLC recommends that public libraries devote, by percent about 4.2, of their nonfiction collection holdings to Dewey Class 610, 3 to Dewey Class 790, and 2.8 to Dewey Class 640. However, as shown in Column 4 of Table 3, the Celebration branch library has percentage holdings in these Dewey classes that are double and triple that recommended in PLC. We find the biggest difference of all in class 610: Medical Sciences. While 13.7 percent of the books in the Celebration library concern topics in the medical sciences, only 4.2 percent of the books mentioned in PLC fall within this category.

Celebration thus has more than triple the number of books in class 610 recommended by PLC, although the eleventh edition of PLC "features extensive revision in the areas of health science and personal finance, and ample coverage

Table 3: Comparison of Most Popular Dewey Topics between
Celebration and the *Public Library Catalog*

Celebration Rank	Dewey Class	Dewey Topic Description	Number and (percent) of Books within Collection (n=1,081)	Number and (percent) of Books within *Public Library Catalog* (n=11,865)
1	610	Medical Sciences	148 (13.7)	494 (4.2)
2	790	Recreational & Performing Arts	92 (8.5)	353 (3)
3	640	Home Economics & Family Living	84 (7.8)	338 (2.8)
4	810	American Literature in English	64 (5.9)	882 (7.4)
5 (tie)	590	Animals	47 (4.4)	170 (1.4)
5 (tie)	970	History of North America	47 (4.4)	427 (3.6)

of cooking and gardening" (vii). Indeed, the percentage weight of five of the top six classes relative to the total nonfiction collection size in Celebration is greater than their respective percentage weights in PLC. The only exception to this is class 810: American Literature. It is also significant that the percentage weight of class 610: Medical Sciences, at the Buenaventura Lakes branch is 5.5, a figure that is much more in line with the recommended 4.2 percent figure of PLC than is Celebration's percentage of 13.7. We are confident in saying that the difference between Celebration and Buenaventura Lakes is a real one in terms of medical science holdings. Whereas Buenaventura Lakes adheres approximately to the recommended weightings of PLC in class 610, Celebration is truly anomalous.

Using the thousands-level DDC schedule, we compared the breakdown of specific topics represented in PLC and in the Celebration library's holdings within each of the top three ranked classes: 610, 790, and 640. Interestingly, in both cases the majority of titles in each of the classes was distributed between the same two topics. These topics are listed in Table 4. Despite this congruence of topics, the actual number of titles per topic—calculated as a percentage of the total holdings for the corresponding hundreds-level class—varies greatly between the Celebration library and PLC. For example, although 649: Child Rearing & Home Care of Persons is the second most represented topic within class 640 in both the Celebration collection and PLC, only 14 percent of PLC titles housed within 640 cover this particular subject. In contrast, 29.8 percent of the Celebration library holdings in class 640 pertain to the topic of Child Rearing & Home Care of Persons. The reverse situation occurs in class 790: Recreational & Performing Arts, where the percentage of PLC titles classified as 791: Public Performances (26.6) is more than double that of the Celebration library's collection (11.9). Nonetheless, as with the hundreds-level distribution shown in Table 3, the most substantial discrepancy pertains to class 610: Medical Sciences. In this instance, the 40.5 percent of books that fall under the topic of 613: Promotion of Health in the Celebration library proves to be significantly greater than the 13.6 percent of books classified within 613 in PLC.

Through the analysis of the three most numerous classes in the Celebration library collection at the thousands level of the DDC schedule, an interesting pattern of topics emerges. The two most heavily represented subclasses of 610, as well as the most populated subclasses of 790 and 640, all contain titles that focus on health and fitness, encompassing the topics of Promotion of Health,

Table 4: Breakdown of Most Popular Dewey Topics in the Thousands-level Schedule

Dewey Class	Dewey Topic Description	Percentage of Celebration Holdings	Percentage of *Public Library Catalog* Titles
613	**Promotion of Health**	40.5	13.6
616	**Diseases**	34.5	44.1
791	**Public Performances**	11.9	26.6
796	**Athletic & Outdoor Sports & Games**	48.9	45.9
641	**Food & Drink**	47.6	63.3
649	**Child Rearing & Home Care of Persons**	29.8	14

Diseases, Athletic & Outdoor Sports & Games, and Food & Drink. An examination of the titles housed within these subclasses supports this interpretation. The first topic, Promotion of Health, is in part defined by the prevention of illness through dietary and lifestyle changes. While some titles present a more general treatment, such as Denise Webb's *Foods for Better Health: Prevention and Healing of Diseases*, other titles target a specific demographic group, such as *Dr. Attwood's Low-Fat Prescription for Kids: A Pediatrician's Program of Preventative Nutrition* by Charles Attwood, and *Fight Fat: A Total Lifestyle Program for Men to Stay Fit and Healthy* by Stephen George. The emphasis on the use of dietary and fitness techniques in disease prevention suggests a holistic approach to health. By the same token, some titles connect the idea of better physical health with that of a healthier life in terms of self-fulfilment. One example is the enormously popular book written by Bob Greene and Oprah Winfrey entitled *Make the Connection: Ten Steps to a Better Body—and a Better Life*. Another example is *Personal Best: The Foremost Philosopher of Fitness Shares Techniques and Tactics for Success and Self-Liberation* by George Sheehan. Some of the more prominent lifestyle books in the Celebration library's collection, such as *Make the Connection* and Andrew Weil's *Eight Weeks to Optimum Health*, are cited by PLC. Yet, of the 60 books classified in 613 in the Celebration branch, only 10 percent are PLC-recommended titles. Many of the Promotion of Health titles not mentioned in PLC focus specifically on weight loss. Moreover, many of these books promote specific programs, such as that of Jenny Craig and *The Hilton Head Diet*.

Similarly, titles contained in subclass 616: Diseases discuss ailments not only from a traditional, medical diagnosis and treatment perspective, but also in terms of alternative health approaches. A primary example is Deepak Chopra's *Healing the Heart: A Spiritual Approach to Reversing Coronary Artery Disease*. Also in common with previous examples is the idea of disease prevention, as opposed to treatment alone, as exemplified by the title *Cancer Free: The Comprehensive Cancer Prevention Program*. While books on sports such as tennis and golf easily fit within the emerging pattern of a health and fitness-focused collection, so do some of the titles contained within the Food & Drink subclass 641. This includes titles on vegetarianism and low-cholesterol and low-calorie cooking. As with a number of examples from 613, some of the books are written by or affiliated with prominent diet programs or exercise mavens, such as Weight Watchers and Richard Simmons.

The overrepresentation of health and fitness books in the Celebration library suggests that some topics are underrepresented. For instance, the highest percentage of books recommended by PLC is biographies (class 920 in the DDC) at 14.4 they represent less than 1 percent of the Celebration library's holdings. At the same time, underrepresented topics occur within a numerous class, such as 610. More than 30 percent of class 610 in both the Celebration library collection and PLC focus on the topic of Diseases (616), see Table 4. Nevertheless, the breakdown of PLC titles classified in 616 reveals that 37.6 percent of these books specifically examine Diseases of the Nervous System & Mental Disorders (616.8). In contrast, 21.6 percent of books in class 616 in the Celebration library focus on these subjects.

To examine what is absent from the Celebration collection, we again compared the shelf list from the Buenaventura Lakes branch library with the Celebration shelf list. As shown in Table 1, the percentage of each library's collection contained within the First Summary classes does not vary to any great extent. Two notable exceptions, by percentage, are 500: Natural Science & Mathematics, which accounts for 11.6 percent of the Celebration collection, but only 4.3 percent of the holdings of Buenaventura Lake, and 900: Geography & History, where Buenaventura Lakes has 19.7 percent of its nonfiction collection, compared with 13.8 percent for Celebration.

Within the second-level DDC summary, however, more subtle distinctions arise. Table 5 lists six topics that receive substantially greater coverage in the collection of Buenaventura Lakes than in the Celebration collection. Buenaventura Lakes has more than double the holdings of Celebration in the top five Dewey classes. For example, by percentage, class 290: Comparative Religions constitutes only .5 of Celebration's nonfiction collection, compared to 1.1 of the nonfiction collection of Buenaventura Lakes; class 320: Political Science constitutes .7 of Celebration's collection, compared with 1.7 in Buenaventura Lakes; and class 330: Economics constitutes only 1.4 of Celebration's nonfiction collection, compared to 2.9 in Buenaventura Lakes. Particularly intriguing is that Buenaventura Lakes has double the holdings of Celebration in class 360: Social Problems and Social Services, perhaps an indication of the ideal community that Celebration theoretically embodies. Both the range of topics and the size of the percentage difference between the two

Table 5: Less Popular Non-Fiction Subject Areas
in Celebration compared with Buenaventura Lakes

Dewey Class	Dewey Topic Description	Percentage of Total Celebration Holdings	Percentage of Total Buenaventura Lakes Holdings
290	Comparative Religions & Other Religions	.5	1.1
320	Political Science	.7	1.7
330	Economics	1.4	2.9
360	Social Problems & Social Services	1.6	3.3
820	English & Old English Literatures	1.3	2.7
910	Geography & Travel	3.8	4.7

branches' coverage of these topics suggest that Celebration's emphasis on health-related books could be at the expense of overall depth and breadth of the nonfiction collection.

The discrepancies between the distribution of titles in the Celebration and Buenaventura Lakes branch libraries also need to be examined in conjunction with the Osceola County Library System's *Collection Development & Materials Selection Policy*. Applicable to all branches in the Osceola system, the policy stresses that "[i]dentifying the community's needs, and meeting or exceeding them, is a fundamental principle and obligation of public library service" (1). Guidelines and criteria are used to meet these needs, including suitability of format and subject, appropriateness of style and level for the intended audience, reviews by critics and staff, reputation of the author and publisher, timeliness or permanence of the material, writing quality, relevance to community needs, price, and appearance of the title in special bibliographies or indexes (3-4). In addition, "substantial demand" is also identified as a reasonable criterion for the acquisition of specific materials (3). Finally, although the library director has "[u]ltimate responsibility for materials selection," he or she is guided by the Library Advisory Committee and by professional staff members, to whom selection responsibility has been delegated based on specific collection area expertise (19).[9]

Arguably, the disparity in the distribution of topics between the Celebration and Buenaventura branches may be construed in terms of the Osceola County library system's particular interpretations of the differing needs of the communities that each branch serves. On the one hand, despite the System's broad mission of "mak[ing] available the widest possible diversity of information, books, and materials" (1), the relative homogeneity of the Celebration collection could be seen to reflect the relative homogeneity of the town. Similarly, the diversity of topics in the Buenaventura Lakes collection could be viewed as reflecting the more diverse community of Kissimmee. On the other hand, this interpretation does not account for the particular focus of the Celebration collection. Certainly, the *Collection Development & Materials Selection Policy* cites "a strong demand for current information on health related issues" and contends that the "area of medical sciences is one of ever changing technologies and needs to be updated on a continuous basis" (43). This recommendation, however, applies to all branches in the Osceola County Library System. The question still remains, then, of why there are so many health-related books in the Celebration library.[10]

Celebrating health

The emphasis on health and fitness exhibited in the Celebration library's nonfiction collection suggests a connection to the concept of wellness—one of the five cornerstones of the community. It is manifested materially in Celebration Health, a combination hospital and wellness facility which opened in November 1997, under the management of Florida Hospital. Designed by Robert A.M.

Stern and situated on 60 acres north of downtown, Celebration Health advertises itself as "a mix of old-fashioned customs and futuristic concepts [where] warm, personal attention is combined with the power of new technology" (Florida Hospital 2000c, ¶ 5). This combination of old traditions and new technology suggests both the prominent role that Celebration Health was intended to play in the community and the means of carrying out that role, which the facility's literature refers to as a "mission" (Florida Hospital 2000b, ¶ 1). Celebration Health contends that "true health is achieved not only by treating the disease, but [also] by addressing lifestyle habits and environmental factors that impact your health" (Florida Hospital 2000a, ¶ 4). Like Celebration itself, the intent of Celebration Health is to create or foster a particular lifestyle—one that "celebrate[s] a happier, healthier you" (Florida Hospital 2000c, ¶ 8). Health is equated with wellness, and wellness with happiness.

For Celebration Health, the process of fostering lifestyle changes is predicated on a holistic approach to wellness that combines state-of-the-art facilities with educational programs. There is the 60,000 square-foot Fitness Center, complete with a full-length basketball court and a warm water pool that accommodates underwater treadmills. In addition, there is the Celebration Health Lifestyle Enhancement Center, offering a number of health education programs. These range from the Rippe Health Assessment—"established to offer high level, comprehensive health, fitness and lifestyle evaluations for men and women executives" (Florida Health 2000b, ¶ 48)—to the Pathways to Potential program—designed to "empower individuals to live with more passion, direction, purpose and peace" (¶ 38). All of the programs offered by Celebration Health reinforce what the institution identifies as "the eight universals of health," which form the acronym CREATION:

> Creation is the first step toward improved health.
> Rest is both a good night's sleep and taking time to relax during the day.
> Environment is what lies outside our bodies yet affects what takes place inside us.
> Activity includes stretching, muscle development and aerobic activity.
> Trust in God speaks to the important relationship between spirituality and healing.
> Interpersonal relationships are important to our well-being.
> Outlook colors our perspective on life, influences our health and impacts progression of disease.
> Nutrition is the fuel that drives our whole system. (¶ 2)

In keeping with the concept of technological innovation, residents of Celebration also have access to Celebration Health programming through the fiber optic network that links this facility to their homes.

The connection between Celebration Health and this holistic and spiritual idea of wellness is not particularly surprising, given that the facility's management by Florida Hospital is under the direction of the Church of the Seventh-Day Adventists. Through their combined emphasis on health reform and spirituality, the Seventh-Day Adventists were an integral part of what Engs (2000) identifies as the First Clean Living Movement, from 1830 to 1860. She defines Clean Living Movements as "broad periods in history when concerns about alcohol, tobacco, other mood-altering substances, sexuality, diet, physical fitness, diseases, and other health-related issues have manifested themselves on multiple fronts" (2). In the mid-nineteenth century, the Seventh Day Adventists focused on a number of these points, advocating vegetarianism, cleanliness, exercise, fresh air, and the avoidance of tobacco, coffee, tea, and doctor-prescribed medications.

Engs (2000) contends that society is in the midst of a Third Clean Living Movement, begun in 1970. In the 1990s it focused on the concept of wellness. The basis of wellness is the viewpoint that health is not simply the absence of illness, but instead can be seen as a personal goal, or as a way of "achieving one's potential" (Goldstein 1992, 18)—an idea encapsulated in Celebration Health's Pathways to Potential Program. The wellness model emphasizes preventative measures through lifestyle changes, rather than physical treatment and medication. While diet and exercise are primary examples of how individuals can alter their personal behavior, wellness also embraces the idea of a mind-body connection. In the words of wellness guru Andrew Weil, "[y]ou cannot look after the needs of your body without addressing the needs of the mind and the spirit" (cited in Engs 2000, 195). This viewpoint underscores the eight universals of health taught by Celebration Health.

The idea of wellness and the means of achieving it have been collectively embraced by both Celebration management and by the town's residents. By February 1998, just three months after it opened, Celebration Health's Fitness Center boasted membership of over 50 percent of the town's residents. According to one Celebration Health executive, "[i]n the average community . . . 10 percent of the residents belong to a fitness center" (Frantz and Collins 1999, 263). Beyond Celebration Health, there is the physical layout of Celebration itself. The topography of the town—the public golf course, the parks that anchor every neighborhood, even the front porches and balconies that adorn most of Celebration's residences—encourages residents to spend time outside. At the same time, the cultivation of healthy people has been promoted through the placement of most of the town's amenities within walking or cycling distance. In keeping with the New Urbanist credo, there is scant distinction made among the residential, commercial, and recreational districts of Celebration. This integration obviates the need for cars within the town, although the maze of surrounding highways makes them a necessity for travelling beyond Celebration's boundaries.

Promoting health, however, produces effects beyond that of personal wellness. Engs (2000) notes that each Clean Living Movement is marked by a period of "moral suasion," characterized by "education and social pressure to change attitudes or behaviours" (xi). Similarly, Callahan (1998) sees a coercive element to wellness, noting "a recognition by individuals that their personal behavior will significantly determine their life-time health prospects and that they have a social obligation to take care of themselves for their own sake as well as that of their neighbor" (176). Healthy living, therefore, extends beyond the personal to include a greater social responsibility. Celebration has not been immune from such social pressure. Observing that "[s]elf-scrutiny was a heady narcotic in a town that had been designed to perform," Ross (1999) relates an incident in which a somewhat portly resident of Celebration was asked "How can you be so fat in such a healthy community?" (262-263). This comment emphasizes the expectation not only that Celebrationites should be healthy, but also that individual healthy (or unhealthy) behavior reflects the health of the community as a whole. In terms of "health moralism" (Ross 1999, 262) the incident suggests that this overweight individual did not adhere to Celebration's expected standard of wellness.

Given Celebration's emphasis on wellness, how, then, should one interpret the relationship between the library and this community cornerstone? To be sure, the library's provision of wellness-related books can be seen as reflective of the "community topography" (Pitts 1996, 49) of Celebration. The range of facilities provided in Celebration and the residents' use of them suggest that wellness is an important factor in the community. Furthermore, both Goldstein (1992) and Engs (2000) note that wellness is a predominantly middle- and upper-middle class phenomenon—as is Celebration. At the same time, this factor could also shed light on the lack of wellness-related material in the Buenaventura Lakes collection, considering the socio-economic profile of Kissimmee. Similarly, Engs also observes that "[i]n all three [Clean Living] movements, fear of foreign immigrants and other 'dangerous classes'—minority groups, poor people, and rebellious youth—was an underlying factor in campaigns against activities engaged in by these individuals" (13-14). Although an interest in wellness obviously should not be equated with a fear of "dangerous classes"; nonetheless, such Clean Living Movements have historically excluded minority groups. While minorities comprise a significant portion of the population of both Kissimmee and of Osceola County, they are underrepresented in Celebration. On the one hand, both of these factors suggest how characteristics of communities are reflected through collection development. On the other hand, that Celebration is the town that Disney built cannot be overlooked. Therefore, an interpretation of the relationship between the concept of wellness and the role of the public library in Celebration first requires an examination of the town as what Ritzer (1999) terms "the new means of consumption."

A town designed to be consumed

Ritzer identifies "the new means of consumption" as the multitude of settings that "allow, encourage, and even compel" individuals to consume any quantity of goods and services (2). Ritzer stresses that the new means of consumption extends beyond traditional markets—shopping malls, the internet, and catalogues—to include casinos, amusement parks, athletic facilities, luxury gated communities, educational settings, and hospitals. The sheer range of these examples reflects its newness—"the dedifferentiation of consumption." Bryman (1999) explains that this dedifferentiation signifies "the general trend whereby the forms of consumption associated with different institutional spheres become interlocked with each other and increasingly difficult to distinguish" (33). In other words, as both the quantity and type of new means of consumption increases, the division between these various settings in terms of how they operate and the goods and services they provide will become increasingly indistinct. Ritzer (1999) provides the example of HealthSouth, "a chain of mainly outpatient rehabilitation and surgery centers" (24). He describes how the chain "uses sports stars to increase its visibility, puts its logo on jogging suits and gym bags, and is in the process of creating a catalog of HealthSouth products" (24). In addition, the idea of "co-branding athletic shoes and nutritional drinks" has also been broached (24-25). As HealthSouth strives to become a brand-name, it simultaneously promotes the idea that health care is simply another "context for shopping" (Bryman 1999, 33).

To "encourage and compel" individuals to consume goods and services (Ritzer 1999, 2), the settings that constitute the new means of consumption have to exert some form of control over their customers. Ritzer explains that these places entice individuals through "the fantasies they promise to fulfil" and secure them "by a variety of rewards and constraints" (29). Credit cards, for instance, reward their best customers with increased credit limits and card upgrades that come with a variety of perquisites. Shopping malls lure visitors not only by their wide range of goods for sale, but also by controlling "the emotion of customers by offering bright, cheery, and upbeat environments" (89). This interplay of rewarding and controlling customers is particularly evident in amusement parks. According to Ritzer,

> Theme parks such as Disney World are notorious . . . for their attempts to control both employees and visitors. Controls over employees tend to be blatant, but controls over visitors, though subtle, are present nonetheless. For example, the parks and the attractions are structured to lead people to do certain kinds of things and not to do others. The paths are set up in such a way that people think they are making free choices when in fact they are generally moving in directions preordained by the designers. (90-91)

In effect, these new means of consumption appear to offer choices but instead control the settings and consumers.

In discussing the theme parks, Ritzer comments that other Disney enterprises such as the Disney Institute and the town of Celebration all are "means of consumption in their own right" (5). Although striving to achieve recognition as a "normal," albeit unique, small American town, Celebration nonetheless occupies a precarious position between a Disney fantasyland and a luxurious gated community. Both of these associations, in fact, bolster the idea of Celebration as an example of the new means of consumption. The seal of the town of Celebration is a silhouette of a pig-tailed girl riding her bicycle past a low picket fence, accompanied by her scampering dog; it is meant to symbolize the town as described in the promotional literature: "A place that recalls the timeless traditions and boundless spirit that are the best parts of who we are" (Ross 1999, 18). Rymer (1996) points out that while the image "is an icon of innocence and freedom," it also "bears a Disney copyright" (67). In addition, that the Celebration seal is "emblazoned on everything from coffee cups to manhole covers" (69) renders it a logo, with both the brand and product being the town itself. Rymer downplays Celebration's pretence to a New Urbanist pedigree, describing the development instead as "a new corporate city" and as "a town off the shelf, meant not to be built but to be consumed by its residents" (76-77). What is being consumed, however, is more than simply houses. Rather, Celebration as a new means of consumption involves the selling of a concept— "the comfortable tradition of a 1930s Main Street with the technology of Tomorrowland" (Clary 1996, A1)—a safe, neighborly, clean, healthy community backed by the assurances of the Disney Corporation.

As with other examples of the new means of consumption, the issue of control arises in the context of Celebration. John Kasarda of the Kenan Institute of Private Enterprise at the University of North Carolina, Chapel Hill, comments that "Disney again has its thumb on the pulse of the American Public—to return to community, to a neighborhood, to a place where they think they have control" (Wilson 1995, A1). This sense of control, in turn, is predicated on the idea of choice. For instance, Celebration Health promotes the concept that health care "starts with you being in control. Making choices, obtaining information and gaining access to the latest and most advanced medical technology and services available" (Florida Health 2000c, ¶ 2). Arguably, Celebration Health itself can be viewed as a new means of consumption, similar to Ritzer's (1999) example of HealthSouth. The equal emphasis placed on fitness and medical treatment blurs the distinction between health club and hospital. This dedifferentiation of consumption is further underscored by the metamorphosis of the hospital cafeteria. As described in the facility's promotional literature, "Hospital food takes on a whole new flavor at the award-winning Seasons café restaurant, which features international cuisine along with a mesquite brick oven" (¶ 50). In addition, the Café sells health-conscious baked goods made and marketed by Florida Hospital. Patrons of Celebration Health, therefore, can make choices and have access to not only advanced medical technology, but also current culinary trends, such as mesquite brick ovens and designer breads.

Perhaps the most crucial component of Kasarda's description of Celebration is that it is "a place where [residents] *think* they have control" (emphasis added) (Wilson 1995, A1). In order to provide an environment to draw people to the town in the first place, Disney has to exert a certain amount of control over that environment and, therefore, over the residents themselves. The Celebration Pattern Book, is a source of such control. Its rules for homeowner conformity, however, are not strictly a Celebration phenomenon. As McKenzie (1994) notes, they are a crucial factor of all Common Interest Developments (CIDs)—a category that includes any planned-unit developments of single-family houses, condominiums, and cooperative apartments. He cites the example of a CID near Philadelphia that required all children's swing sets be constructed of wood. Although residents produced a petition signed by 75 percent of homeowners and an Environmental Protection Agency report citing the dangers of poisonous chemicals used in pressure-treated wood swing sets, a couple was ordered to dismantle their children's metal swing set. The rule reflected a preconceived notion of "what the overall community should look like" (17). Echoing Rymer's (1996) description of Celebration as "a new corporate city," McKenzie views CIDs as "a new kind of community that serves as a monument to privatism" (8) by emphasizing "property values over considerations of individual privacy and freedom" (15).

CIDs implement specific control mechanisms to ensure both compliance with regulations and retention of property values. McKenzie explains that everyone who moves into a CID automatically becomes a member of the community's Homeowner's Association (HOA). Membership is compulsory and is invalidated only when the homeowner sells his or her property. The HOA, in turn, is run by a board of directors that is heavily weighted with Disney development company executives, although there is some community representation. In Celebration, for instance, two of the five board members are reserved for homeowners when 50 to 74 percent of all units are sold. This increases to three memberships when 75 percent of Celebration's units have been sold. The board of directors is responsible for enforcing a development's rules and regulations, referred to as "Covenants, Conditions, and Restrictions" (CC&Rs). Any amendments to CC&Rs are voted on by the HOA as a whole. This voting power, as well as the elected positions to the board of directors, promotes the idea that homeowners have control over the way a CID is managed. The reality, however, is more indicative of an illusion of control. Amendments to CC&Rs require a super majority of 75 percent of *all* HOA members, not just those members who vote (McKenzie 1994, 127). Moreover in mixed owner/ renter developments like Celebration, renters cannot vote. This results in a de facto disfranchisement of an entire subset of the community. In essence, control of the CC&Rs—"the rules of the regime under which, ultimately, the residents will be living" (128)—rests solely with the HOA board of directors. Likening a

CC&R to a "quasi-constitution," McKenzie stresses that a HOA board of directors is in effect "a private government"—one that "[t]hrough private property relations . . . does, indeed, have greater power over its residents than does a city" (20).

The effects of privatization and the illusion of control are particularly pronounced in Celebration. In addition to the 75 percent super majority needed to amend the town's CC&R, the contract signed by all future Celebrationites states that the governing rules cannot be changed "without prior notice to and the written approval of the Celebration Company" (Pollan 1997, 60). In other words, the Celebration Company (i.e., Disney) has, and always will have, the final say in any matters concerning Celebration. And these matters extend beyond town aesthetics. In describing CIDs as private governments, McKenzie (1994) observes that "the words public and private may seem distinct enough—and they are used in popular and political discourse as if they were—but they are not" (123). The division of services in Celebration attests to this increasingly blurred distinction between public and private spheres. For example, Celebration is within the realm of the Osceola County Sheriff's department, yet off-duty officers and private security agents also are paid from HOA fees to patrol the community (Wilson 1997, D2). Similarly, the Celebration School's board of trustees is co-managed by Disney and Osceola County.

Wellness, the Celebration library and "the new means of consumption"

Celebration as the new means of consumption provides an interpretative context for the emphasis on wellness-related materials in the town's library. The Celebration project differs from other CIDs not only in the prominence of the Disney name, but also in the scope of the development. In constructing a community, Disney provided a wide range of facilities for health, education, and security. Yet, at the same time Disney is also selling a community. The facilities and amenities are a means for the company to entice residents and to control the environment of Celebration in order to produce the promised product. As we have seen, wellness is a cornerstone of the Celebration product. Success is to be measured by its residents living healthy lives. It therefore becomes the "responsibility" of Disney to see that the residents live in accordance with the wellness principles. At the same time, however, the emphasis on personal lifestyle choices suggests that the individual is in control of his or her own well-being. The result is an illusion of control that characterizes the new means of consumption.

An analogy can be found in the observation that there is virtually no refuse in Disney World. In fact, Disney has an elaborate system to dispose of the trash generated by the park's daily visitors: constant patrols by costumed street sweepers are supplemented by an underground pneumatic garbage disposal apparatus into which bagged refuse is fed at frequent intervals. Fjellman (1992) explains that "[a] central aspect of Disney's utopian utilization of space is cleanliness, so collection and disposal of this trash are crucial to [Disney World's] control of the environment" (193). He further observes that "Disney people as well as a number of reporters have argued that whether through suggestability or shame, people are trained at [Disney World] in the civility of trash can use" (194). In other words, just as the presence of overflowing trash bins on Disney's Main Street U.S.A. would ruin the utopian effect of the theme park, the presence of overweight people on the streets of Celebration would undermine the image of a healthy and vibrant community. The effect, instead, would challenge Celebration's ability to uphold its cornerstone of wellness. Wellness in Celebration is predicated on the idea that each individual citizen can and should "celebrate a happier, healthier you" (Florida Health 2000c, ¶ 8).

The Celebration library, then, can be seen as contributing to the way in which Celebration operates as a new means of consumption. Given that these settings are characterized by a dedifferentiation of consumption—a scenario in which it is becoming increasingly difficult to distinguish among the products and services offered by various institutions—one could argue that the Celebration library is offering the same goods and services as other facilities in the town. In other words, there is an implosion of the role of the library, the hospital-cum-fitness center, the golf course, even the topography of the town itself, based on the shared emphasis on and promotion of wellness. It should be remembered that the Osceola County library board, not Disney, runs the Celebration library. The original Celebration plan called for a Disney Institute to promote Celebration and a healthy and happy community. Yet CIDs are characterized by a breakdown in the boundary between public and private spheres—an effect that is particularly pronounced in Celebration, given the historically complex relationship between Disney and its local counties. This breakdown, in turn, reflects not only an increasing influence of the private sector on public institutions such as libraries, but also the phenomenon of public institutions serving roles traditionally reserved for the private sector.

In the context of the Celebration library operating as a new means of consumption, the phenomenon of what Bryman (1999) describes as "the dedifferentiation of consumption" has a particularly intriguing final twist. Despite the emphasis that the Osceola County Library System's *Collection Development & Materials Selection Policy* places on determining community needs and ensuring a diverse collection, the basis of the Celebration branch nonfiction collection resulted from weeding the collections of the other branches of the Osceola system.[11] That is to say, those volumes that, for reasons of duplication or lack of shelf space, were deemed surplus at other branches, found their way to Celebration. They were then supplemented by books that have "fast turnover" in such areas as computers, travel, and health. But, as we have seen, a defining feature of the new means of consumption is that, because of the proliferation of "different institutional spheres" where consumption occurs, divisions between these various spheres in terms of operation and the goods or services they provide have become blurred. Even though Celebration's library collection *appears* to be different than the other branches of the Osceola system and PLC, the goods provided by the Celebration branch are, in fact, similar to those offered by other branches, since they have literally been pulled from those other libraries. In the final analysis, this is a delicious tension, a fun-house mirror effect that creates the illusion of difference among a welter of conformity.

Recall, too, that Rymer (1996) refers to Celebration as "a town off the shelf"—a description that takes on ironic force because the Celebration library collection is, for all intents and purposes, off the shelf. Just as residents of Celebration have scant control over their house styles and landscaping options while believing themselves to be in control of their homes—a manifestation of Celebration's precarious position between fantasyland and gated community— they also have little control over what is available for their nonfiction reading pleasure in the Celebration library. Left with only the illusion of control both in their physical and intellectual environments, residents of Celebration facilitate, both willingly and unwittingly, Disney's social and cultural control of their lives. To be sure, the library's emphasis on health-related matters is an accidental representation. Yet, it works hand in glove with the deliberate wellness nexus that Disney markets as a cornerstone of the town. When all is said and done, the library is another aspect of the reification of the prevailing purpose of Celebration, reinforcing the notion of wellness in the same way that its inhabitants embrace and celebrate what they perceive to have been *their* healthy decision to move to Disney's planned community. Accidental or not, the appearance of collection difference in Celebration substantiates the sameness of the totality of goods and services offered to Celebration residents. While Disney claims that its town is different from all others, in essence it is not, since the consumable values on display and for sale in Celebration are extracted from larger social trends and then adroitly packaged as exuding difference. So too is the library collection. Extracted from other collections, the content of the Celebration collection differs significantly from PLC recommendations and from Buenaventura Lakes. Nonetheless, the difference is only a simulacrum insofar as it replicates already existing and well-developed strategies of social control. No matter where they turn, Celebration residents cannot but buy into the concept of wellness, in all its psychological, social, and economic forms. Despite its predominantly accidental origins, the branch library nonfiction collection assumes its place as a locus of control simply because it does not differ from the other consumer items and values that Celebration residents call their own. It is this simulacrum of difference—the seeming difference from all other surrounding towns and the distant communities from which they came—that makes residents of Celebration willing participants in the "new means of consumption" under the illusion that they are exercising control over their lives.

Indeed, there is a historical precedent for the idea of libraries as loci of control—one associated with the development of the public library movement in the nineteenth century. While scholars agree that this movement began with the creation of the Boston Public Library in 1852, the motivations behind the development of the public library system have been subject to debate. Harris (1973) debunks what he refers to as the "public library myth" (2509), a time-honored tale of the creation of the public library as a purely humanitarian exercise with the goal of improving the common man through education. In contrast, Harris argues that a major impetus for the founding of the Boston Public Library was the desire of local elites to exercise control over recent immigrant populations, especially the Irish. Such control would be manifested through the availability of quality books, so that readers could be inculcated with proper habits and ways of thinking—a form of what Harris refers to as "moral stewardship" (2512). Accordingly, one of the central functions of the library was to act as a "stabilizing agent" in society through the provision of "approved" books (2513).

Breisch (1997) notes that, in the decade before Boston Brahmins Edward Everett and George Ticknor formed the Standing Committee of the Boston Public Library, educational reformer Horace Mann suggested the use of public schools as a forum from which to combat "the disintegration of traditional values brought on by large-scale industrialization, urbanization, and immigration" (6). In confirmation of Harris' (1973) theory, Breisch suggests that the Boston Public Library played a similar role. While the goal of the library was the moral and intellectual improvement of the working classes, the underlying motivation was the preservation of societal norms favored by the local gentry. As Garrison (1979) observes, "Like other custodians of culture in this period, [the library planning committee] sought not so much to aid in the assimilation of moral, social, or economic change as to keep the challenge at arms length" (14).

This desire to maintain the status quo was in evidence in the development not only of the Boston Public Library but also of public libraries in such smaller Massachusetts towns as Quincy, Woburn, and Malden. Breisch (1997) points out that each of these towns underwent dramatic demographic and economic shifts that changed both their physical layout and cultural fabric. Industrialization and immigration accompanied growth. It altered the familiar landscape of the town as tenements replaced stand-alone houses, turning rural towns into suburban developments. Fuelled by such changes, the opening of public libraries was fuelled as much by nostalgia as by perceived moral challenges. Evidence of this phenomenon can be found in contemporary librarians' conception of the library as an "appropriate repository for . . . records of the town's early history" (23).

In the case of Celebration, what the Boston Public Library's founders referred to as "healthy general reading" has metamorphosed into general reading about health. Considering the use of "education and social pressure to change attitudes or behaviours" (Engs 2000, xi) that characterizes both Clean Living Movements in general and Celebration's wellness cornerstone in particular, the emphasis on wellness-related material in the Celebration library provides a contemporary example of how the public library assumes the role of a "stabilizing agent" through the provision of approved books. In the process, the Celebration library reinforces a certain homogeneity and conformity that characterizes the community topography of Celebration, thereby promulgating "the spontaneous philosophy which is proper to everyone" (Gramsci 1971, 323). There is, however, a significant distinction between Celebration and its nineteenth-century counterparts. Wiegand (1989) comments that the "goal of American librarianship was obvious—offer library patrons only good reading; buy no bad reading" (100). This maxim was based on a generally held assumption that "good reading led to good social behaviour, bad reading to bad social behaviour" (100). Arguably, the proliferation of wellness-related titles in the Celebration Library also supports the ideology that "good reading [leads] to good behaviour"—in other words, the idea that reading about healthy lifestyles will lead residents to healthy lifestyles. Yet, at the same time, this wellness emphasis in the context of Celebration suggests that the determination of good behavior, and therefore of good reading, is inextricably linked to what is good for the marketability of the town as a whole. Hall (1996) observes that early libraries can be "linked to movements for political, spiritual, and economic empowerment" (26). While the concept of wellness might include the notion of spiritual empowerment, the emphasis on wellness in the Celebration library nonfiction collection suggests the political and economic empowerment of Disney's Celebration more than the empowerment of the residents of the community.

Conclusion

We have presented a case study of how one public library's collection of nonfiction books is a reflection of its community. Collection development practices in public libraries are often perceived as mechanical exercises that do not hold much interest on a socio-cultural level. Yet, as we have tried to show here, public library collections can be interpreted as indicators of "community topography" (Pitts 1996, 49). In general terms, a public library, through its collection, does not deliberately set out to be an ideological formation, but it does have a tendency to become, in the course of time, "a symbol of the values, the governing ideas, the underlying philosophies of a culture" (Meinig 1979, 42-43). To be sure, public libraries become symbols of broad societal values, but they also address, in sometimes surprising ways, the governing ideas of its specific community. In the case of Celebration, an ideology of therapeutic self-help and wellness is a central governing idea. Everyone who lives in Celebration has moved from someplace else. Certainly, the reasons for such a move vary, but, in large part, people are seeking to become "well" by moving away from their current metaphorically "unwell" residence into the wellness of Celebration, as represented by its attention to order, sublime control, and ineffable standardization. In short, they are trying to become whole and to retain that wholeness, once it has been achieved. Of course, Disney is the driving force behind the ideological formation of this community, thus raising intriguing issues about the way in which corporations, as representatives of capital, have become the preferred delivery system for culture. It is therefore logical that the Celebration branch library would emphasize, through its nonfiction collection, values of wellness to a degree not found in another branch library a short distance away and to a degree not found in the *Public Library Catalog*. The Celebration library, a part of the Osceola public system, is therefore an example of the blurred distinction between public space and private corporate interest, where corporate philosophy intrudes on the service and cultural role of the public library.

From a larger perspective, the present study is part of a broad goal to explore public libraries in small towns of the United States with a view towards understanding in detail the extent to which they have become an integral part of the intellectual landscape of their community. Accordingly, we are concerned with the question of how the public library "fits into the larger area of cultural transmission" (Davis and Aho 2001, 26). Our focus is the extent to which collection development practices and choices of a public library reflect the public history of that particular community. Ultimately, these practices and choices result in libraries becoming (very) selective repositories of cultural heritage, with different emphases. In a real sense, library collections assume a political force insofar as they help in filtering the world for the patrons of that community. The interaction of that selectiveness with larger socio-cultural currents can therefore contribute to understanding the history of a specific community and its intellectual trajectory.

Notes

1. For example, Nardini, Getchell, and Cheever (1996), analyzing the books supplied on approval by a single vendor over a one-year period to two research libraries and two medium-sized academic libraries, found that when the titles received by the four libraries were compared, only 6 percent were acquired in common. St. Clair and Treadwell (1989), examining the approval selections supplied by four vendors in response to a science and technology profile, found that only 4 percent of the titles would have been supplied by all four vendors and concluded that "the diversity of titles that would have been supplied by different vendors using the same profile makes the selection of a vendor (and careful construction of a profile) even more serious" (387).

2. A donation of $250 was made to the Osceola County Library system in return for their kindness in producing these two computerized shelf lists. We would like to extend heartfelt thanks to the former Director of the Osceola Library System, Bill Johnson, as well as to Sharon Pesante, Technical Services, for their help with these shelf lists.

3. These figures should be compared with Blair (2001). Blair states that census figures show 2,376 residents in Celebration, with a white population of 88 percent. However, a document entitled Census 2000 Redistricting Data, available at www.floridacensus.com/census/summaries/place.summary.txt, shows the population of Celebration as 2,736.

4. As of September 2001, this is the latest available income data available at the city level for Kissimmee. Income data for states and cities based on Census 2000 data is projected to be released in the middle of 2002. To be sure, national income data showed that the median household income in 2000 was $42,148. For African Americans, this figure was $30,439; for Hispanics, $33,447. Seelye (2001) provides a succinct overview. These figures represent an increase from comparable 1990 figures, and it is therefore to be expected that median income in Kissimmee will follow national trends.

5. The base volume includes recommended books published in or before 1998. The yearly supplements typically include books published in the year of their spine date.

6. The total number of titles contained in PLC is readily accessible from the publisher and printed information contained in the volumes themselves. The number of titles listed in each Dewey class and subclass can be determined by simply counting them. Dividing the number of recommended titles in a certain Dewey class by the total number of titles in PLC provides information about the relative percentage weight that a certain Dewey class should assume in a library's total collection. For example, if PLC contained a total of 5,000 recommended titles and

250 of these titles were listed under Dewey Class XYZ, a library would understand that its collection of Dewey Class XYZ should be approximately 5 percent of its total collection.

7. We used the latest available print version of the DDC, published in 1996 by Forest Press. The electronic version of DDC, available at http://www.oclc.org/dewey, contains slight modifications to the wording of Dewey topic descriptions. Editors of DDC occasionally change the wording in topic descriptions, but the underlying categorizations remain the same. These modifications in no way detract from our argument. The modifications are as follows: 000 Computers, Information, & General Reference; 290 Other Religions; 360 Social Problems & Social Services; 610 Medicine; 640 Home & Family Management; 700 Arts & Recreation; 790 Sports, Games & Entertainment; and 900 History & Geography.

8. Because the shelf lists for Celebration and Buenaventura Lakes were generated in October 2000, we used the PLC eleventh edition base volume and the 1999 and 2000 supplements. The 1999 supplement covers books published in 1998, and the 2000 supplement covers books published in 1999. The total number of PLC titles was therefore calculated as 11,865. We added together the number of titles listed in the eleventh edition base volume (9,424) and in the 1999 and 2000 supplements (1,401 and 1,040, respectively). The figure for the eleventh edition was provided by Mr. Phil Taylor, Director of Customer Relations for the H.W. Wilson Co., publisher of PLC, who observed that the statement in the introduction to the base volume of PLC to the effect that it contained "over 8,000 volumes" was slightly understated (private email dated September 6, 2001). Each of the supplements supplied the total number of listed titles in its introduction.

9. We would like to thank the current director of the Osceola County Library System, Mr. Ed Kilroy, for sending us a copy of the Osceola County Library collection development handbook.

10. It would have been appropriate to examine Celebration circulation data to see whether health-related books circulated more than other titles. However, the Celebration Library does not keep track of circulation according to Dewey classes, limiting itself to circulation statistics in terms of nonfiction, biography, fiction, mystery, easy, and rental books.

11. We would like to thank Ms. Joyce Gibson, currently manager of Human Resources for the Osceola County Library System, for taking the time to speak to us about the development of the Celebration branch collection on September 7, 2001. Ms. Gibson was chiefly responsible for implementing the Celebration branch and ensuring that there were books available at Celebration. During our phone conversation, Ms. Gibson stated that the nonfiction collection came about as a result of weeding the collections of other Osceola branches, with particular attention to duplicate copies, surplus copies, and the lack of shelf space at those other branches. The assembled collection was then supplemented by "new orders of computer, travel, and health books that have fast turnover."

Works Cited

Blair, Jayson. 2001. "Failed Disney Vision: Integrated City." *New York Times,* 23 September , A21.

Breisch, Kenneth A. 1997. *Henry Hobson Richardson and the Small Public Library in America: A Study in Typology.* Cambridge, Mass.

Bryman, Alan. 1999. "The Disneyization of Society." *The Sociological Review* 47 (1): 25-47.

Callahan, Daniel. 1998. *False Hopes: Why America's Quest for Perfect Health is a Recipe for Failure.* New York.

Clary, Mike. 1996. "A Disney You Can Go Home To." *Los Angeles Times,* 27 September, A1+.

Cyzyk, Mark. 1993. "Canon Formation, Library Collections, and the Dilemma of Collection Development." *College & Research Libraries* 54 (January): 58-65.

Davis, Donald G., Jr., and Jon Arvid Aho. 2001. "Whither Library History? A Critical Essay on Black's Model for the Future of Library History, with Some Additional Options." *Library History* 17 (March): 21-36.

Engs, Ruth Clifford. 2000. *Clean Living Movements: American Cycles of Health Reform.* Westport, Conn.

Fjellman, Stephen M. 1992. *Vinyl Leaves: Walt Disney World and America.* Boulder, Colo.

Florida Health. 2000a. *Celebration Health Lifestyle Enhancement Center.* Retrieved July 19, 2001, from http://www.celebrationhealth.com/chstory.

Florida Health. 2000b. *Celebration Health Programs and Services.* Retrieved July 19, 2001, from http://www.celebrationhealth.com/chstory.

Florida Health. 2000c. *Welcome to Celebration Health.* Retrieved July 19, 2001, from http://www.celebrationhealth.com/overview.

Frantz, Douglas, and Catherine Collins. 1999. *Celebration, U.S.A.: Living in Disney's Brave New Town.* New York.

Garrison, Dee. 1979. *Apostles of Culture: The Public Librarian and American Society, 1876-1920.* New York.

Goldstein, Michael. 1992. *The Health Movement: Promoting Fitness in America.* New York.

Gramsci, Antonio. 1971. *Selections from the Prison Notebooks.* New York.

Hall, Peter Dobkin. 1996. ""To Make Us Bold and Learn To Read – To Be Friends to Each Other, and Friends to the World': Libraries and the Origins of Civil Society in the United States." *Libraries & Culture* 31 (Winter): 14-35.

Harris, Michael. 1973. "The Purpose of the American Public Library: A Revisionist Interpretation of History." *Library Journal* 98 (September 15): 2509-2514.

Lewis, Peirce F. 1979. "Axioms for Reading the Landscape." In *The Interpretation of Ordinary Landscapes: Geographical Essays*, edited by D.W. Meinig (8-24). New York.

McKenzie, Evan. 1994. *Privatopia: Homeowner Associations and the Rise of Residential Private Government.* New Haven, Conn.

Meinig, Donald W. 1979. "The Beholding Eye: Ten Versions of the Same Scene." In *The Interpretation of Ordinary Landscapes: Geographical Essays.* (33-48). New York.

Nardini, Robert F., Charles M. Getchell, Jr., and Thomas E. Cheever. 1996. "Approval Plan Overlap: A Study of Four Libraries." *Acquisitions Librarian* 16: 75-97.

Pitts, Francis Murdock. 1996. "What to Read When Building a Library (Or, Is That a Mastodon in the Choir Loft?)." *American Libraries* 27 (April): 48-50.

Pollan, Michael. 1997. "Town-Building is no Mickey Mouse Operation." *New York Times Magazine,* 14 December, 56-63.

Public Library Catalog. 1999. Edited by Juliette Yaakov. 11th edition. New York.

Quinn, Brian. 1995. "Some Implications of the Canon Debate for Collection Development." *Collection Building* 14 (1): 1-10.

Ritzer, George. 1999. *Enchanting a Disenchanted World: Revolutionizing the Means of Consumption.* Thousand Oaks, Calif.

Ross, Andrew. 1999. *The Celebration Chronicles: Life, Liberty, and the Pursuit of Property Value in Disney's New Town.* New York.

Rymer, Russ. 1996. "Back to the Future: Disney Reinvents the Company Town." *Harper's* 293 (October): 65-78.

Scully, Vincent. 1996. "Disney: Theme and Reality." In *Building a Dream: The Art of Disney Architecture*, edited by Beth Dunlop (4-11). New York.

Seelye, Katherine Q. 2001. "Poverty Rates Fell in 2000, but Income was Stagnant." *New York Times,* 26 September, A12.

St. Clair, Gloriana, and Jane Treadwell. 1989. "Science and Technology Approval Plans Compared." *Library Resources & Technical Services* 33 (October): 379-390.

Wiegand, Wayne. 1989. "The Development of Librarianship in the United States." *Libraries & Culture* 24 (Winter): 99-109.

Wiegand, Wayne. 1999. "Tunnel Vision and Blind Spots: What the Past Tells Us about the Present; Reflections on the Twentieth-Century History of American Librarianship." *Library Quarterly* 69 (January): 1-32.

Wilson, Craig. 1995. "Mickey Builds a Town: Celebration Puts Disney in Reality's Realm." *USA Today*, 18 October, A1+.

Wilson, Craig. 1997. "The town that Disney Built: Celebration Sells a Family Lifestyle." *USA Today*, 3 July, D1+.

Exploring the American Idea at the New York Public Library

Jean L. Preer

In the aftermath of the Second World War, as American society adjusted to the political and international landscape of the early Cold War, librarians examined the role of libraries as agencies of culture. With mounting fears about Communist expansion, government agencies, foundations, and the mass media undertook efforts to educate citizens about the meaning of democracy. Librarians, following intense wartime activity, returned to questions about the public library's appropriate clientele and collections. At the New York Public Library a new reading and discussion group, "Exploring the American Idea" (EAI), merged these strands of societal and professional concerns. Focused on the meaning of the American democratic tradition in turbulent times, EAI can be viewed as part of the postwar effort to create a liberal consensus around democratic values. An adult education program based on the Great Books model, EAI can be regarded as the embodiment of the library as an agency of culture providing serious works to an educated elite. A closer look, however, suggests that as it developed, Exploring the American Idea gave participants room to question the liberal consensus and offered the library a means to expand its audience beyond its traditional base.

In the decade before the war, librarians struggled to define their role in the burgeoning adult education movement. The American Library Association (ALA) had been a charter member of the American Association of Adult Education (AAAE) founded in 1926 with the support of the Carnegie Corporation, and among the myriad religious, farm, university, and civic groups involved in adult education only librarians served whole communities and supported the spec-

0026-3079/2001/4203-135$2.50/0   American Studies, 42:3 (Fall 2001): 135-154

trum of adult educators. Through the 1930s, however, the profession was divided between those who questioned the educational role of the library and those who welcomed the role and believed librarians should be in the lead. In 1941 Ralph Beals observed that the scope and functions of the American public library were in dispute, even among librarians. While agreeing on the role of libraries as conservators of culture and as "service stations for the ready supply of answers to miscellaneous questions," many were skeptical of education as an ultimate objective of the library.[1]

At the New York Public Library (NYPL), however, the adult education concept infused the approach to adult services.[2] Since 1928, when Jennie Flexner established the Readers' Adviser's Office, the library had sought to offer services to adults comparable to that offered to children and other specialized clientele. Through individual consultations, the office suggested courses of readings to meet the interests and goals of each reader. Under Flexner's leadership, the office also developed extensive group services to the unemployed during the Depression and to immigrants fleeing Europe in the late 1930s. Bibliographies prepared for such radio shows as "Town Meeting of the Air" extended the reach of the library, but in a supportive rather than independent role.

With the outbreak of war, librarians turned their attention from parochial professional debates to the practical matter of supporting the war effort. Other professional priorities, including the nascent quest for federal funding, were put on hold as librarians plunged into the Victory Bond campaign and turned their libraries into War Information Centers. The war heightened rhetoric about library and democracy. Speakers from Librarian of Congress Archibald MacLeish to President Franklin Delano Roosevelt equated libraries and democracy, heralding the role of libraries in creating the informed citizenry and preserving the cultural heritage that would win the war.[3] Seeking a role comparable to the Library War Service that had boosted the visibility of libraries during World War I, public libraries emphasized their role as community information centers rather than as cultural agencies.[4]

Following the war, the tension between the library as an agency of adult education meeting the needs of a well-educated few and as a political agency undergirding the democratic process became more apparent. Picking up the pieces of the national plan for library service developed in 1943, librarians resumed lobbying for federal assistance to support the creation of public libraries in underserved, largely rural areas. Proposed by Emily Taft Douglas in 1946, the Public Library Service Demonstration Bill echoed the democratic rhetoric of the war years, with supporters ritually heralding the library as the embodiment of democratic values.[5] Indeed, the library extension effort was premised on the belief that democracy required and depended on libraries within the reach of all citizens.

While federal support for rural libraries suggested the widest possible reach for library service, librarians in urban areas in 1946 adopted a new adult education initiative based on the Great Books curriculum and aimed at a limited, self-selected audience. This approach assumed that the classic texts of western civilization could profitably be read by anyone with an interest, regardless of their educational background. Small groups of about thirty were to meet every two weeks with lay leaders trained in the Socratic method. Public libraries in Chicago and Cleveland led the way, drawing serious readers to the library for discussion and debate.

Beginning also in 1946, the Public Library Inquiry joined questions about the public library's role as an agency of adult education with doubts about the profession's faith in the library as an embodiment of democratic values.[6] Undertaken at first to examine personnel issues, the inquiry grew into a full-blown study of the current status of virtually every aspect of American public libraries, including not only staffing, but also funding, governance, and how libraries were actually being used by the American public. Funded by the Carnegie Corporation, the study was conducted by the Social Science Research Council and led by Robert Leigh heading a team of social scientists and advised by a committee including Ralph A. Beals of the New York Public Library.[7]

Ralph Beals, appointed NYPL director in 1946, was connected to several of these strands of library concern and activity. An early proponent of library adult education, he had served on the staff of the American Association for Adult Education from 1933 to 1939. As Assistant Director of the District of Columbia Public Library, from 1940 to 1942, he had spearheaded the library's war activities, transforming his office into a War Information Center and heading the ALA's War Service Committee on Information and Education.[8] Beals had then served as director of the library and dean of the Graduate Library School at the University of Chicago. While there, he had become a close associate of Robert M. Hutchins, president of the university and proponent, with Mortimer Adler, of the Great Books approach to learning. Beals joined the board of the Great Books Foundation when it was created in 1947.[9]

Beals's scholarly background and his interest in community outreach matched the dual identity of the New York Public Library as both a privately endowed, research institution and a metropolitan public library. The library's internal organization reflected this division. The Reference Department maintained the research collections and served the clientele of the Central Library at Fifth Avenue and 42nd Street; the Circulation Department oversaw the library's Carnegie branches funded by the city budget. Similarly, NYPL seemed to have found a middle ground in the debate over whether the public library should meet the more serious educational needs of its users or cater to their more popular reading demands. The library assumed its readers would be interested in the best works and able to appreciate them. At the 1936 conference of the American Library Association, Esther Johnston, head of the NYPL Central Circulation Branch, warned against underestimating the taste and intelligence of borrowers. Making a plea for "the reader of apparently ordinary tastes whose potentialities are apt to be overlooked," she argued against lowering standards by too much popularizing.[10] The introduction of the Great Books program, at Beals's suggestion in 1947,[11] demonstrated this confidence in readers. Open to anyone interested, the Great Books program had no special educational qualifications, but as described in an NYPL brochure, put the burden on the participant:

> This type of social reading requires your active participation.
> . . . The trained leaders will not tell you what you should think about the books. You will express your own understanding of what you read and will exchange your views with those of other members of the group. The leaders will not deliver lectures on the authors or the books; they will simply help the discussion by asking questions.[12]

In the first three series of Great Books, only *The Federalist Papers* and works by Thoreau were by Americans, although several, including those by John Locke, John Stuart Mill, and Adam Smith, had significantly influenced American political thought.

In the aftermath of World War II and the early years of the Cold War, interest in the meaning of democracy was widespread. Using programs and exhibits, the NYPL responded to this interest and used it to promote the library. The journey of the Freedom Train from September 1947 to January 1949 spurred such activity. Funded by the new, non-partisan American Heritage Foundation, comprised largely of business and media executives, the train displayed important documents of United States history from Columbus's discovery of America to the 1945 United Nations Charter.[13] A library brochure showed a toy train heading up the steps of the Central Building where the library displayed copies of documents on the train and related materials from its own collections.[14] In each of the exhibited documents, "there [was] to be found a principle—a thread of history—which was to become an essential part of the American tradition."[15] A "Heritage of Freedom" brochure for Staten Island branches invited additional reading on the heritage theme including biographies of George Washington, Abraham Lincoln, and Abigail Adams, *John Brown's Body*, *Leaves of Grass*, *O Pioneers!* and *Folk Song U.S.A.* by John Lomax.[16]

After the Freedom Train departed, the NYPL's *Branch Library Book News*, continued the heritage theme with a lengthy bibliographic essay, "Exploring the American Mind" by Margaret E. Monroe, assistant readers' adviser.[17] Mixing historical monographs, biographies, novels, poetry, folklore, and government reports, Monroe's list included works by dissenters from the American tradition, notably Henry George and Eugene V. Debs, and those excluded from its privileges, notably women and the poor, represented by Jane Addams and Lillian Wald. Surprisingly, given the library's own notable Schomberg Collection and its interest in race relations,[18] there were no African American writers on the list, although it included Gunnar Myrdal's *An American Dilemma* and Gustave Myers's *A History of Bigotry in the United States*. The issue also included lists of American historical novels,[19] books by and about women,[20] and information

Figure 1: A brochure invited the public to follow a visit to the Freedom Train with a trip to the New York Public Library. "The Freedom Train Leads to the Library." *Courtesy of New York Public Library Archives, The New York Public Library, Astor, Lenox and Tilden Foundations.*

on upcoming programs on the library's radio show, "Treasury of the Spoken Word," including Ralph Bellamy reading from "Leaves of Grass," Donald Crisp on Longfellow's poems, and Clifton Fadiman on Patrick Henry.

As pressures from censors and anti-communist politicians increased in the late 1940s, the library had its own interest in the interpretation of basic democratic values. Books in New York City school libraries had been challenged, and the New York Public Library itself faced concerns about owning or lending controversial works. When a New York state court in November 1946 declared Edmund Wilson's *Memoirs of Hecate County* to be obscene, the library removed the book from circulation and informed readers on the waiting list that it was no longer available.[21] In 1948, the New York City schools had banned *The Nation* because of Paul Blanshard's articles criticizing the Catholic Church.[22] Meeting in Atlantic City in June 1948, the American Library Association, under its president Paul North Rice, chief of the NYPL Reference Department, condemned censorship as a threat to democracy and reaffirmed the Library Bill of Rights, adopted originally in 1939. Describing the library as "an institution of education for democratic living," it stated that "the library should welcome the use of its meeting rooms for socially useful and cultural activities and discussion of current public questions" with meeting rooms available on equal terms regardless of the beliefs and affiliations of their members.[23]

With the meaning of the American democracy a practical as well as a scholarly matter, Beals convened a Committee on the American Tradition, in fall 1949, at the library to develop a plan to "provide an environment favorable to reading and reflection on what the American way of life is."[24] After reading and discussing numerous works, the committee in February 1950 unanimously endorsed implementation of a reading and discussion project at the library to promote the understanding of American democracy:

> We look upon this series of readings and discussions . . . as an attempt to find the living tradition of America. It is an attempt to analyze the ideas important in the development of this tradition and to relate them to the present. It is an intellectual adventure in which the ideals of our culture—sometimes unattained or disregarded—are reexamined through writings expressive of fundamental viewpoints which are now a part of our heritage.[25]

The committee's tentative reading list included the Declaration of Independence and the Constitution, Thomas Paine's *The Age of Reason*, Alexis de Tocqueville's *Democracy in America*, writings by Henry David Thoreau, Abraham Lincoln, Walt Whitman ("On Ontario's Blue Shore"), William V. Moody ("Ode in Time of Hesitation"), John Dewey and Woodrow Wilson. Recent works included the *Report* of the President's Committee on Civil Rights, the United Nations' Universal Declaration of Human Rights, and a selection by

David Lilienthal, former head of the Tennessee Valley Authority and current chair of the Atomic Energy Commission. The committee had also considered works by Ben Franklin, Ralph Waldo Emerson, Henry Adams, Lincoln Steffens, John Woolman, and James Bryce and continued to refine its list. In May 1950 the committee recommended to Beals that the readings be tested in two or three experimental groups using the Great Books model. "By this we mean the following: Two leaders who use the Socratic method. Small groups of approximately 15-20 members. Two hour meetings every other week."[26] The committee presented a fully developed reading list. Paine, Moody, and Dewey had been removed, while George Washington, Thomas Jefferson, and Oliver Wendell Holmes had been added. The list included background information on each reading, questions for discussion, and information on the document's availability.[27]

Tellingly, the committee used as the program theme a quotation from the foreword of *This I Do Believe* by David Lilienthal, published by Harper & Brothers in 1949. "What as individuals can we do to safeguard and nourish this great inheritance?" Lilienthal asked. "I say: Search our minds and our souls and find out what it is we believe about democracy and about America."[28] To anyone following the rightward tilt of Congress, the use of this quotation seemed to signal where the library stood in the debates over the meaning of democracy. As former head of TVA, Lilienthal was associated with New Deal government now seen by some as socialism tending toward Communism. Lilienthal had written this statement of his political faith after a tense confirmation hearing before the Joint Congressional Committee on Atomic Energy, in February 1947, when Senator Kenneth D. McKellar (D-Tenn.) accused him of having leftist sympathies and demanded to know his convictions on Communist doctrine. In this foreshadowing of McCarthyism, Lilienthal's passionate defense of democracy as an affirmative doctrine built on the rights of the individual attracted widespread attention.

The initial EAI texts and questions for discussion reflected the liberal consensus of postwar values. Based on rights to life, liberty, and the pursuit of happiness, guarded by freedom of religion and speech, this view assumed the need of a strong central government to protect individual liberty, accomplish the nation's purposes, and work toward the realization of American ideals. This strong government must be balanced by active citizen participation and resistance to tyranny through the constitutional process. For a discussion of the Declaration of Independence, the EAI reading list suggested, among others, these questions: "In what ways are men equal? Why are governments instituted? May a government be overthrown? In the list of abuses are there any we would accept without protest today?"[29] Throughout, democracy was seen as the means to solve the problems of democracy.

Thus Exploring the American Idea implicitly challenged the idea of American society as one of pluralistic harmony and widely shared consensus. Indeed, the proposed questions suggested that major differences could exist on the fundamental nature of American democracy. Unlike the Freedom Train, which al-

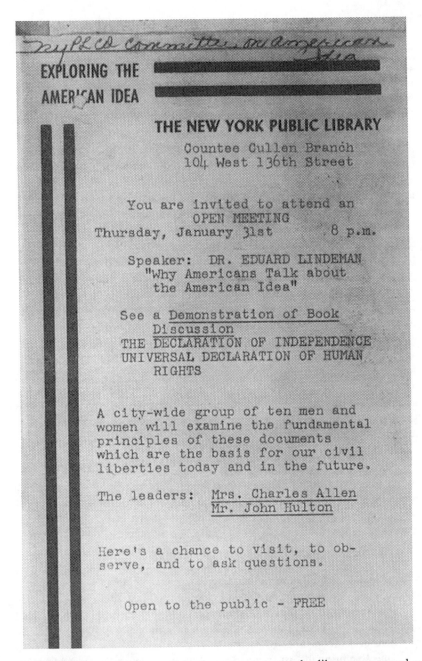

nyPLCd committee on american idea

**EXPLORING THE
AMERICAN IDEA**

THE NEW YORK PUBLIC LIBRARY
Countee Cullen Branch
104 West 136th Street

You are invited to attend an
OPEN MEETING
Thursday, January 31st   8 p.m.

Speaker: DR. EDUARD LINDEMAN
"Why Americans Talk about
the American Idea"

See a Demonstration of Book
    Discussion
THE DECLARATION OF INDEPENDENCE
UNIVERSAL DECLARATION OF HUMAN
    RIGHTS

A city-wide group of ten men and
women will examine the fundamental
principles of these documents
which are the basis for our civil
liberties today and in the future.

The leaders: Mrs. Charles Allen
              Mr. John Hulton

Here's a chance to visit, to ob-
serve, and to ask questions.

Open to the public - FREE

Figure 2: To generate interest in the new program, the library sponsored a demonstration of group discussion at the Countee Cullen Branch. "Exploring the American Idea-memo." *Courtesy of New York Public Library Archives, The New York Public Library, Astor, Lenox and Tilden Foundations.*

lowed a brief glimpse of documents to the crowds filing through the exhibit, EAI required active engagement with the meaning of the texts. Rather than a prepackaged interpretation of the meaning of the American democratic tradition, the reading and discussion format of EAI put that interpretation up for consideration. It suggested that difference and dissent were part of not only the American past but also the American present and that citizenship involved questioning as well as accepting the basis of that tradition.

Although the Great Books influence on Exploring the American Idea was apparent, the two programs diverged on the extent to which they allowed participants to challenge the set curriculum. They shared a belief that the discussion method of free and full investigation of ideas was the only proper basis for decision and that in the realm of ideas all decisions could be re-examined. Both used challenging primary texts and were open to all wishing to read the selections and to consider, in discussion, their major ideas. A single brochure advertised both discussion groups for fall 1950,[30] and their leader training sessions met jointly. Among the first group of EAI leaders were two community people who had led Great Books discussions.

But the Great Books reading courses were formulated by the Great Books Foundation in Chicago, with the same unchanging sequential series used by groups all over the country. EAI was based on this model with readings and discussion questions selected by librarians. Even in the experimental year, however, EAI groups chose their own topics and decided on their own readings. Mildred Mathews reported that at the Central Library two groups, largely made up of professional people, and a group in the Bronx, mostly housewives, followed the prescribed program. In contrast, a more diverse group in West New Brighton branch on Staten Island, jettisoned many of the readings as "too heavy going" and instead added essays by Ralph Waldo Emerson, Lincoln Steffen's *Autobiography*, various plays, poems, and *Manhattan Transfer*, a novel by John Dos Passos.[31] The use of a flexible reading list, democratically selected, including popular works as well as classics, became the hallmark of Exploring the American Idea groups. The act of reading and discussion became as important as the specific selections on democracy; the democratic process undergirded consideration of it.

While adapting the Great Books model to the local library, Exploring the American Idea served as the model for a national program of reading and discussion on the meaning of the American democratic tradition. Historically, libraries had acted as cultural agents in local communities. A coincidence of events in spring and summer of 1951, however, transformed Exploring the American Idea from a local program of the New York Public Library to a national program of the American Library Association. Planning its seventy-fifth anniversary, ALA had appointed an anniversary committee, chaired by Ralph Ellsworth, librarian of the State University of Iowa, to develop a theme and program. Sensing that the country's perils presented both dangers and opportunities for America's libraries, the committee proposed the theme: "The Heritage of the

United States in a Time of Crisis." Ellsworth was aware of the NYPL program and in December 1950 had asked Ralph Beals if he might share the preliminary report of the Committee on the American Tradition with his group. He had already secured $10,000 from Gardner Cowles, publisher of *Look* magazine and a major supporter of the Freedom Train and had arranged for Harper and Brothers to issue two books on the American heritage theme in October 1951. Journalist Gerald W. Johnson was to write a popular volume on six important problems facing the nation, while historian Henry Steele Commager was to edit a sourcebook of documents.

Exploring the American Idea had also attracted the attention of C. Scott Fletcher, head of the new Fund for Adult Education (FAE). Created by the Ford Foundation in its effort to settle its tax status with the Internal Revenue Service, the fund had a particular interest in civic and adult education. Working behind the scenes with Carl Milam, departing executive director of ALA, and his successor John Mackenzie Cory, Fletcher indicated the fund's interest in supporting reading and discussion groups modeled on NYPL's fledgling program. On July 13, 1951, he informed Cory that the FAE board had formally approved a $150,000 grant to ALA for "the promotion and demonstration of adult community discussion programs on the American heritage and its contemporary application, to be undertaken by means of a continuing program through the agency of public libraries."[32] ALA was to coordinate and support local program activities, select six demonstration areas, conduct a training program, and seek the guidance of other national groups. The grant's size, huge compared to other foundation support of ALA, and the program's national scope promised a greatly expanded audience for the public library as an independent agent of adult education.

Since FAE had specified that ALA base its training and promotional materials on the New York Public Library experience,[33] New York City was named one of the six initial sites along with Athens, Georgia, the state of Vermont, La Crosse, Wisconsin, Denver, Colorado, and Los Angeles County, California. In October 1951, librarians from the participating libraries attended a week-long orientation in New York City where they observed a model group discussion of the Declaration of Independence led by Margaret Monroe and Ida Goshkin, head of training for the American Heritage Project, and a Great Books group at the 96th Street branch.

The American Heritage Project was ALA's first national adult education program to be centralized in both theme and implementation. The Great Issues program, introduced as part of the Four Year Goals in 1948, had promoted the discussion of serious current issues in libraries but went no further than book lists on the selected issues, including world government, civil rights, and inflation, programming suggestions, and posters.[34] Although discussion groups were suggested, few were organized. Librarians had little support for the effort, and it was generally regarded as unsuccessful.[35] In contrast, the American Heritage Project provided reading materials through its office in Chicago along with train-

Figure 3: As part of the ALA's American Heritage Project, the Exploring the American Idea program used the AHP logo of the Statue of Liberty in its publicity materials. "Exploring the American Idea-title page." *Courtesy of New York Public Library Archives, The New York Public Library, Astor, Lenox and Tilden Foundations.*

ing and follow-up consultation by project staff. Nonetheless, AHP displayed the same local autonomy and flexibility that characterized Exploring the American Idea. ALA's position that the choice of topics, readings, and pace would be left not just to local communities but to individual discussion groups enabled it to deflect potential criticism of the project from political conservatives.[36]

Like its use of the Lilienthal quotation, the program's links to Commager and Johnson put the program squarely within the bounds of the liberal democratic consensus. The format of Commager's *Living Ideas in America*, with primary documents grouped around issues appropriate for discussion, allowed groups to choose their own topics and readings. Heavy on writings of the Founding Fathers and New Dealers, it offered a more diverse array than earlier EAI readings. It included works by African Americans W. E. B. Du Bois and Booker T. Washington and suffragists Elizabeth Cady Stanton and Susan B. Anthony and omitted writings by utopians, anarchists, Wobblies, and union leaders. Excerpts by Jane Addams, Catherine Beecher, and Dorothy Canfield Fisher confined women's voices to social welfare and education issues. Commager himself was on hand at the training institute in New York to discuss the materials.[37] In contrast to Commager's selection of primary documents, Gerald W. Johnson's *This American People* presented the view of one writer, an unabashed New Dealer and enthusiast of democracy.[38] Written to stimulate discussion, it emphasized that hard work and courage were necessary to sustain democracy and was used in conjunction with study guides prepared by such groups as the General Federation of Women's Clubs.

Discussion groups gave libraries an opportunity to expand their potential as agencies of adult education and to enlarge their audience for serious works on current issues. In this, both EAI and AHP seemed to fulfill the recommendations appearing in the studies of the Public Library Inquiry published by Columbia University Press from 1949 to 1951. Finding that only a small fraction of the public used the public library and tended to seek popular, ephemeral material, the PLI challenged the notion of the library as bulwark of democracy. Libraries, they concluded, were limited by the self-selected nature of their audience and the emergent competition of the mass media. In light of this, libraries should concentrate on reaching local communications elites with serious, controversial works of long-lasting interest.[39]

The evolution of Exploring the American Idea, however, suggests that the library went beyond this role to reach an expanded audience outside the library. The use of new media became crucial to this outreach effort. Based on the Great Books model, EAI had not included film in its design, although as early as spring 1950 NYPL had begun training film discussion leaders and conducting separate film discussion series. Nor had the use of film been mentioned in planning the American Heritage Project. The Fund for Adult Education had a strong interest in film, however, through its president, Scott Fletcher, former head of Encyclopaedia Britannica Films, and Grace Stevenson, head of the American Heritage Project, a pioneer in the use of films at the Seattle Public Library.[40]

Films were an integral part of the American Heritage training session in New York in October 1951, with Ida Goshkin showing "Due Process of Law Denied" based on *The Oxbow Incident* and leading discussion on the issues it raised.

Planned before joining the American Heritage Project, the second year of Exploring the American Idea seemed much like the first, but AHP funding changed the program's size and composition. The 1951-1952 brochure again announced both EAI and Great Books groups and used the same quotation from David Lilienthal. EAI expanded to fifteen groups, met at additional branches, and used program materials produced by ALA. The major difference lay in the addition of film discussion groups in six branches with newly purchased movies and equipment.[41] A brochure resembling a piece of film advertised the program as:

> A film review of our heritage. An adult discussion series to investigate basic principles of our society through motion pic- tures. At this critical time we seek democratic solutions to democracy's problems. Come to your neighborhood branch library once in two weeks. 8 P.M. FREE[42]

Films were central to extending the library's reach.[43] They promised to expand the library's audience but, used without readings, they changed the dynamic of group discussion. Film audiences were larger, more anonymous, and changed from week to week. They required little or no advance preparation. With increased emphasis on group service and the use of films, EAI discussion groups moved away from individual interaction with text and small group consideration of them. In extending its reach as an agency of culture, the library assumed a new role as adult educator using non-print media but lessened the opportunity for individual engagement. Participants became more passive than active, the program more entertainment than education.

At the end of the 1951-52 project year, Mildred Mathews reported overall success far exceeding the library's hopes. The flexibility of the program, necessitated by the diversity of the city, was seen as a major strength. Reporting to ALA, she described New York as a series of disconnected communities with wide variations in racial and economic status that caused tensions as neighborhoods changed. "Any program," she observed, "that is designed for New York City (from rural Staten Island, to footloose central Manhattan, to kaleidoscopic Bronx) must be extremely flexible in methods and materials." The program's ability to reflect this heterogeneity was a key interest of project staff. In her report, Mathews commented,

> The quality and content of the discussion is unusually good. This is due not only to the leaders and materials, but also to the great variety in the educational, religious, and racial backgrounds of the participants as well as in their occupations.

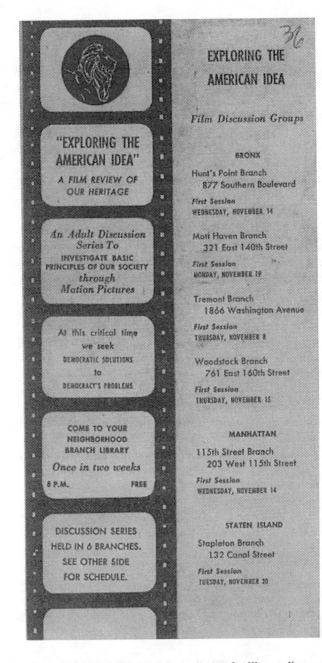

Figure 4: The use of film broadened the audience for library discussion groups. "Exploring the American Idea-film discussion groups." *Courtesy of New York Public Library Archives, The New York Public Library, Astor, Lenox and Tilden Foundations.*

> There are old and new Americans, Puerto Ricans, American
> Negroes, Europeans, lawyers, actors. Clerks, Catholics, Jews
> and Protestants, high school graduates and others with ad-
> vanced degrees, young adults and some not so young, etc.[44]

Mathews reported that thirteen groups had used the original list from the Committee on the American Tradition; one advanced group used a second series of readings, selected by leaders. Six film discussion groups used different combinations of books, films, and pamphlets, each using film in a different way. "There has been," she concluded, "no rigid overall pattern." Thus, as the group members increasingly made decisions about the topics and works to be discussed, the role of the librarian as book expert and arbiter of taste was diminished in an increasingly democratic selection process.

While there were quantifiable indicators of success, including an increase in the numbers of participants and groups and in the proportion of groups led by community volunteers, many benefits were intangible.[45] Librarians and participants profited from enhanced leadership skills, enrichment from sharing ideas with others, the opportunity to read new and sometimes challenging works, and to meet and work with new people. In addition, the program had given the library greater visibility, attracting non-users and calling the library to the attention of other institutions in the city, including the Board of Education, New York University, and the League of Women Voters. Most importantly, the library had defined itself as a safe place in which important matters could be discussed. Mathews reported,

> In this time of increasing tension, loyalty oaths, and fear to
> speak one's mind, many people coming to these American Idea
> groups have exclaimed: " I had no idea we could speak so
> freely! Almost anywhere else it's impossible." The growing
> taboo on the discussion of basic principles of democracy (aris-
> ing from a mistaken method of fighting communism) has made
> it socially incorrect in many areas (radio, schools) [and] eco-
> nomically unwise to inquire into the basis for our democratic
> government. This discussion program makes such inquiry once
> more "respectable", and puts a foot in the door that was gradu-
> ally closing. This program, small as it is, has generated a force
> to help stop the development of a dangerous taboo that no
> democracy can afford.[46]

In her report on the 1951-52 program year, Mathews noted numerous requests for assistance from organizations wishing to conduct an American Idea group,[47] so while fine-tuning the EAI reading list for 1952-53, and adding a new series on the American Character, NYPL staff proposed a greater emphasis on group service. Ralph Beals explained that community organizations would benefit from the library's resources and experience while the library could reach a larger number of people in this way than it could reach directly with the same expenditure.[48] The library's 1952-53 report to ALA demonstrated the impact of these changes on the program's content and reach. The new series on the American Character, including biography, fiction, and films, had proven even more popular than the original American Idea series which was also losing ground to Great Books. Mildred Mathews observed,

> Great Books is not only a larger established program, but it also seems to have a self-improvement or even a "snob appeal" aspect which seems to be lacking in the American Ideas series. Perhaps advertising the latter as the Great Books of America might have an effect. Numbers of people who come to this office to inquire about discussion groups, when presented with both programs, choose the Great Books.[49]

The most dramatic increases, however, were in film attendance and group service. The five film discussion groups at library branches held 42 meetings with average attendance of more than 21, and, unlike other groups, included more men than women. The library also helped community organizations plan and conduct their own American Heritage programs. Nine church groups used films and pamphlets consistently; seven community centers adapted American Heritage programs for adult discussion groups; and six homes for the aged had begun programs. Overall the library helped plan programs and supplied films and materials to 60 organizations and circulated 217 films to audiences totaling 26,003.[50]

Of particular note was the library's response to the interests of a group of elderly Chinese gentlemen. Because they did not speak English, a Chinese assistant from the Chatham Square branch had read to this Golden Age Club each week for two years. When the group wanted to know more about America and American history, the Office of Adult Services arranged to show films acquired for the American Idea series, including "The Declaration of Independence," "America, the Beautiful," "Due Process of Law Denied," and "Grandma Moses." With an enrollment of 51, attendance over six meetings totaled 253 and averaged 39. The library's report concluded:

> "Exploring the American Idea in Chinese" has brought library service to a group which could not have been reached as effectively in any other way. Here was an adult group and an expressed need, with language and educational barriers to communication. The use of specially selected films and other materials and the encouragement of free discussion have been

one effective means of meeting The New York Public Library's
responsibility to the Chinese community in New York City.[51]

The use of films and group services as part of the American Idea program
peaked in 1953-54, the last year in which it received FAE support. While enrollment in Great Books increased from 411 to 454, participation in the American
Idea series declined again, from 344 to 303. Average attendance dropped from
13.5 to 10. Nonetheless, the library planned another series of readings, focused
on the American Scene, using novels, drama, and poetry. The audience for films
provided by the library seemed secure, increasing by 50 percent over the previous year to 39,994. The number of films circulated increased from 217 to 625,
and the number of groups served up from 60 to 110, nearly exceeding the library's
ability to meet the demand.[52] Like the library, these organizations were short-
staffed and often required more assistance than the library could provide.

At the same time, many discussion groups turned their attention to affairs in
their local communities. Early descriptions of the Exploring the American Idea
stressed that it was a discussion not an action program. But, particularly in the
film discussion groups, participants moved from talk to action. With themes
often related to community issues, such as "Who's Delinquent?" on troubled
youth or "The City" on urban planning, films led to "constructive action for
neighborhood betterment." Discussion at the Tremont, Bronx, branch, for example, prompted creation of a neighborhood committee to get better police and
sanitation services. Discussion of the film "Our Better Tomorrow" by a group at
the Morrisania, Bronx, branch, including local PTA members, was credited with
greater understanding of community school issues. On Staten Island, a film program led to the organization of a book discussion group on "Mental Health in
the Community" led by a local psychiatrist and regional librarian.[53]

In the postwar world, librarians sought to define the role of public libraries
in adult education and to respond to the crisis of American democracy posed by
the Cold War. Exploring the American Idea merged these strands, adapting the
Great Books model to the public library setting for reading and discussion groups
on the American democratic tradition. Beginning in New York City and then
across the nation, the program enabled public libraries to fulfill the role advocated by the Public Library Inquiry, meeting the needs of well-educated and
serious readers to consider the issues of the day. At the same time, however, the
format of discussion, involving lay leadership, close reading of the text, and a
questioning of fundamental ideas, challenged the notion of a fixed set of democratic values or a widely shared, unaltered consensus. As the program evolved,
with greater group involvement in the selection of topics and reading and a
more community and action-oriented focus, the group setting offered an experience of democracy as well as a consideration of it. The introduction of film
discussion moved the groups further away from the Great Books model. As
participation became more anonymous and more passive, the entertainment as-

pect partly eclipsed the education function. At the same time, however, film enabled the library to expand its reach and inspired action among community organizations and ethnic groups whose members might never have joined a book discussion group or been considered part of a community's educated elite. While embodying the postwar notion of democratic consensus, EAI gave scope for questioning it. While embodying the Public Library Inquiry vision for public library service, EAI provided a way for libraries to extend their reach to the broader public beyond their traditional base.

Notes

1. Ralph A. Beals and Leon Brody, *The Literature of Adult Education* (New York, 1941), 356.

2. Margaret E. Monroe, *Library Adult Education: The Biography of an Idea* (New York, 1963). Monroe provides a history of adult education at the NYPL and observes that even those libraries most actively engaged in adult education activities rarely referred to them as such. The author wishes to thank Dr. Monroe for reading and commenting on an earlier draft of this article.

3. Archibald MacLeish, "The Librarian and the Democratic Process," *ALA Bulletin* 34 (June 1940): 385-388, 421-422; Franklin D. Roosevelt, "A Message to the Sixty-fourth Annual Conference of the American Library Association, Milwaukee, June 26, 1942," *ALA Bulletin* 36 (July 1942): [422]

4. "Libraries and the War," *ALA Bulletin* 36 (January 1942): 3-5. A statement adopted unanimously by the Council of the American Library Association on December 29, 1941 read, "Every library must organize its services and expenditures without delay to meet the necessities of a nation at war. Every library activity must stand a triple scrutiny. Will it contribute to victory? Will it help to make a better America? Will it help to make a better world?"

5. "The Library Demonstration Bill," *ALA Bulletin* 40 (May 1946): 157-159; Emily Taft Douglas, "Rural Libraries in America," *ALA Bulletin* 40 (September 1946): 269-272 [address to Second General Session, American Library Association annual conference, Buffalo, June 18, 1946].

6. For an extended discussion, see Douglas Raber, *Librarianship and Legitimacy: The Ideology of the Public Library Inquiry* (Westport, Conn., 1997).

7. Leslie I. Poste, "The Public Library Inquiry," *Library Journal* 74 (1 September 1949): 1162.

8. Emily Miller Danton, "Public Library War Information Centers," *ALA Bulletin* 36 (August 1942): 501; Ralph A. Beals, "Public Libraries and the War," *ALA Bulletin* 36 (August 1942): 476-479; "Chairmen of ALA War Service Committees," *ALA Bulletin* 36 (April 1942): 230. For further biographical information on Beals, see Jesse Shera, "Beals, Ralph Albert (1899-1954)," in *Dictionary of American Library Biography* (Littleton, Colo., 1978), 17-20.

9. "Chicago University Experiment Develops into Great Books Foundation," *Library Journal* 72 (15 June 1947): 916.

10. "Richmond Conference," *Library Journal* 61 (15 June 1936): 491. Minutes of the Order and Book Selection Round Table reported by W. T. Purdum, Secretary.

11. "The New York Public Library Launches Great Books Program," *Library Journal* 72 (1 September 1947): 1174. Beals claimed that the first Great Books discussion in a library was held at the New York Public shortly after John Erskine first taught his course on Classics of the Western World at Columbia University.

12. "Groups Discussion of Great Books on Basic Problems 1949-1950: Announcing a Reading and Discussion Program in the New York Public Library," NYPL Archives, RG 6 Public Relations, Pro Samples 1949-1951 [hereafter Pro Samples].

13. James Gregory Bradsher, "Taking America's Heritage to the People: The Freedom Train Story," *Prologue* 17.4 (1985): 229-245; Stuart J. Little, "The Freedom Train: Citizenship and Post War Political Culture 1946-1949," *American Studies* 34 (Spring 1993): 35-68.

14. "The Freedom Train Leads to the Library," [brochure] Pro Samples 1949-1951.

15. "The American Tradition; Letters and Documents Selected by the Staff of the Manuscript Division," *Branch Library Book News* 26.2-3 (1949): 43-48.

16. Pro Samples 1949-1951, RG 6 /3-4.

17. Margaret E. Monroe, "Exploring the American Mind," *Branch Library Book News* 26.2-3 (1949): 39-40, 50-53. Monroe began her essay with the central question being debated by scholars in the newly developing interdisciplinary field of American studies:

Three hundred years of blending peoples and cultures have produced a unique character in the American people. Europeans, Orientals, South Americans look curiously at the United States to see what makes it a nation. And we, inquisitively and sometimes self-consciously, search out the essential forms that are American, the molding forces that make us a people distinct from other peoples.

For a look at how ideological issues afftected the development of American Studies at Yale and elsewhere, see Michael Holzman, "The Ideological Origins of American Studies at Yale," *American Studies* 40 (Summer 1999): 71-99.

18. The library's Honor Roll of Race Relations honored African Americans and whites each year who had contributed to the betterment of race relations in America.

19. Katherine O'Brien, "American Historical Novels," *Branch Library Book News* 26.2-3 (1949): 41-42, 53.

20. Marion E. Lang, "The Distaff Side of American History," *Branch Library Book News* 26.2-3 (1949): 49.

21. Memorandum to Branch Librarians from Esther Johnston, Supervisor of Branches, 6 December 1946, NYPL Archives, RG 8 Office of Branch Libraries, Memo Scrapbook 1946. The case, *Doubleday & Co. v. New York*, 335 U.S. 848 (1948), began when four plainclothes police, acting on a tip from the New York Society for the Suppression of Vice, raided four Doubleday Book Shops in Manhattan. The Court of Special Sessions of the City of New York found that the book violated the New York State obscenity statute. The Appellate Division of the New York Supreme Court, the New York Court of Appeals, and the Supreme Court of the United States upheld this decision. The beginning and end of the saga are reported at "Police Here Seize Book as Obscene; 4 Doubleday Shops Entered in Vice Society's Action against 'Memoirs of Hecate County'," *New York Times*, 9 July 1946, 19; "High Court Backs New York Book Ban; State Ruling Is Upheld on the Obscenity of 'Memoirs of Hecate County'," *New York Times*, 26 October 1948, 33. Announced without an opinion, the Supreme Court's 4 to 4 tie vote let stand the state court conviction.

22. David K. Berninghausen, "Ban of the *Nation*," *Wilson Library Bulletin* 23 (September 1948): 20-21; David K. Berninghausen, "The Case of the *Nation*," *The American Scholar* 19 (January 1950): 44-55.

23. Benjamin Fine, "Library Association Asks Support for Fight against Various Forms of Censorship," *New York Times*, 20 June 1948, sec. 4, p. 9; "Library Bill of Rights," *ALA Bulletin* 42 (July-August 1948): 285. For a history of ALA's policy on intellectual freedom during this period, see Louise S. Robbins, *Censorship and the American Library: The American Library Association's Response to Threats to Intellectual Freedom* (Westport, Conn., 1996).

24. Mildred V. D. Mathews, "Exploring the American Idea," *Library Journal* 76 (1951): 985.

25. Preliminary Report, Committee on American Tradition, NYPL Archives, RG 6 Director's Office, CD American Heritage, Box 30. [Hereafter CD American Heritage] The committee name varied from American tradition to American idea or heritage. In addition to Mildred Mathews, committee members included Robert Henderson, chief of the Main Reading Room, Loda Hopkins, librarian of the 96th Street Branch, Gerald McDonald, head of the American History Division, and Lilian Wilson, librarian of the Bronx Reference Center.

26. Report, Committee on American Tradition. 3 May 1950, CD American Heritage.

27. The brochure announcing the fall 1950 organization of experimental reading and discussion groups on the theme of "Exploring the American Idea" included a partial list of readings. Before publishing the final list, Beals hoped to convene a symposium of outside lay people and library staff for a general review of the projected program. Declining Mathews's suggestion that he approve the titles, he wrote, "A determination of the list should rest primarily in the hands of your committee not mine." Although Beals and Mathews each suggested possible participants, including Judge Learned Hand and *Saturday Review* editor Norman Cousins, and Beals drafted an invitation, the symposium was not convened. Mathews to Beals, 19 June 1950, CD American Heritage; "Draft of Letter to Be Sent to Persons on Attached List," Ralph A. Beals, Director, CD American Heritage. A penciled note indicates "not sent." The program went ahead relying on the experience of the library in group reading and discussion and the judgment of its librarians on appropriate readings. While such an outside group might have warned against undertaking such a program in the chilling political climate, it might have also questioned the omission of any works by women or African Americans from the proposed reading list.

28. "Group Discussion of Books 1950-1951" [Brochure] Pro Samples 1949-1951.

29. CD American Heritage, [Exploring the American Idea 1950-51 Table of Contents, List of Readings, Discussion Guide]. See also, "The Library Leads to Learning," *Branch Library Book News* 27.7 (September 1950): 91.

30. "Group Discussion of Books 1950-51."

31. Mathews, "Exploring the American Idea," 987-988.

32. Fletcher to Cory, 13 July 1951, American Library Association Archives, Executive Board and Executive Director, Grace T. Stevenson Papers, 2/4/21, Box 1, University of Illinois. [Hereafter ALA Archives 2/4/21]

33. *Ibid.* Interestingly, given the origin of the NYPL project, Ralph Ellsworth strongly opposed the Great Books method, writing in a marginal note on a copy of Fletcher's letter, "Stay away from Great Books technique—Ellsworth."

34. "Four Year Goals; Statement of Policy Adopted by Council, January 31, 1948," *ALA Bulletin* 42 (March 1948): 121-122. "The Great Issues," *The Booklist* 44 (August 1948): 397-422. Book lists included: "How Much World Government?" "Inflation and Deflation," "Labor-Management Relations," "Civil Rights," and "U.S.-Russian Relations." The list on U.S.-Russian Relations was prepared by Dr. Avrahm Yarmolinsky, Chief of the Slavonic Division, and Margaret E. Monroe, Assistant Readers' Adviser, at the New York Public Library.

35. For Lester Asheim's evaluation, see "Response to the Great Issues Program," *ALA Bulletin* 44 (July-August 1950): 285-289.

36. Grace Thomas Stevenson, "ALA American Heritage Project Report to Council," January 1952, ALA Archives, 2/4/21, American Heritage Project Reports 1951-1955.

37. Henry Steele Commager, ed. *Living Ideas in America*, (New York, 1951). Ellsworth had resisted Harper's choice of Commager as editor, but his book proved useful, and Commager became an active participant in the American Heritage Project. Margaret Monroe reported that when Senator Joseph McCarthy charged that Commager was a Communist, ALA dealt with these "startling defamations" by ignoring them. Neil Jumonville's intellectual history of Commager, *Henry Steele Commager: Midcentury Liberalism and the History of the Present*, (Chapel Hill, 1999) does not mention Commager's connection with the American Heritage Project.

38. Gerald W. Johnson, *This American People* (New York, 1951).

39. The volumes making this case most strongly were Bernard Berelson, *The Library's Public* (New York, 1949) and the Inquiry's summary volume, Robert D. Leigh, *The Public Library in the United States: The General Report of the Public Library Inquiry* (New York, 1950).

40. Benjamin Fine, "Education in Review: Film Discussion Groups Are Carrying Out a Novel Experiment in Adult Education, *New York Times*, 30 March 1952, sec. 4, p. 11. In 1951 the Fund also sponsored the Experimental Film Discussion Project to test films, along with specially prepared essays and guides, as the basis of adult discussion groups. Some libraries participated in this film project, using Encyclopaedia Britannica films on "American Statesmen" to discuss the theme "Great Men and Great Issues in Our American Heritage."

41. "Group Discussion of Books 1951-1952. Announcing Reading and Discussion Programs in The New York Public Library." Pro Samples 1949-1951.

42. Pro Samples, 1949-1952.

43. Cory to Clift, 29 August 1952, CD American Heritage. American Heritage Funds also enabled NYPL to undertake its first public circulation of films, although necessarily limited for the present to films on American heritage themes.

44. Report 1951-1952 [responding to undated memorandum to all supervisors of American Heritage Programs from Grace Stevenson], NYPL Archives, RG 8 Branch Libraries, Office of Adult Services, Annual/Monthly Reports, 1951-52. [Hereafter cited, Office of Adult Services, Report 1951-52]

45. Annual Report Readers' Adviser's Office and Office of Adult Services, July 1, 1952-June 30, 1953 [Submitted by Mildred V. D. Mathews, Superintendent of Adult Services, dated 24 June 1953], Office of Adult Services. [Hereafter Office of Adult Services, Annual Report 1952-53]

46. *Ibid.*, Insertion, 8.

47. Office of Adult Services, Annual Report 1951-52, 4.

48. Beals to Clift, 26 May 1952, CD American Heritage.

49. *Ibid.*, 4.

50. Office of Adult Services, Annual Report, 1952-53.

51. "Exploring the American Idea in Chinese," Office of Adult Services, Annual Report 1952-53.

52. The New York Public Library Adult Group Specialist Report 1953-1954, Office of Adult Services.

53. *Ibid.*, 2.

"We Have Become Too Tender-Hearted": The Language of Gender in the Public Library, 1880-1920

Jacalyn Eddy

Gender in library history has customarily been conflated with the battle between men and women over wages, professional advancement, and employment discrimination. Clearly, women both endured discrimination and made important contributions to the library. A valuable social history has begun to emerge that restores women's contributions to library service by demonstrating that women both resisted and accommodated library politics. Yet gender was a component of library history not only as a "battle of the sexes," but also as a linguistic code in the institution's past. As a potent rhetorical strategy, gender was consistently employed by librarians in debates over the library's nature and role in American culture. As such, gender became a critical mechanism of complex negotiation not merely related to biological circumstance. The questions of interest to historians are thus not simply "how did men feel about women?" or "what did women accomplish despite job discrimination?" but rather, how was gender employed—consciously or not—to construct the politics and future of the library? What did the presence of "female" signal in the library, space at once public *and* private? How did concepts of gender provide an interpretive framework for defining the meaning of the public library? The idea of "uplift" evident in primary sources demonstrates that the development of the public library was a class issue, but gender was also a central factor.

The library, along with other organizations and institutions emerging in the late nineteenth century, reflected profound changes in American society. Its search for ways to express anxieties about those changes resulted, significantly, in a discourse that utilized gender, a dominant trope of the time. The way in

0026-3079/2001/4203-155$2.50/0   American Studies, 42:3 (Fall 2001): 155-172

which the institution engaged gender deserves attention because it reveals gender as a cultural rather than merely biological fact of library life, thus enhancing our understanding of the library's nature. Discussions about "female" in library history are more richly understood at a metaphoric level, for it was on that level—rather than through explicit conflict—that gender became an important vehicle to define the library's ideology, plan its future, defend its funding requirements, consider its functions, and establish its institutional credibility.[1]

Between the 1880s and 1920 the library's official forum, the *Library Journal*, engaged in gender politics by utilizing rhetoric that reinforced gender norms, reflecting the low status of librarians in American culture.[2] In fact, however, the story was not quite that simple. The library's language reinforced gender norms, but it also mirrored deep, culture-wide ambivalence about gender. When the library is viewed in the gendered terms of its own debate, an essential tension becomes evident: women were desirable as librarians to enhance institutional claims to authority at precisely the same moment gender language was used to express fear that female influence would compromise those claims. The concern about "female" expressed in the debate represents an important and neglected, if minority, opinion among early library leaders.

The Library and Women

Situated in the broader context of a burgeoning nationwide organizational matrix, democratized education, and a heightened interest in scientific expertise, the public library was "up for grabs" between 1880 and 1920, caught among competing visions of its proper role in American culture. If, as many librarians envisioned, the library were to take its place as a powerful institution, it needed to reflect assumed "male" values such as strength and serious intellectual pursuit. If, on the other hand, the library should offer leadership in cultural matters, the library should exhibit "female" traits such as morality and virtue. For many librarians, some combination of the two was ideal; that is, the library could and should evidence institutional characteristics associated with "maleness," and others associated with female identity.

Such thinking reflected the way in which gender assumptions evolved in America throughout the nineteenth century. Gender jurisdiction, particularly in middle-class culture, was frequently divided into "spheres," associating private with female and public with male. Well-defined and broadly accepted, these differences limited women's access to formal political life and prescribed the circumstances of their civic engagement, particularly during the antebellum years.[3]

On closer inspection, however, the simplicity of this trope obscures a highly complicated gender dynamic in American social life. The construction of spheres, in fact, should be understood less literally than as a metaphoric infrastructure of complex negotiation. Far from being confined to their homes in any literal sense, women participated substantially in organizational activity and entered professions such as teaching and social work in increasing numbers. As the end of the century approached, the "spheres" seemed less apt than ever since gender relations, now in a pronounced state of flux, were hardly as tidy as the concept implied. The workplace thus became a logical and primary site of gender negotiation, but the process by no means led to the abandonment of notions about what constituted women's proper work. Women were admitted to education and social work, for example, because those professions had the welfare of children and families as their primary focus and, thus, did not challenge accepted gender norms.[4] Typically, women who rejected these options and pursued non-traditional careers faced formidable social disapproval. In addition, women continued to labor under multiple, and sometimes contradictory, cultural expectations; the demand for "submissive helpmates" and "pillars of strength" sent an uncertain message to women about their role in American culture.[5]

Whether or not "spheres" accurately reflected gender relations, however, the notion retained its appeal for the middle class because it simultaneously engaged the concept of space.[6] Although the distinction between public and private space existed before the middle of the nineteenth century, it carried special significance by the latter half, representative of power and success in a complex world.[7] Both literally and symbolically, space became increasingly associated with distinct functions, consistent with the modern notion that specialization confirmed progress.[8] If specialized space was proof of progress, then, by implication, so were specialized tasks. As professional tasks were defined, gender was prominently situated on the cultural fault line.

Space and specialization achieved this level of importance, in part, from nagging anxieties about modern life, including a perceived loss of moral and intellectual fortitude. During the 1880s, those anxieties coincided with the appearance of the New Woman, a new phenomenon on the American social scene. In profile, the New Woman was less often married and aspired to greater educational and economic opportunities than did her mother or grandmother. Gradually, she inhabited public, male space traditionally off-limits to her while retaining claims to typically female space within genteel middle-class society.[9] Her emergence not only contributed to a sense of social upheaval but also resulted in allegations of cultural feminization. Gender thus served as a flashpoint for a middle-class critique of modern life, regarded by some as an age of uncertainty, moral and otherwise.[10] As old beliefs were disrupted, torn from their traditional moorings by rapid social, industrial, and economic change, many worried that authentic experience had been the cost of modern conveniences.[11] Perceiving themselves to be in a crisis of authority, such individuals sought to establish institutions that would uphold and reinforce traditional social and cultural beliefs.[12] Gender was therefore intimately connected to questions of authority and, unsurprisingly, the library engaged with gender when considering those questions.

The Library and Print Culture

By the time the American Library Association was created in 1876, print was fast becoming a critical technology for many Americans. This gave a new degree of power to print.[13] As America's "primary social currency," words offered a perfect basis for the library's claims to authority, adding new and urgent legitimacy to the institution. As an obvious broker of words, the library could logically anticipate the realization of its goal to become one of America's premier cultural institutions.[14] Along with the support of benefactors like Andrew Carnegie, space had been made available by increased municipal funding. Together with the acknowledged power of print, the library seemed fortuitously poised for success. But several obstacles stood between the library and the authority it desired. Its voluntary nature, the presence of amateur librarians, the institution's inability to offer academic degrees, and challenges to the library's traditional texts upon which its authority historically rested, all complicated the acquisition of authority.[15]

To circumvent such obstacles, library leaders employed several strategies, including myth creation about the importance of such things as literacy, to persuade the reading public of the library's indispensability. Readers, the library insisted, were more "civilized" and stood a better chance at upward social mobility than nonreaders.[16] Moreover, one of the library's most powerful early myths portrayed the library as essential for civic-minded citizens interested in serious self-education, thereby linking intellectual development to active citizenship.[17] Time and again, enthusiastic library advocates assured the American reading public that the fulfillment of democratic ideals could be achieved by utilizing library resources. Democratic reading was potentially a "vital part of civic life, essential for complete public as well as private development."[18] Its overarching goal was community building, and librarians often spoke proudly of inspiring and encouraging citizens' use of the library to create a "reading democracy," providing an indispensable foundation for citizenship, because books were believed to humanize and civilize readers.[19] If "weeded" of sentimentality (understood to be a female trait) the "rich soil" of books would surely create better people.[20] "We want citizens," one contributor to the *Library Journal* quipped, "and the public school and the public library are the places where citizens are made. . . . If this were an absolute monarchy, and we had a peasant class, [the public library] would not be necessary. But it is not a monarchy, and we have no peasant class."[21] Samuel Thurber, a high school principal in Massachusetts, praised the library, noting that "our teachers and pupils throng the Library, and there acquire the habit of investigation, and of independent, well-grounded opinion on a multitude of subjects of the utmost importance to citizens in a republican State. . . . Without the Library, the desire for knowledge constantly awakened in the school would have to go unsatisfied."[22]

The library's connection to and support for republican ideology is further evidence of its strategies for coping with cultural crisis and with gender. Ongoing predictions that republics eventually succumb to "an irresponsible leisure class and a vicious urban mob" served as a cautionary tale of the consequences of loss of intellectual rigor and vigorous political involvement ("maleness").[23] The powerful, intimate link between the library and formal political participation, from which women, at the time, remained largely disconnected, constituted a *de facto* claim concerning the nature of library space: its most fundamental aspects would be, by definition, "male."[24]

Ironically, however, librarianship was rapidly feminizing at the precise moment that the library advertised itself as the appropriate space for developing mental and political skills. Only two years after the ALA was founded, two-thirds of the nation's librarians were women. By 1910, the percentage had risen to 78.5 percent; by 1920, fully 90 percent of America's librarians were women.[25]

The astounding pace of feminization in librarianship suggests that women were granted admission to the profession unchallenged.[26] Solid reasons existed for allowing women into the field. Chronic labor shortages and modest library funding made it difficult to refuse female applicants who would work for less in the rapidly growing number of public libraries. Of equal or greater importance, however, was the widespread belief in the innate moral superiority of women, an invaluable asset to an institution whose self-determined mission was tied to supervising the integrity of the public's reading taste.[27] The editor Montrose Moses compared the library to a "temple of treasures," wherein the librarian functioned as the "high priestess."[28] To most librarians, women made perfectly appropriate guardians of the public's reading selections insofar as the library wished to exert moral influence over those selections.

But the rush to embrace women into librarianship did not occur without misgivings.[29] While the presence of women may have been relatively uncontested, the presence of "female" was not. Women might be willing to work for less pay, and they were acceptable cultural guardians. But what was the consequence of too much female influence in public space? To the extent that the modern library stood for serious learning, civic duty, or democratic opportunity, the library continued to be "male" space, and the individuals who staffed it should exemplify those attributes and beliefs. Moral influence and smaller paychecks, while desirable, were insufficient to induce library leaders to embrace women unreservedly. Librarians would have to be educated, thoroughly knowledgeable about books, and prepared to respond to patrons' needs and questions. Americans increasingly looked to experts as signposts of explanation in the modern world, but few women at the time had the kind of broad education that its founders saw as important to assist the library in its goal of achieving cultural authority.[30]

To bring "female" qualities (morality and good character) and "male" qualities (discipline, education, strength) into proper balance, the trend was inexorably toward formal library training. Such training, it was hoped, would mitigate women's assumed tendencies to nurture and sentimentalize, qualities that might signal to the public that the library had become too "female."[31] Professionalization thus became critical to the library's development, and a powerful authority-gaining strategy. Because space and words were key ingredients in the acquisition of legitimate authority, the library, as specialized space, was now obliged to develop a professional culture that included specialized training, a body of expert knowledge, and defined standards.[32]

The ALA, therefore, placed consistent emphasis on professional education. By 1902, for example, the New York State Library School, then located in Albany, was placed on a graduate footing, requiring all applicants to have completed a course of study at colleges registered by the University of the State of New York. James Wyer, president of the school when he wrote its history in 1926, recalled this decision as a "pioneer step" for librarianship.[33] Employment success derived from formal training, he argued, and explained the high demand for Albany graduates throughout the country. Wyer boasted that Albany graduates directed roughly half the libraries in American cities with populations exceeding 100,000; headed libraries at thirty colleges, including thirteen state university systems; were state librarians in California, Ohio, and New Hampshire; furnished five presidents to the ALA; and directed or were on the faculty of twenty library schools.[34] Education, he reassuringly reported, paid off for librarians.

Not everyone was pleased with the ALA's educational initiatives. In 1891 the *New York Sun*, for example, expressed indignation over the NYS Library School's educational plan by engaging gender directly.

> The subject of cooking is a great deal more important to the community at large than this new science of Mr. Melvil Dewey's; and the Regents of the University might just as properly establish a State cooking school at Albany, and confer degrees in that important branch of knowledge. . . . The scheme is nonsensical and the degrees originating in this manner and proceeding from such a source will be ridiculous.[35]

Given the contemporary animus against female professionalism, the overwhelming presence of women in the school—now potential candidates for advanced educational opportunities—undoubtedly served as the catalyst for such complaints. In any event, critics of the library's plan to accumulate cultural authority by educating rank and file librarians made use of gender language by comparing librarianship and food preparation, traditionally among the most basic of female occupations.

The Library and Fiction

While the ALA struggled to persuade the public of its usefulness in creating citizens, and to develop a staff of competent professionals, some library leaders feared that the growing presence of fiction on library shelves threatened to undermine the library's authority. Deeply rooted in Puritan anxieties about recreation and books that were not "true," such concerns centered specifically on the dilution of the library's function by luring patrons to books for pleasure rather than for civic duty or self-education. Worse, the growing desire for fiction suggested to some an emasculated reading public suffering from a loss of independence; bookish individuals were increasingly associated with effeminate qualities.[36] Not all fiction was "bad," but tolerance of it frequently represented the hope that it would be a steppingstone to improved reading selections.[37]

The well-known, protracted debate over fiction among librarians offers excellent examples of the ways in which gendered language was used to negotiate the meaning of the library. The fiction question has often been interpreted as a class issue: i.e., the "better" sort of people encouraged the "lower" sort of people to appreciate the "better" sort of books. But the fiction question may also be understood metaphorically, wherein fiction was associated with "female" traits that library leaders preferred to minimize.[38] That the majority of librarians were women obviously connected fiction with female because librarians stocked the library's fiction. Consistent attempts to persuade librarians to reduce the amount of fiction on their shelves produced mixed results.[39] Women, however, not only stocked fiction, they were assumed to be its major consumers. Publishers, for example, took it as a matter of course that reading taste was driven by gender. The lack of factual data to support this assumption did not deter publishers from targeting markets by gender as early as the mid-nineteenth century.[40] Finally, the didactic and sentimental fiction characteristic of the first half of the nineteenth century, often (though by no means exclusively) written by women, had fallen precipitously from grace.

Fiction, therefore, was historically and intimately connected with "female" on the surface of the debate, but discussions about it were gendered on a deeper level as well, and related to questions of institutional authority. In 1916, Henry N. Sanborn, secretary for the public library commission of Indiana, complained that "our public libraries are far from interesting men as we should like. . . . Too many of our libraries select their books...almost wholly for women and children. . . ."[41] Sanborn urged librarians to stock their shelves with more books appealing to "the masculine mind."[42]

> women are more emotional, certainly more sentimental, than men. . . . We naturally expect women to read more...fiction, more poetry, and more literature devoted to alleviating undesirable social conditions. But some librarian says: 'It is the women and not the men in my town who want books on eugenics, world politics, history, economics, industrial education.' . . . The average woman—not the specially college

> trained woman—reads these books because her club is study-
> ing the subject or because she feels she should know some-
> thing of these subjects to attain her desired goal of intellectual
> breadth and culture. A man . . . reads these books . . . because
> the subject itself interests him . . . a man gets information
> because he loves the subject, but a woman gets information
> because she loves to have information. . . .[43]

Sanborn explicitly connected fiction (substandard reading) with "female" traits.

> Women are more interested in mental vivisection than are men,
> at least in psychological studies that tend to the morbid, the
> abnormal, or the degenerate. . . . Men do not object to psy-
> chology if it depicts men and women who are optimistic, and
> morally on the upward path in life. The characters may be
> criminals, degenerates, or undesirables of any kind, as long as
> the chief interest is in their strong, good, healthy characteris-
> tics. Nothing can do more to convince the men of a town that
> the library is something more than a *feminized institution* than
> to have material which will be of use to them. . . . As a general
> statement, it can be safely said that men will read heavier and
> more serious books than women. . . . Sentimental stories are
> for women . . . [44] (italics mine)

This passage associates "female" with emotionalism, sentimentality, and fiction. Sanborn's references to morbidity, abnormality, and degeneracy reflected
his attention to the new field of psychology. As traditional frameworks of meaning weakened, the vacuum was filled with a therapeutic orientation, the primary
vehicle of which was introspection. This obsessive self-scrutiny, sometimes regarded as the prime characteristic of the modern age, produced a preoccupation
with self considered by some to be "morbid."[45] Neurasthenia, the new psychic
malady of the late-nineteenth century, was generally understood to be rooted in
fear, and neurasthenics the pale offspring of hardy ancestors.[46] While neurasthenia affected both men and women, the condition was nonetheless frequently
associated with women attempting to escape their responsibilities.[47] At the same
time, behaviorists like G. Stanley Hall and John B. Watson warned Americans of
the effect of excessive female influence. As an intellectual trend, therefore, psychology tended to encourage privatization (associated with "female") perceived
to endanger republican civic-mindedness (associated with "male").

On the other hand, Sanborn equated "male" with optimism, strength, good-
ness, health, and serious study. His deeper worry was that feminization would
result in diminished status and compromised potential for the library as an American cultural institution. Traditional assumptions about gender provided

Sanborn both with an ideological basis and the metaphoric language for his concern.

The Library and Work with Children

By 1900, debates about the nature and role of the library had produced significant changes within the ALA. After a long struggle, several outspoken women members had finally succeeded in convincing the organization to provide formal support for children's work in public libraries. Support for work with children stemmed partially from middle-class concern over the consequences of recent social trends: industrialization, urbanization, and immigration. But support also drew on a belief in children as unique individuals requiring special care (and special space) in libraries.[48] Just as the child-centeredness of teaching and social work placed those professions securely in the hands of women, library work with children provided women with an especially acceptable point of entry into professional authority. Since women were already acknowledged experts on the subject of children, children could become the legitimate concern of women in library service.

The organization's support for children's work contained many layers, some intended to benefit adults as much as children. Segregating children from adults conveniently confined them to a particular space in the library, leaving adult spaces free for serious study. Whatever the motivations, age segregation represented a sharp break with the previous literary training of American children, who traditionally had been encouraged to read adult literature as early as possible. In any case, all agreed that women were the logical choice to supervise children in public space of the library, just as they did in the private space of the home. It was conventional wisdom that "a sympathetic and sane-minded woman . . . will have a strong, fine far-reaching influence over children's lives."[49]

Thus, children's space became women's space in the public library. Indeed, supervisors of children's work like Anne Carroll Moore (New York Public Library) and Alice Jordan (Boston Public Library) infused space devoted to children in their libraries with soft ambiance—pastel wall colors, soothing art work, and exhibits of interest to children—all of which succeeded in encouraging children to come to the library. Emphasis was placed on hands-on activities, offering children a visceral experience with books.[50] For children's librarians, reading represented a "near-sacred communion between reader and text."[51] Story hours, poetry readings, and special celebrations, heretofore unknown in the public library, became stock in trade for children's librarians after the turn of the century.[52]

The response of children to these efforts was impressive. By 1911, NYPL alone circulated over two-and-a-half-million books in its children's rooms.[53] But while acknowledging responsibility for supporting this work, library boards did not wish to be misunderstood: the primary purpose of the library, even for children, was education and citizenship. In 1895, for example, the Examining

Committee at the Boston Public Library declared that the children's room "should be the most important place in the city for the training of those readers without whom the Library is a mere ornament . . . instead of the nursery of good citizenship which it was meant to be."[54] In its statement, the Committee recognized the contribution of "female" influence (nursery) to the "male" outcome (citizenship). Library administrators like Arthur Bostwick genuinely supported this work (and the feminized milieu that resulted), but support was not always unqualified. Bostwick worried that children's rooms would become overly feminized, failing to represent "the masculine point of view," and urged measures designed to offset maternalizing temptations.[55] Discipline was routinely recommended. As Bostwick put it, "assistants who are 'fond of children' are often the very worst person to do work in a children's room."[56] The message, if not always the method, was clear: supervise children without suffocating them with motherly attention that might rob them (particularly boys) of natural curiosity and independence.[57]

But nurturing curiosity was not intended to conflict with reality-based learning. Fiction was bad enough, but outright fantasy—talking animals or dancing flowers—pushed the limit of tolerance for some library leaders who accused children's librarians of using fantasy to shield children from the realities of life.[58] As with fiction, gender became the mechanism and language to express concern. Helen Haines claimed that

> children's work is a cult apart . . . producing a sort of sentimentalized, devitalized mind-training . . . turning away from literature . . . with strong moral or dramatic appeal. . . . Delicately fanciful stories of baby bees and friendly flowers, will not satisfy a child's sturdy common-sense. You remember the children's librarians whose story-hour dealt with the coming of spring. She told of the pretty little birds chirping, and the pretty little sunbeams beaming, and the joyous little breezes frolicking about the passers-by. . . . [A boy] unconsciously demands something for his mind and his intelligence to grow upon [rather than] thin-spun, super-feminized fancies. . . . Our best hope lies in our work with children, provided it . . . inspir[es] strength as well as sweetness.[59]

The passage opens by comparing children's work to a cult, suggesting first that women were susceptible to bizarre fringe beliefs stemming from emotionalism. That being the case, women supervising children in special space outside the mainstream of the library's business might lose perspective about the serious purpose of the library. Haines' portrayal of the children's librarian as "female" was, as already noted, accurate. Her portrayal of the child in search of mind development as "male," however, is more revealing, resting on gender assumptions consistent with those of other librarians. The librarian was realistically assumed to be female, while the reality-oriented patron who wisely insisted on mental development was male. In this scenario, the young boy had a more solid grasp on the purpose of the library than the adult female librarian. Obviously, the use of plural pronouns could have avoided gender altogether, but those notwithstanding, "super-feminized fancies" threatened to devitalize the boy's mind, just as fiction threatened to devitalize the library.

The Library and Progressivism

Enthusiasm for Progressive reform translated into expanded activities for children's librarians. Refusing to remain confined to traditional tasks in formal library space—"irksome minutiae" that NYPL Director Edwin Andersen compared to "crochet work"—librarians embraced activities like home, hospital, and settlement house visitation.[60] While these activities undoubtedly carried the usual multivalent, overlapping, and sometimes confusing ambitions often associated with Progressivism, they nonetheless became a significant part of the librarian's routine. One of the first orders of business for a new librarian was to familiarize herself with the neighborhood in which the library was situated, often by contacting organizations with whom she could establish cooperative working relationships. Cities were often divided into territories, assigning them to branch librarians for investigation about community life—schools, clubs, associations, churches, hospitals, factories, and ethnic composition—in short, whatever might affect the community's social life. Librarians at the Logan branch of the Minneapolis Public Library, for example, sometimes went shopping with children, recommended books containing medical advice, assisted with finding jobs for homeless individuals, provided instruction on mothering skills, attended PTA meetings, advised wives about intemperate husbands, counseled children about their spiritual lives, and even offered fashion advice.[61]

Such street networking represented not only an expansion but also the feminization of the library. Unwilling to wait for readers to come to the dignified halls of the library, women librarians were out and about in the very ordinariness of America's city streets, expanding the definition of library space in ways that were distinctly "female," strengthening both the library's connection to the home and librarians' connection to readers. This behavior permanently altered the library's image. In 1903, for example, the *Library Journal* had declared that, unlike teachers, librarians could never hope to have "a personal interest and knowledge of each child."[62] Only ten years later, Arthur Bostwick spoke easily of "personal relations between librarian and reader."[63]

Nowhere in the library world were women more visible and more powerful than in children's rooms. Judson Jennings, in the 1924 ALA presidential address, alluded to activities in children's rooms to complain about the feminization of the public library.

We have secured books and money for our libraries thru pink teas and lotteries, by concerts, picnics, plays and exhibitions, somewhat as funds are raised for missionary work. . . . Meeting these difficulties and overcoming these handicaps has developed in librarians something of a spirit of the missionary. . . . In going about my own library, I have at different times found exhibits of dolls, or embroidery, or bird houses or even a collection of dead birds. . . . We are all interested in music. . . . But why stop here, we have said. Why not buy and lend music scores. . . . And so we buy scores . . . then we add music rolls and phonograph records. . . . And next we install pianos and victrolas in order that Mrs. Music Lover may test one of Harry Lauder's masterpieces before she makes the mistake of taking it home. . . . Then again we have supplied Mrs. Jones with a book on the care of the baby and we have lent Mrs. Jones a book on vegetable gardening. It is only a step further actually to assist in caring for the baby or the garden. And in these ways we have acquired the attitude of the welfare worker. We have taken a motherly interest in our readers. . . . We have become too tender-hearted. . . . It is partly because of this missionary spirit . . . that a number of . . . features have been gradually grafted on to library work. . . . Perhaps we have gone too far. . . . Since our libraries lend cook books, should we not provide cook stoves in order that the anxious young housewife may test Mrs. Farmer's recipes?"[64]

Jennings made it clear that he did not view the library as an appropriate place for dolls, embroidery, motherly interest, tender-heartedness, welfare work, missionaries, or anxious young housewives—all allusions to female interests and occupations that compromised the potential of the library for the more valuable work of citizenship training and civic responsibility. In short, he employed gendered language to complain about the library's actual or potential loss of authority.

It has been suggested that librarianship rapidly diminished by mimicking the traditional sphere of women's influence.[65] This is true, in a sense. Women's activities in the library did assume "homelike" qualities. But this passage reveals that, in reality, some library leaders feared that the library had expanded too far. Women did not merely take home to work, passively and uncritically accepting their assigned roles, or simply transfer their domestic responsibilities to the workplace. Instead, women used traditional skills and authority already established in the private sphere as a point of entry in their search for professional identity and satisfaction. This search constituted a new awareness of "female" on the part of women who intended to become upwardly mobile.[66]

The Library and the First World War

As America prepared for war in 1917, so did the public library. The war was, in fact, a "watershed event" in its development.[67] So long as the war remained a European affair, librarians generally complied with Woodrow Wilson's request for neutrality.[68] Following the declaration of war in April 1917, the library, along with other institutions, responded with enthusiastic patriotism.[69] The library, anxious to be of service to the state, supported the supposedly selfless aim of securing democratic process for the rest of the world,[70] engaging in a variety of activities, including dissemination of government information about the war, Liberty Bond drive support, book collection, and food conservation campaigns.[71] Women met in libraries to knit for soldiers and to rehearse patriotic community celebrations. The library was a drop-off point for canned goods, nurses were recruited there, and clothes for war orphans were sewn on the premises.[72] Such response to the war reflected not only eagerness to enhance its image in the eyes of the public (thus strengthening its influence) but also opportunity to fulfill some of its oldest and most cherished goals: serious study and civic participation. Demand for nonfiction titles was up; Americans were now interested in military science and organizations, map reading, and drill manuals.[73]

The organization viewed the war as a service opportunity to America's armed forces as well, since "these armies of this world war are reading men."[74] Even fighting men would want to read, the ALA assumed, and developed an initiative to provide books for them, both in camps and hospitals on the homefront as well as overseas. At the request of the War Department, the ALA began book collection drives that, during the eighteen months of war, resulted in the donation of five million dollars and three million books.[75] And what would soldiers like to read? "Some thoughtful, simple devotional books," suggested the *Journal*, "forward movements in social welfare and civic betterment. . . . Books on citizenship, patriotism and thrift are well to include."[76]

But the ALA intended to send librarians as well as books to America's troops. During the summer of 1918, the *Journal* ran a series of articles aimed at preparing librarians for war work. They also revealed the continued use of gender as an interpretive framework, reminding librarians to conduct themselves with "certain traits of character," enumerated as dignity, maturity, and loyalty. After all, one contributor remarked, "we women were not invited to enter this world of men and if we do intrude we must bear ourselves as good soldiers and not complain of hard beds, soiled table linen, lack of bathrooms, suffocating heat and dust in summers, freezing cold in winter, and tobacco smoke all the time."[77] Librarians, therefore, were admonished to behave in "male" (soldierly) ways, guarding against "petty jealousies, gossip, scandal, and quarrels . . . [and] able to take orders and accept a reprimand in a soldierly spirit. . . . The common soldier is not supposed to think for himself but he is trained to obey orders. . . .

[The librarian] must not be sensitive and she must not be sentimental. Sympathy the boys want, but how they do hate to be wept over!"[78]

Aside from observing decorum, the librarian was encouraged to "sing, draw, paint, play games, get up impromptu entertainments on rainy days or dull evenings" to make herself a "treasure." Such ability, claimed the *Journal*, was actually more important than formal library training.[79] Further, librarians were informed that men in hospitals wanted "detective and 'wild West' stories, adventure, romance and poetry when they are sick . . . [later] they demand books on gas engines, turbines, radio and wireless, trigonometries, all sorts of things a woman knows little about."[80]

Miriam E. Carey was even more direct. In a paper delivered to the ALA conference at Saratoga in July 1918, she informed librarians that

> the doctors say that there is nothing really the matter with most of the sick soldiers except sheer homesickness. What does a home-sick man choose for his reading? Probably what he craves is an old-fashioned love story . . . *the man who is sick is more like his mother than his father.*"[81] (italics mine)

Carey used gender to create a continuum of convalescence, where the reading selections of soldiers evolved from "female" (fiction) to "male" (nonfiction); the closer the soldier to recovery, the more "male" (healthy) his reading tastes became. Carey was not as interested in criticizing the reading habits of women as in communicating realistic expectations to inexperienced librarians by employing rhetorical strategies comparing male/female to health/illness.

Summary

Space, gender, and language converged in the public library in ways that both reinforced and challenged prevalent cultural beliefs during the early years of its development. Differences between word and deed—what the library *said* and what it *did*—created unique tensions, making the library an important agency of culture between 1880 and 1920. By using gender as a linguistic code, the library expressed misgivings about "female," reinforcing cultural norms by reaffirming the notion that men and women were essentially dissimilar and that excessive female influence endangered public space. Its official rhetoric rested on the broadly accepted belief that women presided over a cultural/moral/private domain while men presided over an intellectual/civic participatory/public domain.

At the same time, the library did not simply reflect and perpetuate gender norms wholesale. The admission of women to librarianship in substantial numbers—whatever the motives—placed the library in the advance guard of the lengthy process to alter those norms. The increased visibility of women in libraries—public and professional space—blurred and, gradually, helped to unhinge the connection between public/private and male/female. The shift in urban "sexual geography," however, did not signal fairness in the work place because allowing women in public space was not, by itself, equivalent to granting them power. [82] Still, at a time when only one percent of the nation's lawyers and six percent of the nation's physicians were female[83], those professions that feminized early are noteworthy for the cultural change they both portended and affected by their overall institutional behavior, if not their words. The consequence of *not* recognizing the importance of gender as metaphor in the library is to regard the library as an abstract, disembodied concept distant from society in a moment of dynamic social change, rather than as an active shaper of those changes. In this sense, at least, the library indeed accomplished its goal of becoming one of America's leading cultural institutions.

Notes

1. In *Gender and the Politics of History* (New York, 1988), Joan Wallach Scott argues that gender is a "deep structure" of history. Beneath the surface of "what happened" lies a critical substructure of rhetorical devices that serve as shorthand for expressing cultural attitudes. Certain characteristics—say, strength or courage—have traditionall been "male," while others—like sentimentalism or nurturing—have been associated with "female." In *Disorderly Conduct: Visions of Gender in Victorian America* (New York, 1985) Carroll Smith-Rosenberg argues that the battle of the sexes cannot be understood until the language surrounding it is decoded. Sexual language, she suggests, "functions as political metaphor," converting "flesh-and-blood creature[s] into a condensed symbol of disorder and rebellion"(246-247). See especially the chapter "The New Woman as Androgyne: Social Disorder and Gender Crisis 1870-1936."

2. As Wayne Wiegand has noted, the American Library Association never claimed a majority of librarians as members. See for example, *The Politics of an Emerging Profession: The American Library Association, 1876-1917* (Westport, Conn., 1986). This article, however, is less concerned with *Library Journal* circulation figures than with the status and influence it enjoyed as the profession's official journal. As such, it is a critical site of professional discourse.

3. As Linda Kerber and other historians have noted, the distinction between public and private and its link to gender is not uniquely American but predates Western culture. See "Separate Spheres, Female Worlds, Woman's Place: The Rhetoric of Women's History" in *Toward an Intellectual History of Women* (Chapel Hill, 1997).

4. In *The Feminization of American Culture* (New York, 1977), Ann Douglas argues that women used the home to "sanction rather than limit" the search for professional identity as part of a "new self-conscious sense of upward mobility"(78).

5. T.J Jackson Lears, *No Place of Grace: Antimodernism and the Transformation of American Culture, 1880-1920* (Chicago, 1981), 16. "Separate spheres" requires qualification. Historians have debated its meaning since the 1960s, historiographically outlined by Linda Kerber in "Separate Spheres, Female Worlds, Woman's Place: The Rhetoric of Women's History." In brief, early interpretations of separate spheres were essentially attempts at giving the concept a central location in women's historical experience. By the late-1970s, historians' views of separate spheres had become more complex, including claims for a distinct woman's culture in the nineteenth century (Smith-Rosenberg) as well as viewing the spheres as a necessary precondition for modern feminism (Cott). Historians of female labor (Kessler-Harris, Blewett, Levine, Milkman, Buhle, Stansell) suggest that the labor market is segregated by gender, but that the patterns of segregation are constantly renegotiated.

6. Burton Bledstein, *The Culture of Professionalism: The Middle Class and the Development of Higher Education in America* (New York, 1976), 56. Bledstein argues that space was actually one of the Victorians' most fundamental concepts.

7. *Ibid.*, 56.

8. *Ibid.*, 61-64.

9. Smith-Rosenberg, *Disorderly Conduct*, 245.

10. Lears, *No Place of Grace*, 4-5,46. See also Ann Douglas, *The Feminization of American Culture.*

11. Lears, *No Place of Grace*, 303.

12. Bledstein, *Culture of Professionalism*, 53. For discussions of the importance of gender politics in America, see also, Kristin Hoganson, *Fighting for American Manhood: How Gender*

Politics Provoked the Spanish-American and Philippine-American Wars (New Haven, 1998) and Gail Bederman, *Manliness & Civilization: A Cultural History of Gender and Race in the United States, 1880-1917* (Chicago, 1995).

13. Christine Pawley, *Reading on the Middle Border* (Amherst, Mass., 2001): 6,7. For a discussion of the early years of the ALA, see Wiegand, *The Politics of an Emerging Profession.*

14. Bledstein, *Culture of Professionalism*, 70. Joan Shelley Rubin argues that the spread of print "could subvert as well as consolidate . . . authority . . . by grabbing up 'trash.'" *The Making of Middlebrow Culture* (Chapel Hill, 1992): 18.

15. Wayne A. Wiegand, *"An Active Instrument for Propaganda": The American Public Library During World War I* (New York, 1989): 3.

16. Pawley, *Reading on the Middle Border*, 7.

17. Phyllis Dain, *The New York Public Library: A History of Its Founding and Early Years* (New York, 1972): 32. Republican themes, of course, were not new. I connect this rhetoric to the library as "myth" only insofar as the library insisted on its centrality to the fulfillment of republican ideals.

18. Jessie Carson, "The Children's Share in a Public Library," *Library Journal*, 37, (May 1912): 254.

19. Montrose Moses, *Children's Books and Reading* (New York, 1907): 5,8. As Christine Pawley (*Reading on the Middle Border*) has pointed out, librarians frequently stressed the "civilizing" effects of reading. By extension, then, the library was a "civilizing" institution. The idea of "civilized" is complex. Part of the critique of modern life, as Bledstein notes, was precisely that life had become overly civilized. The library, therefore, walked a fine line between "civilizing" and "overcivilization." See also Rubin, *The Making of Middlebrow Culture* for a discussion of this topic.

20. Carson, "The Children's Share," 256.

21. Winston Churchill, *Library Journal*, 28, (March 1903): 115-116.

22. S.S. Green, "The Relation of the Public Library to the Public School," *Library Journal*, 5: 9-10, (September-October, 1880): 238.

23. Lears, *No Place of Grace*, 27.

24. While women remained largely disenfranchised from electoral politics, large numbers were, as already noted, actively engaged in various aspects of political life, including reform movements and the campaign for suffrage. In some states and territories, limited suffrage was granted to women.

25. Dee Garrison, *Apostles of Culture: The Public Librarian and American Society, 1876-1920* (New York, 1979): 173. In *Cultural Crusaders: Women Librarians in the American West, 1900-1917* (Albuquerque, 1994) Joanne Passet shows that in terms of wages, librarians at the turn of the century earned roughly $700 a year for a 42.5 hour work week. By 1913, wages were up approximately 36 percent to $1,100 per year at a time when subsistence wages were $400-520 per year. Librarians' wages were generally in keeping with those of public health nurses, who earned $600-$1,020 per year, while teachers' earnings remained less than $600. Women librarians were less likely to marry than women in other professions. Garrison reports that as late as 1920, only 7.4 percent of librarians married. Only stenographers and typists had a lower marriage rate.

26. In *Apostles of Culture*, Garrison argues that male librarians offered "no opposition" to the feminization of librarianship (174).

27. Rubin, *Middlebrow Culture*, 17. Rubin identifies a genteel "ideology of culture," which throughout the nineteenth century increasingly linked "culture" to character and moral stature rather than to financial means or social status. The "democratization of gentility" had as its goal the greatest exposure of individuals to culture, "spreading the 'best' throughout society," often by establishing standards. In the library, this translated into what has been called "the library faith," that is, getting the "best" books to the greatest number of people. Recommended reading lists were frequently the institution's method of standard setting.

28. Moses, *Children's Books*, 5.

29. Among those misgivings was a concern over women's supposedly fragile health. One argument against allowing women into professions was that it would result in race suicide, that is, that women would sacrifice their reproductive abilities by taxing their physical and mental energies. See Carroll Smith-Rosenberg, "The New Woman as Androgyne."

30. Bledstein, *Culture of Professionalism*, 78. Ironically, according to Bledstein, the very abundance of the printed word became a contributing factor to the anxiety and confusion of modern life, necessitating experts to mediate.

31. See, for example, Christopher Lasch, *The Culture of Narcissism: American Life in an Age of Diminishing Expectations* (New York, 1979): 161.

32. Bledstein, *Culture of Professionalism*, 57, 79.

33. James Wyer, *New York State Library School, 1887-1920* (New York, 1926).

34. *Ibid.*

35. *New York Sun*, reprinted in the *Library Journal*, 16, (March 1891): 9.

36. Lears, *No Place of Grace*, 104.

37. One method for coping with the public's taste for fiction was to limit the amount of fiction a patron could borrow at one time. By 1915, only one of the four books allowed to be charged at the New York Public Library could be fiction (Dain, *The New York Public Library*, 286).

38. In *Reading on the Middle Border*, Pawley challenges the validity of claims that reading was as gendered as librarians assumed. Her study of library records of the Sage Library in Osage, Iowa during the late-nineteenth century indicates that fiction reading was much more equally distributed between men and women than librarians assumed. This finding makes an understanding of gender as a linguistic code all the more important in order to appreciate why fiction was so persistently associated with "female."

39. It is important to note that while rank and file librarians were often treated to anti-fiction rhetoric, they continued to place book orders for their libraries that included a significant amount of fiction. According to Douglas (*The Feminization of American Culture*) only 3 percent of American books were fiction in the 1680s (108). By the end of the nineteenth century, the percentage was closer to fifty percent. Librarians who actually did the book ordering in towns and cities across the nation responded to library patrons by stocking books they knew would draw readers to the library. Christine Pawley's findings in *Reading on the Middle Border* reinforce the idea that librarians continued to stock fiction in large numbers, often to facilitate the absorption of middle-class values by immigrant and working class populations (78). In *Reading the Romance: Women, Patriarchy, and Popular Literature* (Chapel Hill, 1984), Janice Radway suggests that fiction reading might be construed as oppositional or as a "female ritual" by which women "explore the consequences of their common social conditions"(212, 220). She observes that explanations for the increase in fiction consumption are technological as well as sociological; advances in print technology made mass book production possible (19-20). Likewise, the development of formulaic fiction enhanced fiction sales by establishing a "permanent conduit" between publishers and readers (24).

40. Pawley, *Reading on the Middle Border*, 106.

41. Henry N. Sanborn, "Books for Men,"*Library Journal*, 41, (March 1916): 165.

42. *Ibid.*, 166.

43. *Ibid.*, 166-69.

44. *Ibid.*

45. Lears, *No Place of Grace*, 49.

46. *Ibid.*, 50.

47. *Ibid.*, 51. See also Bledstein, *Culture of Professionalism*, 46-49. In *The Feminization of American Culture*, Ann Douglas notes that women "talked about ill health more than they experienced it in order to palliate not only their failures in society, but their successes. Feminine modesty, broadly conceived, was an apology for new strength. It assured its public that its possessors, if they had come so far, would come no further" (93). Men were also affected by neurasthenia. See, for example, George Cotkin, *William James: Public Philosopher* (Baltimore, 1990).

48. By the end of the nineteenth century, childhood was recognized as a distinct time of life. The romantic attitude toward children, according to Anne Scott MacLeod, altered the relationships between children and adults, prompting culture-wide efforts to protect the innocence of children. As MacLeod puts it, "children's innocence, emotionality, and imagination became qualities to be preserved rather than overcome; a child's sojourn in childhood was to be protected, not hastened." *American Childhood: Essays on Children's Literature of the Nineteenth and Twentieth Centuries* (Athens, Georgia, 1994): 156. Christine Jenkins, "Precepts and Practices," *Horn Book* (September/October 1999): 549. Jenkins describes children's work as a "religion" whose tenets of faith included a belief in the primacy and uniqueness of the individual child; a belief in the critical importance of individual choice in young people's reading; a belief in the strength and resilience of young people; a perception of the children's room as an egalitarian republic of readers; a belief in literature as a positive force for understanding not only between individuals, but also between groups, and nations; a friendly and unsentimental older sister's attitude toward children; and an assumption that children's librarians would inevitably face and prevail over adversity in the performance of their professional work. In domesticating the workplace, Ann Douglas contends that women were "making the best of a bad situation" (*The Feminization of Culture*, 78).

49. Carson, "The Children's Share," 253.

50. Frances Clarke Sayers, *Anne Carroll Moore: A Biography* (New York, 1972): 72.

51. Jenkins, "Precepts and Practices," 551.

52. Douglas argues that "barred from the manifest spoils...of office, women understandably sought less legitimate rewards for their very real energies: psychological, emotional, what they called 'moral' or 'religious' control over the minds of their actual or symbolic offspring" (*The Feminization of American Culture*, 76).

53. Carson, "The Children's Share," 256.

54. Dianne Farrell, notes, Robb Lecture (May 24, 1989), Alice Mabel Jordan Box, Archives and Special Collections, Boston Public Library.

55. Arthur Elmore Bostwick, *The American Public Library* (New York, 1929): 91.

56. *Ibid.*, 93.

57. Bostwick's support for children's work is made clear in an open letter to NYPL's staff on the occasion of Moore's twenty-fifth anniversary with the library. Despite whatever ambivalence Bostwick may have had about feminized space in the library, he wanted it remembered that developing children's services at NYPL had been his idea. Arthur Bostwick to ACM, letter, 10/10/31, Box 1, Anne Carroll Moore Papers, Special Collections, New York Public Library.

58. Somewhat later, the so-called "fairy tale wars" emerged between those who advocated stories that indulged children's imaginations and those who favored a more reality-based children's literature. Anne Carroll Moore would serve as an example of the former, and Lucy Sprague Mitchell (the "Here and Now" books) as an example of the latter. See Christine Jenkins, "Precepts and Practices."

59. Helen Haines, "A Commentary on Catchwords," *Library Journal,* 42, (December 1917): 941.

60. Edwin Andersen, "Training for Library Service," *Library Journal,* 49, (May 15, 1924): 464.

61. Raymond L. Walkley, "All in the Day's Work," *Library Journal,* 43, (March 1918): 159-163.

62. "Library Institute Held at Plainfield, NJ," *Library Journal,* 28, (March 1903): 120.

63. Arthur Bostwick, "Library Circulation at Long Range," *Library Journal,* 38, (July 1913): 392. Joanne Passet has observed that librarianship at this time shifted from a "collection oriented to a client oriented" outlook. (*Cultural Crusaders,* xiii).

64. Judson Jennings, "Sticking to Our Last," *Library Journal,* 49, (July 1924): 614.

65. Garrison, *Apostles of Culture,* 176.

66. Douglas, *Feminization of American Culture,* 78. Smith-Rosenberg argues that women created power and legitimacy from their Progressive reform efforts (*Disorderly Conduct,* 256).

67. Wiegand, *"An Active Instrument For Propaganda,"* 1. See also Arthur Young, *Books for Sammies: The American Library Association and the First World War* (Pittsburgh, 1981).

68. *Ibid.,* 8.

69. *Ibid.,* 31.

70. *Ibid.,* 30.

71. *Ibid.,* 5.

72. *Ibid.,* 38-41.

73. *Ibid.,* 35-36.

74. Edith Kathleen Jones, "What a Base Hospital Librarian Should Know—Outline of a Course of Training," *Library Journal,* 43, (August 1918): 568.

75. Wiegand, *An Active Instrument For Propaganda,* 62-64.

76. "Plans for War Service by the ALA," *Library Journal,* 42, (August 1918): 566.

77. Jones, "What a Base Hospital Librarian Should Know," 570.

78. *Ibid.*

79. *Ibid.,* 570-571.

80. *Ibid.,* 571.

81. Miriam E. Carey, "What A Man Reads In Hospital," *Library Journal,* 43, (August 1918): 566.

82. Sarah Deutsch, *Gender, Space, and Power in Boston, 1870-1940* (New York, 2000): 12, 26. Deutsch explores the ways in which Boston women confronted gender ideology in that city. See also Mary Ryan, *Women in Public: Between Banners and Ballots, 1825-1880* (Baltimore, 1990) and *Civic Wars: Democracy and Public Life in the American City during the Nineteenth Century* (Berkeley, 1997).

83. Passet, *Cultural Crusades,* 2.

The Roosevelt Presidential Library:
A Shift in Commemoration

Benjamin Hufbauer

On April 12, 1937, Franklin D. Roosevelt made a sketch of the first federally administered presidential library, a new kind of institution that shifted presidential commemoration into the realms of the archive and museum. Roosevelt
drew a two-story Dutch-colonial style building faced in stone with a full-length
porch, small windows, and a steeply pitched roof, like the houses he remembered from his childhood in New York State (figures 1 and 2). He labeled the
two views "Ground Plan" and "Front Elevation," and signed the drawing with a
flourish, "FDR."[1] Roosevelt had collected many things since his childhood, from
books to stuffed birds, from model ships to millions of government documents
relating to his public service. As a student of history, he knew the danger of
leaving the fate of these collections to chance. They needed an archive in order
to remain intact after his death and thereby remain a testament to his life. To
appeal to the public, FDR wanted a tourist-friendly history museum to be part of
his library, and he hoped that it would draw "an appalling number of sightse-
ers."[2]

On viewing Egypt's pyramids during the Second World War, Roosevelt
commented that "man's desire to be remembered is colossal,"[3] and what he
observed about the pharaohs was true of himself. Roosevelt so desired to be
remembered, and to be remembered in a particular way, that he altered the essential terms of commemoration for the American presidency. No previous president had presumed to memorialize himself; self-aggrandizing monuments were
thought to be for monarchs, not the elected leader of the United States. Ameri-

0026-3079/2001/4203-173$2.50/0   American Studies, 42:3 (Fall 2001): 173-193

Figure 1: President Roosevelt with a plan for the Roosevelt Library in Hyde Park, New York, 1939. *Courtesy of the Roosevelt Library.*

can leaders submitted their bid for immortality to posterity, and some were commemorated with statues, preserved homes, obelisks, and even temples, while others within a few generations were nearly obliterated from public memory. Never before had a president designed his own national memorial. Compared in size to the monuments with which previous leaders in world history have been commemorated, the Roosevelt Library is relatively modest. But it was audacious in its ambition to preserve not just the Roosevelt name, but also a narrative of the man's life, and a vast variety of relics for as long as the United States remains in existence.[4]

Roosevelt's library, the first federal presidential library, set a precedent. Currently ten presidential libraries run by the National Archives and Records

Figure 2: Roosevelt speaking at the opening ceremony at the Roosevelt Library, 1940. *Courtesy of the Roosevelt Library.*

Administration draw thousands of scholars and over a million tourists each year.[5] The eleventh, the William Jefferson Clinton Library in Little Rock, Arkansas, is under construction and scheduled to open in 2004. The national cultural impact of the presidential library today directly flows from Roosevelt's plans for self-commemoration.

As an intervention in public memory, the presidential library functions in several ways. For tourists, a presidential library presents an ideologically charged narrative that valorizes a presidential life. Informing and validating a presidential library's museum are archives that preserve documents and other presidential possessions as national relics. Finally, presidential libraries through their sites project an aura of the sacred by entwining an individual's life with national history to create a narrative circuit that concludes with a presidential grave. Presidential libraries as institutions help create narratives about national history not only through their sites and museums, but through the accessibility of their archives. This accessibility, as will be seen, Roosevelt secretly hoped to prevent even as he publicly brought it about.

Sites of memory, like presidential libraries, have come under increasing scrutiny by scholars who examine the landscape of public memory.[6] As John Bodnar has written, "Public memory is produced from a political discussion that involves . . . fundamental issues about the entire existence of a society: its organization, structure of power, and the very meaning of its past and present."[7] As sites of memory, presidential libraries have embedded within them an ideology that attempts to reify reverence for the presidency. This article explains why and how this new site of memory was created, and examines its cultural effects.

Presidential Records and Relics

One of FDR's goals in creating a federally administered Roosevelt Library was to escape a pattern of destruction and disbursement that had affected presidential records since George Washington's death. The private ownership of presidential papers was a peculiar national tradition established when Washington, at the end of his second term, shipped all of his documents to Mount Vernon.[8] During retirement, Washington wanted to erect a stone building at Mount Vernon "for the accommodation and security of my Military, Civil and private Papers which are voluminous and may be interesting."[9] Washington had in mind a precursor to the presidential library, but he was unable to carry out his plan, and on his death his papers went to his nephew, Bushrod Washington.[10] Bushrod lent large portions of the papers to Chief Justice of the United States John Marshall, who confessed that after many years they were "extensively mutilated by rats and otherwise injured by damp."[11] The remains of Washington's papers, like the remains of most presidential papers, were eventually purchased by the Library of Congress, but only after many were lost forever. Even some presidential papers that found their way to the Library of Congress had unusual restrictions placed on them. For instance, many of Abraham Lincoln's papers were sealed and unavailable to historians until 1947.[12]

Webb Hayes, the son of late-nineteenth-century President Rutherford B. Hayes, created an institution that provided a model for Roosevelt's library. In 1910, Hayes deeded his parents' 25-acre estate, Spiegel Grove, to the state of Ohio under the condition that "a suitable fireproof building" be erected "for the purpose of preserving and forever keeping" the records and relics of his parents.[13] The Hayes family and the Ohio Legislature provided the money for the neo-classical library, privately administered by the Ohio Historical Society and the Hayes Foundation. Until Franklin Roosevelt, however, no president seems to have looked to the Hayes Library as a model for preserving presidential papers and collections. President Roosevelt instructed the Director of the National Archives, Robert Connor, to investigate the Hayes Library and learned that it was "a veritable gold mine for historical scholars."[14]

Even before Roosevelt investigated the Hayes model, however, I believe two other commemorative events helped shape his vision of presidential commemoration. The first was the founding of the National Gallery of Art by Andrew Mellon, which gave Roosevelt a lesson in how to build an institution from scratch and persuade the federal government to administer it in perpetuity. The second was the controversy surrounding the design and building of the neoclassical Jefferson Memorial, which may have led Roosevelt to create his library outside the capital, using a domestic architectural idiom.

Mellon's National Gallery and the Jefferson Memorial

Andrew Mellon, treasury secretary for three Republican presidents during the booming 1920s, epitomized the mysteries of public and private finance for that era.[15] At the 1924 Democratic National Convention, Franklin Roosevelt said, "Calvin Coolidge would like to have God on his side, but he *must* have Mellon."[16] When the Great Depression hit, however, Mellon's reputation became as tarnished as it had been bright. His son, Paul Mellon, recalled reading a scrawled poem above a urinal in 1934 that illustrated how far his father's reputation had fallen:

> Hoover blew the whistle
> Mellon rang the bell
> Wall Street gave the signal
> And the country went to hell[17]

After Roosevelt became president, his administration launched a highly-publicized investigation into Mellon's taxes, charging that the former Treasury Secretary had violated the very laws he was pledged to uphold. Mellon had for years deducted from his income on his tax returns the purchase prices of many expensive works of art—including paintings by Raphael, Titian, Vermeer, and Rembrandt.[18] Mellon claimed that the prices of his masterpieces could be deducted because the art was officially owned by a non-profit trust.

On December 22, 1936, during the Roosevelt Administration's investigation against him, the 81-year-old Mellon wrote Roosevelt a letter offering to donate his collection to the United States in order to found a "National Gallery of Art." Roosevelt was delighted with Mellon's proposal to give to the nation a priceless art collection, and also pay for the construction of a massive museum in which it and future donations could be displayed. All Mellon wanted in return was for the National Gallery to be supported by annual appropriations from Congress, and to be chartered by the Smithsonian Institution, assuring Mellon a form of immortality. Mellon was later asked why he would give his art collection to the very government that was attacking him. "Every man wants to connect his life with something he thinks eternal," he said.[19]

In a letter marked "Personal and Confidential," Attorney General Homer Cummings told Roosevelt that under the proposal, Mellon's trustees would outnumber government appointees, and would appoint their successors. "The net result is that they will control the management of the Gallery, the site, and the contents thereof for all time. . . . The anomaly is therefore presented of government property being managed by a private group."[20] Roosevelt did not see this concern as serious. In fact, it appears that FDR tried to follow this precedent in creating his presidential library.[21] Cummings also objected that in the proposal "the faith of the United States is pledged" to support the National Gallery. "A question of taste and propriety is raised by this phraseology, but it was a form insisted upon by Mr. Mellon's attorney."[22] Roosevelt insisted on similar language when he deeded his presidential library to the United States.[23]

While the National Gallery provided Roosevelt with an institutional framework to follow in preserving his collections with assistance from the federal government, the relative failure of the Thomas Jefferson Memorial, the last great neo-classical presidential monument built in Washington, may have spurred Roosevelt's presidential library as well. The Jefferson Memorial was authorized by Congress during the height of the New Deal to give Democrats something approaching equal commemorative space with Republican Abraham Lincoln. Designed by John Russell Pope, also architect of Mellon's National Gallery, the Jefferson Memorial was based on ancient Rome's Pantheon, a form particularly suited to the commemoration of the classically minded Jefferson, who had used the domed temple as his model for Monticello.[24]

But while the neoclassic design of the Lincoln Memorial was hailed two decades earlier, many advocates of modern design considered neoclassicism anachronistic in the late 1930s. The *Magazine of Art* criticized Pope's design with an open letter to President Roosevelt:

> An enlightened government must realize that the stir which the announcement of the proposed Jefferson Memorial has occasioned, is not due solely to the Jefferson Memorial itself, but is due in large measure to the pent up feeling against a long series of dreary, costly, pretentious, inefficient, and dishonest buildings.[25]

Moreover, several of Washington's famous cherry trees had to be destroyed during construction. As a supporter of the Jefferson Memorial and an avid reader of the *New York Times*, FDR was probably chagrined to read on April 8, 1937, as the controversy moved to its height: "Plan for Jefferson Memorial Under Attack; New Site and Design Urged Upon Congress."[26] Although construction of the Jefferson Memorial continued, in spite of stiff opposition, Roosevelt was concerned with how he himself would be commemorated. Four days later, FDR was thinking about a different kind of presidential commemoration as he sketched his library.

FDR and the First Presidential Library

Roosevelt's library was, like the National Gallery, to be privately constructed, but operated by the federal government. In late 1937 Roosevelt asked architect Henry J. Toombs, a personal friend with whom he had previously worked on small architectural projects, to draw up a design based on his sketch for a new building next to his family home at Hyde Park, New York.[27] Toombs soon sent the plans, remarking in the enclosed letter that

> I tried to arrange a plan as closely as possible to the plan you
> sketched for me. . . . The stack area will take care of your
> files and while it has been very difficult to arrive at the proper
> amount of exhibition space, I think what I have is about
> right.[28]

Roosevelt replied that Toombs had not taken into account the number of tourists
that would visit the site. FDR thought that in the summer there might be as many
as 3,000 visitors a day:

> That is an appalling number of sightseers to handle, and these
> visitors would have to go in and pass through the rooms and
> exhibition halls and out again on regular tour. That makes
> me think that what we call a reading room would not be a
> reading room at all for students but rather a very carefully
> designed living room which would contain portraits, sev-
> eral of my favorite paintings and perhaps a thousand of my
> books . . . [with] visitors to pass in one door and out another
> through an isle formed by stanchions and ropes. This room,
> incidentally, I could use myself in the work of preparing the
> collections during hours when the public was not admitted.[29]

FDR's desire to convert the research room into a display room for paintings and
books shows Roosevelt's understanding of the need to appeal to tourists, even if
it meant sacrificing facilities for researchers.

Roosevelt understood that most tourists would have little interest in using
the archive, even if it was what validated the site and informed the displays. The
research room was instead to become a subsidiary presidential workspace, a
room where Roosevelt could lavish attention on the objects he proposed to display in the museum and store in the archive. FDR's papers and collections were
to be stored mostly out of sight, in a National Archives' repository that was to be
part of the building. In terms of display, and thus of the relationship between
most visitors and the archive, many of the traces of presidential labor were to be
hidden. And the building itself was even larger than it appeared, for Roosevelt
as designer had minimized the apparent size of the library by drawing upon
domestic architectural metaphors. The Roosevelt Library's design included a
full basement and a steeply pitched roof that made it a three-story building of
approximately 40,000 square feet—twenty times the size of a comfortable middle-
class home.[30] Although no one would easily connect the Roosevelt Library with
the overtly magnificent Jefferson Memorial, it was actually larger in square
footage.

As important as the public display of his collections and memorabilia was
to Roosevelt's plans, the museum alone was not enough to justify creating the
first federal presidential library. FDR knew that every government activity re-

quires a coalition of groups who will benefit and will therefore lend political support. After deciding on Hyde Park as the site and himself as master designer, FDR wooed professional historians, perhaps the most important constituency for his plans. One of the first approached was Samuel Eliot Morison, a professor of history at the President's alma mater, Harvard. Roosevelt told Morison that

> My own papers should, under the old method, be divided among the Navy Department, the Library of Congress, the New York State Historical Division in Albany, the New York City Historical Society, Harvard University, and various members of my family. . . . If anything is done in the way of assembling a fairly complete collection in one place, the effort should start now, but it should have the sanction of scholars.[31]

Morison replied that he liked the idea for what he called the "New Deal Archives," but still thought that Roosevelt's official state papers should be deposited in the National Archives in Washington, D.C.[32] Roosevelt was undeterred, however, and wrote to another professor that "the creation of a center devoted to the history of this period must have the support of the fraternity of historians."[33]

On July 4, 1938, Roosevelt met at the White House with National Archives Director Robert Connor to enlist help in creating his new institution. Roosevelt told Connor that he had ruled out the Library of Congress and the National Archives for his papers. Moreover, he warned, concentration in Washington could lead to a disaster for national records if war broke out and the capital were attacked. FDR described how the national archives of Spain had been severely damaged during the recent Spanish Civil War, and he related the anxiety French government officials had expressed to him about the concentration of France's national records in Paris with war looming in Europe.[34] Roosevelt proposed constructing a combined archive and museum in Hyde Park with private funds, and then making the building a branch of the National Archives. But to start this process, FDR needed to begin a private fund-raising campaign to build the facility. Well-off though he was, FDR did not have the personal wealth needed to build an impressive memorial. Eventually $400,000 came from 28,000 donors to build the Roosevelt Library.[35]

The loss of many presidential records, and the limited access granted to some of those that remained, gave Roosevelt a compelling rationale for creating his archive. Professional historians, Roosevelt judged, would come around to his plan if they could be made to see its advantages for their profession. On November 1, 1938, Roosevelt invited a select group of historians and archivists to lunch at the White House on December tenth:

> I am asking a small group of people from different parts of the country to come together to discuss with me a matter

> which lies very close to my heart. . . . I am enclosing a short
> and very sketchy memorandum which I hope you will be
> thinking over.[36]

The two-page single-spaced memorandum that FDR included was actually a detailed summary of the variety of papers and other collections that he had gathered over his life. Roosevelt stated that with the new facility, his collections would remain "whole and intact in their original condition, available to scholars of the future."[37]

The historians discussed with Roosevelt his planned archive, and after lunch FDR called a press conference to announce his plans. Professor Morison, who had been won over, stood near him to show the historians' support. Professor Morison said to the press, "President Roosevelt has proposed, for the first time, to keep all of his files intact . . . under the administration of the National Archives so that . . . they will be under public control and will not be subject to dilapidation or destruction or anything else."[38] The President needed to create this impression to gain press support, which in turn would garner congressional support. On the following day, the *New York Times* headline announced: "ROOSEVELT ESTATE TO HOUSE ARCHIVES, GO TO PUBLIC LATER," and beneath, "Historians Back Idea."[39]

Not all reaction was positive, however. The *Chicago Tribune* printed an editorial cartoon captioned, "He Did His Shopping Early," showing a rotund FDR dressed up as Santa Claus leaving a weighty present in a stocking. The stocking is marked, "Hyde Park Memorial to Franklin D. Roosevelt, to be enlarged by public subscription and forever maintained at government expense. To be grander than Mount Vernon or Monticello." At the far left of the cartoon FDR as Santa walks away and says, "Won't he be Surprised—Bless His Heart," as he looks back at his card, which is engraved "To Pres. Roosevelt from F.D.R."[40]

Unmoved by the criticism, Roosevelt appointed a committee composed mainly of professors and archivists to make recommendations about the organization of the facility. On December 17, 1938, the committee decided to name the site the Franklin D. Roosevelt Library.[41] The term library was chosen over archive because it was thought that it would seem less alien to the public. The Library was to include Roosevelt's extensive collection of books, but that was only a small portion of its proposed contents. The name was also chosen because of the precedent established by the Rutherford B. Hayes Library. After the morning session, the committee reconvened at the White House for lunch with President Roosevelt. FDR, almost certainly with Andrew Mellon's National Gallery in mind, wondered if some designation could be found that did not use the Roosevelt name. "What about the Hyde Park Library?" Roosevelt asked, at which some committee members scoffed.[42] FDR eventually agreed to the name "Roosevelt Library" because, as the committee stated, "the President's personal and official papers . . . constitute the principal reason for establishing the Library."[43]

A draft of the legislation by the Justice Department establishing the Roosevelt Library as part of the National Archives was submitted to Congress four days after the library committee's first meeting.[44] The legislation languished in Congress for some months, however, and one Republican congressman complained that "only an egocentric maniac would have the nerve to ask for such a measure."[45] Columnist John T. Flynn compared Roosevelt to a glory-mad Egyptian pharaoh, and said FDR wanted a "Yankee Pyramid."[46] Nevertheless, the legislation finally passed Congress in July of 1939, which at that time had a substantial majority of Democrats in both houses of Congress. Roosevelt, following Andrew Mellon's example, was able to insert language into the bill promising that the federal government would "provide such funds as may be necessary . . . so that the said Library shall be at all times properly maintained."[47]

At the cornerstone-laying ceremony on November 19, 1939 (figure 3), FDR said:

> Of the papers which will come to rest here, I personally attach less importance to the documents of those who have occupied high public or private office than I do the spontaneous letters which have come to me . . . from men, from

Figure 3: President Roosevelt spreading mortar for the cornerstone laying ceremony of the Roosevelt Library, 1939. *Courtesy of the Roosevelt Library.*

> women, and from children in every part of the United States,
> telling me of their conditions and problems and giving me
> their own opinions.[48]

Roosevelt did value expressions of popular opinion, but his statement screened his desire to prevent access to many of his own sensitive papers.

We see this in FDR's desire to select his close advisor Harry Hopkins as the Library's first director, which would have given Roosevelt indirect control of his sensitive archival materials. National Archivist Robert Connor wrote in his diary, "Wow! Was that a blow!"[49] Connor convinced the President that an archivist would be better for the position, but only after Supreme Court Justice Felix Frankfurter, one of FDR's appointees, warned Roosevelt against choosing a "court historian." Connor instead recommended professional archivist Fred Shipman, and Roosevelt acquiesced. By 1941, when the museum portion of the Roosevelt Library opened to the public, Connor confided in his diary, "The President still thinks of the library as his personal property."[50]

Indeed Roosevelt did. In 1943, he wrote a memo to Director Shipman that revealed his intentions. Roosevelt, like Andrew Mellon with the National Gallery, wanted to exercise some control over his institution even after his death, through people of his own choosing:

> Before any of my personal or confidential files are trans-
> ferred to the Library at Hyde Park, I wish to go through them
> and select those which are never to be made
> public. . . . If by reason of death or incapacity I am unable to
> do this, I wish that function to be performed by a Commit-
> tee of three, namely, Samuel I. Rosenman, Harry L. Hopkins
> and Grace Tully, or the survivors thereof.
>
> With respect to the file known as "Famous People File,"
> the same procedure should be followed. Those which are
> official letters may be turned over to the Library, but those
> which are in effect personal such as, for example, the long-
> hand letters between the King of England and myself, are to
> be retained by me or my Estate and should never be made
> public.[51]

Roosevelt, five years after he began selling his new institution as an accessible archive, here privately revealed that access to sensitive materials was to be almost the opposite of his public statements. In 1947, however, after Roosevelt's death, New York Judge Frederick S. Quintero ruled that Roosevelt's public utterances were a "valid and effective *gift* of all of his papers . . . to be placed, maintained, and preserved in the Franklin D. Roosevelt Library."[52]

The ruling eventually gave the public access to all of the materials in the Roosevelt Library's archives consistent with respect for the feelings of living persons and the requirements of national security. Roosevelt ended up creating, in spite of his contrary private desires, an institution that fulfilled the roles that he publicly advertised for it, providing unprecedented public access to sensitive government materials decades sooner than they otherwise would have been available. In no other major nation can citizens so easily obtain access to previously secret, sensitive, personal, as well as banal documents and collections as one can in a presidential library.[53] British citizens wishing to see the hand-written correspondence between King George VI and President Roosevelt, for instance, would find this difficult in England. But at the Roosevelt Library, within half an hour of entering the library's archive, a researcher assisted by professional archivists would be able to see copies of documents that Roosevelt thought should be sealed forever.

A Commemorative Shift

On April 12, 1945, as the Second World War was drawing to a close, President Roosevelt died of a cerebral hemorrhage in Warm Springs, Georgia. The President's body was taken by train to Washington, D.C., and then on to Hyde Park, and during the journey thousands of people lined the tracks to pay their last respects to the President. Roosevelt was laid to rest near the Roosevelt Library, where his grave completed the monument that he had created for himself. The library helped to insure the continuance of Roosevelt's memory after his death through his museum and archive, which would help to project his life and image into the future. At the Roosevelt Library, FDR thought of himself as a tourist object, and placed himself within a narrative circuit of the settings and objects that framed his life, from the Roosevelt family mansion in which he grew up (figure 4), to his personal collections, to his presidential work, and, finally, to the large stone that he had designed for his grave (figure 5). The narrative generated confers authenticity on the complex through the telling of a cyclical story, which concludes by returning Roosevelt to sacred American soil.

The narrative circuit that Roosevelt designed for himself is structured around the idea of mystified presidential labor. As Dean MacCannell has written, many tourist sites, such as the pyramids of Egypt or Saint Peters in Rome, are opulent displays of stored labor power that present the production and storage of work as a form of collectable authenticity.[54] The Roosevelt Library is meant to store and display every preservable trace of Roosevelt's life and labor for as long as possible. The archived traces of Roosevelt's labor become the sacra of the presidency at the site, and are meant to possess an almost religious essence. The mystified quality of this labor is emphasized by Roosevelt's plan to restrict access to the archive, which was to be seen even more than it was to be used.

The commemorative transition that the presidential library represents may be described in part as a shift from a classical to a Christian mode of commemoration. In classical commemoration, an abstract or representational monument, such as the Washington Monument or the Lincoln Memorial, visually attests to

Figure 4: The Roosevelt family home in Hyde Park, New York. *Courtesy of Bess Reed.*

Figure 5: The graves of Franklin and Eleanor Roosevelt near the Roosevelt Library. *Courtesy of Bess Reed.*

the heroism of a president. In presidential libraries, a comparatively Christian mode of commemoration, objects used by a president become relics, and are stored and displayed in a federal facility that affirms a heroism that is supposedly already accepted. In other words, the touch of a president potentially transforms any object into a relic to be kept by a presidential library. Royal Cortissoz, author of the inscription inside the Lincoln Memorial, foresaw this transformation of presidential belongings into relics and feared it. Cortissoz wrote to the architect of the Lincoln Memorial, Henry Bacon, and warned against "turning the [Lincoln Memorial] into a miscellaneous, museumy place for the army to deposit 'relics' in."[55] Yet the process of creating an archival form of commemoration that displayed relics in museums was not to be repressed. National presidential commemoration embraced relics, validated itself through archives, and became a newly personalized, arguably mundane form of American commemoration in the presidential library.

Roosevelt was able to conceive of an archival memorial in part because of shifts in media technology and culture that occurred before and during the twentieth century.[56] These shifts increased the importance of archives for preserving new forms of memory, making it possible for Roosevelt to think of an archival commemoration. Donald M. Lowe and others have analyzed how shifts in media technology layer different modes of perception:

> Culture can be conceived of as oral, chirographic, typographic, or electronic, in accordance with the communications media which sustain it. Each of these four types of culture organizes and frames knowledge qualitatively in an entirely different manner than the other three. And . . . each subsequent type is superimposed on the previous one.[57]

Roosevelt's political career stretched from a typographic culture characterized by print media, to the beginnings of a culture that relied more on such media as "telegraph, telephone, phonograph, radio, film, television, audio-video tape and disc, computer, plus others yet to come."[58]

The presidential library that Roosevelt designed was capable of storing and displaying both old and new forms of memory. In addition to its millions of government documents, it also preserves thousands of photographs, miles of film and audio tape, and every relic of Roosevelt's experience that he thought significant, down to a horseshoe that he found in the Sahara desert during the Second World War.[59] Collections, forms of relics, can be a way to project an ego ideal—for instance, a collection of paintings, such as Andrew Mellon's, can represent a collector's aesthetic sensibility, intelligence, and wealth.[60] The Roosevelt Library took this process one step further by combining a museum with a personal and national archive. Through the organization of his presidential library into a tourist site and museum, Roosevelt was able to elevate the idiosyncrasy of his collections to the level of national relics.[61]

The Roosevelt Library's Life Cycle

Changes in cultural technology made possible—and have continued to affect—the presidential library as an institution. Through FDR's live radio "fireside chats," to his nearly weekly appearances in filmed newsreels, to the previously unprecedented reproduction of his images throughout American culture, Roosevelt was able to become an effective shaper of his image in the mass media.[62] Herbert Hoover, while he was President, received at most 600 letters a day, while FDR sometimes received as many as 6,000.[63] This proliferation of letters, many of which are stored at the Roosevelt Library, is evidence that FDR forged a more powerful connection with the public through the mass media than did most of his predecessors. Some Americans, inspired by Roosevelt's image, even created folk-art representations of the President that are stored at the library. One, a sphinx with Roosevelt's face and characteristic cigarette holder that was part of the Roosevelt Library's early displays, manifests a popular appreciation for the mystery of FDR's political success, a mystery connected to Roosevelt's mastery of new media technologies (figure 6).

The Roosevelt Library was first opened to the public in 1941, but wartime restrictions on travel held down admissions until the second half of the 1940s. From 1947 to 1986, however, admissions averaged nearly 200,000 annually, an impressive figure for an institution that is a substantial drive from any large city.

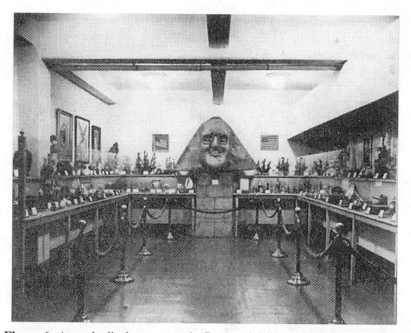

Figure 6: An early display room at the Roosevelt Library, featuring a portrait of FDR as sphinx. *Courtesy of the Roosevelt Library.*

By the late 1980s, a slow and steady decline had set in, and by 1994 admissions had dropped to 136,000.[64] The displays of Roosevelt's relics, from his christening gown to his extensive political memorabilia, began to lose some of their appeal as living memory of Franklin Roosevelt passed away. As Pierre Nora has written, sites of memory can become "like shells left on the shore when the sea of living memory has receded."[65] As the tide of living memory that Nora refers to withdrew in the early 1990s, the Roosevelt Library faced what its director Verne Newton called "a demographic crisis."[66] To reach a new generation of patrons who "processed information in a fundamentally different way," Newton believed that "the Roosevelt Library would have to reinvent itself or eventually die."

When Newton became director, the exhibits had only been revised twice since the library had opened, and were largely static displays of relics in glass cases accompanied by extensive wall text. Newton observed visitors in the Roosevelt Library's museum, and found that although the declining numbers of older tourists were engaged, younger visitors were restless and bored. He stated that "the way this new generation receives its information is through interactive video and audio displays, and this was our guiding philosophy as we redesigned the museum." Newton had the library create its own video game that confronts visitors with the same information FDR had as President, for instance about whether to send destroyers to Britain during the early days of the Second World War, and the visitor must choose between various options. Younger audiences are more interested in this game than in Roosevelt's relics, and the library even contemplated expanding the computer game so that it could be marketed nationwide. Another new display recreates the White House's wartime map room, and uses a visitor-activated recording of a voice actor to create an imagined fragment of one of Roosevelt's workdays during the war. The game and recreation were meant to make a president who seems almost as distant for some younger visitors as the founding fathers seem more relevant. Newton stated that the Roosevelt Library, in order to survive, "must become a mini-Disneyland. It needs to entertain, educate, and even create a marketable product."

The Roosevelt Library, like succeeding presidential libraries, has gone through a life-cycle in its displays, and also in the way its archive is used. A presidential library is born as the culmination of a huge fund-raising drive, its museum is opened to tourists, and then its archive is opened to scholars.[67] In a presidential library's early years, there is immense work behind the scenes as archivists painstakingly catalog and organize presidential materials, which are slowly declassified and released for use by scholars, who then write histories and monographs. Often, just as tourist interest begins to wane, best-selling biographies are published that make use of the unprecedented scope of materials and access a presidential library provides. They often revive interest in a presidential library's subject, even if they sometimes create unflattering portraits of presidential lives.[68] Since 1950, hundreds of books on Roosevelt, the depression, and the Second World War have been written by making use of the Roosevelt Library's archive. When eventually the interest of scholars, as with tourists, subsides, it becomes a continuing challenge for presidential libraries to justify their existence. The Roosevelt Library, like many presidential libraries, currently has a successful program to encourage the use of its archive by high school and grade school students.[69] President Roosevelt, who originally wanted to eliminate the room at the library for researchers, and thought many papers should be preserved but sealed forever, might be disquieted by the sight of students working with the raw materials of his history at the Roosevelt Library.

The Presidential Library

The unusual hybrid commemorative institution that Franklin Roosevelt invented came to seem natural and necessary to his successors, and every president since has had a hand in the creation of his own presidential library. Presidential libraries have increased dramatically in size and cost, but have not changed essentially from the model laid out by FDR. The presidential library as an institution is one reflection of what Arthur Schlesinger called the "Imperial Presidency." Schlesinger identified Roosevelt as the first in a long line of presidents who took on, and sometimes abused, increased powers that resulted from the Second World War, the Korean and Vietnam Wars, and the Cold War. Not only did those who occupied the presidency since the 1930s have greater power than nearly all of their predecessors, but the role of former presidents was also dramatically enhanced. The presidential library has come to function as the base for what Senator William Roth has called "the Imperial ex-Presidency."[70] Presidential libraries, especially since Lyndon Johnson's was opened in 1971, have increasingly functioned as policy centers as well as archives. One example is the Carter Center, associated with the Carter Library, from which Jimmy and Rosalynn Carter have launched extensive philanthropic activities. The presidential library also functions as the most important institution for the expansion of the civil religion of the American presidency, continuing in a new form the structure of reverence initiated by the creation and use of such memorials as the Washington Monument and the Lincoln Memorial. With the presidential library, however, every president—not merely the exceptional—has a national monument. Presidential libraries reify the ideology that claims all presidents as exceptional human beings and leaders worthy of reverential commemoration.

The presidential library is based upon the idea of the archive as *the* effective storage system for contemporary memory. As Pierre Nora has written,

> Modern memory is first of all archival. It relies entirely on
> the specificity of the trace, the materiality of the vestige, the
> concreteness of the recording, the visibility of the image . . .
> [for] society as a whole has acquired the religion of preser-
> vation and archivalization.[71]

Yet while presidential libraries are part of a societal urge for archives that has been called archive "fever" or "sickness,"[72] the displays in presidential libraries, while continuing to construct a veneration for presidential relics, increasingly revolve around recreations and simulations. Relics provide the authenticating foundation on which replicas and recreations have been built in the commemorative space of presidential libraries.[73] Although the Roosevelt Library did not originally have any replicated presidential spaces, its recent remodeling has given it three: its World War II map room, a recreation of a fragment of Roosevelt's Oval Office, and a recreation of part of Eleanor Roosevelt's post-White House office.[74] Recently some presidential libraries, such as Ronald Reagan's in Simi Valley, California, have created a simulated "meet the President" display, using interactive CD-ROM technology.

Presidential libraries, with their museum collections, archival holdings, houses, and graves, mark a shift in commemoration reflective of changing technologies of memory. They are constructed to high standards and are designed to last for many hundreds of years. Inside, rather than unchanging permanence, however, are museum displays of presidential stories and American history that change over time. Each generation of presidential library directors, curators, and archivists—who might be thought of as priests and priestesses within contemporary archival temples—reconstructs the story of their president for every new generation of visitors. The technology of display changes as well, from glass cases filled with relics, to computer controlled exhibits that simulate a visitor's meeting with a president. Especially as living memory of a president passes away, a library's most important commemorative work is to transform presidential labor into history and myth and give it seemingly transcendent value.

Notes

I would like to thank Bess Reed, Carol Krinsky, Verne Newton, John Ferris, Sally and Karl Hufbauer, and the readers for *American Studies* for their invaluable assistance. I would also like to thank James Grubola, chair of the Fine Arts Department of the University of Louisville, for a course release which allowed time to work on this article. Finally, I would like to thank the University of Louisville's College of Arts and Sciences for generously providing me with a Project Completion Grant.

1. This drawing is in the collections of the Roosevelt Library in Hyde Park, New York. FDR had for some time considered building his own archive. In 1934 he wrote to a Hyde Park neighbor that he wanted to build a "fireproof building in Hyde Park in which historical documents can be safely kept." FDR to Dr. Edward J. Wynkoop, 15 October 1934, Library file, Franklin D. Roosevelt Library.

2. FDR to Henry J. Tombs, 22 November 1937, Library File, FDRL.

3. Michael F. Reilly, *Reilly of the White House* (New York, 1947), 170. Reilly was one of the Secret Service agents assigned to protect FDR, and he accompanied the President to Egypt during the Second World War.

4. For the earlier literature on the Roosevelt Library, which tends to be factual rather than interpretive, see esp. Donald R. McCoy, "The Beginnings of the Franklin D. Roosevelt Library," *Prologue* 7 (Fall 1975), 137-150; Frank L. Schick with Renee Schick and Mark Carroll, *Records of the Presidency: Presidential Papers and Libraries from Washington to Reagan* (Phoenix, Ariz., 1989), 159-167; Geoffrey Ward, "Future Historians Will Curse as Well as Praise Me," *Smithsonian* 20 (December 1989), 58-69; and Curt Smith, *Windows on the White House: The Story of Presidential Libraries* (South Bend, Ind., 1997), 41-58.

5. Data: Office of Presidential Libraries, National Archives and Records Administration, Washington, D.C., 20408. Annual admissions to all presidential libraries generally totals about 1.5 million a year.

6. Some excellent examples of the literature on memory and commemoration are: Pierre Nora, Editor, *Realms of Memory: The Counstruction of the French Pact*, vol. 1, *Conflicts and Divisions*, translated by Arthur Goldhammer (New York, 1996-1998); John R. Gillis, Editor, *Commemorations: The Politics of National Identity*, (Princeton, N.J., 1994); Kristin Ann Hass, *Carried to the Wall: American Memory and the Vietnam Veterans Memorial* (Berkeley, 1998); and Kirk Savage, *Standing Soldiers, Kneeling Slaves: Race, War, and Monument in Nineteenth-Century America* (Princeton, N.J., 1997).

7. John Bodnar, *Remaking America: Public Memory, Commemoration, and Patriotism in the Twentieth Century* (Princeton, N.J., 1992), 14.

8. Presidential papers were privately owned until the Presidency of Richard Nixon. In 1974, during the Watergate crisis, Congress seized President Richard Nixon's presidential papers, and the Presidential Records Act of 1978 ended the private ownership of presidential papers. See Schick, *Records of the Presidency*, 17, 242.

9. Washington to James McHenry, 3 April 1797, *George Washington: Writings* (New York, 1996), 993.

10. Washington, "Last Will and Testament," *Writings*, 1029.

11. John D. Knowlton, "Properly Arranged and So Correctly Recorded," *American Archivist* 27 (July 1964), 372.

12. David Herbert Donald, *Lincoln* (New York, 1995), 14.

13. "Dedication of the Hayes Memorial Library," *Ohio Archaeological and Historical Quarterly*, 25 (Oct. 1916), 401.

14. Donald W. Wilson, "Presidential Libraries: Developing to Maturity," *Presidential Studies Quarterly* 21 (Fall 1991), 771.

15. On Andrew Mellon, see Arthur M. Schlessinger, Jr., *The Age of Roosevelt: The Crisis of the Old Order* (Boston, 1957), esp. 62, and Burton Hersh, *The Mellon Family: A Fortune in History* (New York, 1978).

16. Emphasis in original. Geoffrey C. Ward, *A First-Class Temperament: The Emergence of Franklin Roosevelt* (New York, 1989), 752.

17. Hersh, *The Mellon Family*, 349.

18. In spite of his impressive collection, Mellon was inarticulate on the subject of art, but he would stare at his canvases with such intensity that his aide John Walker believed that a profound connection existed between Mellon and his paintings. John Walker, *Self-Portrait with Donors* (Boston, 1974), 106.

19. Walker, *Self-Portrait with Donors*, 132.

20. Homer Cummings to FDR, 15 January 1937, National Gallery file, FDRL.

21. When I mentioned the probable influence of the National Gallery on FDR's creation of his Library to Richard A. Jacobs, then Director of the Office of Presidential Libraries in Washington, D.C., he said that he had believed for many years that Franklin Roosevelt got the idea to create the first presidential library largely from Andrew Mellon's gift to the nation of the National Gallery. Jacobs, personal communication, 18 August 1995.

22. Homer Cummings to FDR, 15 January 1937, National Gallery file, FDRL

23. Statutes at Large 1062-1066.

24. On Jefferson's admiration for classical architecture, see Jack McLaughlin, *Jefferson and Monticello: The Biography of a Builder* (New York, 1990).

25. William Lescaze, "America is Outgrowing Imitation Greek Architecture," *Magazine of Art* 30 (June 1937), 375.

26. *New York Times*, 8 April 1937, 2.

27. On FDR's relationship with Tombs, see Ward, *A First-Class Temperament*, esp. 736.

28. Toombs to FDR, 13 November 1937, Library File, FDRL.

29. In this letter FDR wrote, "Before you and I die we will have revived Hudson River Dutch." FDR to Toombs, 22 November 1937, Library File, FDRL.

30. For the square footage of the FDR Library, see Schick, *Records of the Presidency*, 254. Since its original construction the Roosevelt Library has been expanded to over 50,000 square feet. Other more recent presidential libraries, such as the Johnson and Reagan Libraries, are well over 100,000 square feet.

31. FDR to Morison, 28 February 1938, Waldo Gifford Leland Papers, FDRL.

32. Morison to FDR, 11 March 1938, Library Files, FDRL.

33. FDR to Keith Morgan, 25 May 1938, Library Files, FDRL.

34. Journal of Robert D.W. Connor, 4 July 1938, Southern Historical Collection, University of North Carolina Library.

35. Schick, *Records of the Presidency*, 157.

36. FDR to Beard, 1 November 1938, Library File, FDRL. Other letters sent out that day were similar. Roosevelt got Professor Morrison to assist him in drawing up the list of invitees.

37. Press Release, 10 December 1938, Library File, FDRL.

38. Press Release, 10 December 1938, Library File, FDRL.

39. *New York Times*, 11 December 1938, 1.

40. Library File, FDRL. *Chicago Tribune*, 13 December 1938.

41. Minutes, First Meeting of the Executive Committee of the President's Records and Historical Collections, 17 December 1938, Library File, FDRL.

42. McCoy, "The Beginnings of the Franklin D. Roosevelt Library," 142.

43. Minutes, 17 December 1938, Library File, FDRL, 2-3.

44. Minutes, 17 December 1938, Library File, FDRL, 3.

45. Ward, "Future Historians," 58-69.

46. *Ibid.*

47. Statutes at Large, 1062-1066.

48. *New York Times*, 20 November 1939.

49. Connor Journal, 7 April 1940, and Robert E. Sherwood, *Roosevelt and Hopkins: An Intimate History* (New York, 1948), 171-172.

50. Connor Journal, 30 June 1941.

51. FDR to Director of the Franklin D. Roosevelt Library, 16 July 1943, FDR Case File, R.G. 44, FDRL.

52. Judge Quintero's ruling was made in July 1947. See letter from National Archivist Solon J. Buck to Senator Owen Brewster, 25 July 1947, FDR Library Case File, R.G. 44, FDRL, italics added.

53. Foreign researchers often come to the Roosevelt Library and its successors for access to documents that they are unable to obtain in their home countries. For an example, see, Martin M. Teasley, "The Eisenhower Library at Thirty-something," *Government Information Quarterly*, 12:1 (1995), 85, and Schick, *Records of the Presidency*.

54. See esp. Dean MacCannell, *The Tourist: A New Theory of the Leisure Class* (New York, 1976, 1989), 2-14.

55. Cortissoz to Bacon, 28 August 1911, quoted in Christopher Alexander Thomas, "The Lincoln Memorial and its Architect, Henry Bacon (1866-1924)," (Ph.D. diss., Yale University, 1990), 482.

56. See Walter J. Ong, *Orality and Literacy: The Technologizing of the Word* (London, 1982). Ong writes, "The shift from orality to literacy and on to electronic processing engages social, economic, political, religious, and other structures." (3), and Marshall McLuhan, *Understanding Media: The Extensions of Man* (Cambridge, Mass., 1994).

57. Donald M. Lowe, *History of Bourgeois Perception* (Chicago, 1982), 2. See also James W. Carrey, *Communication as Culture: Essays on Media and Society* (Boston, 1988).

58. Lowe, *History of Bourgeois Perception*, 4.

59. This horseshoe is now in the archive of the Roosevelt Library.

60. For instance, see Werner Muensterberger, *Collecting: An Unruly Passion* (Princeton, N.J., 1994), 10-12, 139; Russell W. Belk *Collecting in a Consumer Society* (London and New York, 1975), Jean Baudrillard, *A System of Objects,* translated by James Benedict (London and New York, 1996), and John Elsner and Roger Cardinal, *The Cultures of Collecting* (Cambridge, Mass., 1984).

61. Verne Newton, personal communication, 21 August 1995.

62. The number of films, sound recordings, and photographs of Roosevelt was substantially greater than that generated for any previous twentieth-century president For instance there about 42,000 still pictures in the Hoover Library, (which was build after the Roosevelt Library and based on its example), but over 134,000 still pictures in the FDR Library. Data from the Hoover and Roosevelt Libraries.

63. Fred Shipman, "What do You Know About the Franklin D. Roosevelt Library," 3, Library File, FDRL.

64. Data: Office of Presidential Libraries, Washington, D.C. Since 1994, admissions to the Roosevelt Library have increased.

65. Nora, *Realms of Memory: The Construction of the French Past,* 1:7.

66. This and all subsequent quotes of Verne Newton in the following two paragraphs are: Roosevelt Library Director Verne Newton, personal communication, 21 August 1995.

67. For a discussion of the life-cycle of presidential libraries, see Don W. Wilson, "Presidential Libraries Developing to Maturity," *Presidential Studies Quarterly* 21 (Fall 1991).

68. An example is provided by Robert A. Caro's multi-volume biography *The Years of Lyndon Johnson* (New York, 1982-), which has used materials in the Johnson Library to create a fascinating and disturbing account of the life of the 36th president.

69. Acknowledging changing demographic factors and technology, the Library also teamed with nearby Marist College to create a searchable on-line finding aid system and a digitized database featuring typed and facsimile versions of 13,000 documents from the archive.

70. Senator William V. Roth, Jr. "Ex-Presidential Perks Are Way Out of Hand," *USA Today*, 28 March 1984.

71. Nora, "Between Memory and History," 8.

72. Jacques Derrida, *Archive Fever: A Freudian Impression*, translated by Eric Prenowitz (Chicago, 1996), 91.

73. Roosevelt's successor, Harry S. Truman, created the most significant change in presidential libraries by recreating the Oval Office at the Truman Library in Independence, Missouri, which opened in 1957. This replicated Oval Office is the most popular display at the museum, and additional replicas of the Oval Office now draw tourists at the Kennedy, Johnson, Ford, Carter, and Reagan Libraries, while another is planned for the Clinton Library.

74. Presidential monuments in Washington, D.C., prior to the advent of the presidential library represent the president alone. Since the invention of the presidential library, first ladies have been commemorated as keepers of the domestic environment of the White House and as policy advocates. This process of incorporating the first lady within the commemorative and archival framework of presidential libraries culminated in 1972, when a new Eleanor Roosevelt gallery was added to the FDR Library. The displays at the library include materials on her work as first lady as well as her work after FDR's death.

Research Note

Antebellum Libraries in Richmond and New Orleans and the Search for the Practices and Preferences of "Real" Readers

Emily B. Todd

The Virginia Historical Society, in Richmond, and the New Orleans Public Library both house extensive borrowing records from antebellum libraries once based in those two cities. At the Virginia Historical Society, three dusty ledgers list the names of Richmond Library Company (and Mercantile Association) patrons and the titles of the books they borrowed from 1839 to 1860.[1] In New Orleans, the microfilmed borrowing records of the Lyceum and Library Society contain the names and the reading histories for hundreds of New Orleans readers who visited the library from 1854 to 1867.[2] Despite the details in these ledgers—thousands of book titles and hundreds of names—these two antebellum institutions neither have been the subject of detailed scholarship nor have their records been widely used in studies of reading history.[3]

For the scholar interested in discovering "real" readers, such library borrowing records represent excellent, if largely untapped, sources for interdisciplinary work on reading and intellectual history. A few scholars, of course, have drawn on library borrowing records in studies of particular reading communities: a chapter in Ronald Zboray's *A Fictive People* analyzes the borrowing habits of men and women who visited the New York Society Library in the

0026-3079/2001/4202-195$2.50/0   American Studies, 42:3 (Fall 2001): 195-209

1850s, and Christine Pawley's *Reading on the Middle Border* uses the records from Sage Library in Osage, Iowa, to recreate the reading practices of late-nine-teenth-century Midwesterners.[4] But the neglected records from the Richmond and New Orleans libraries suggest the extent to which library borrowing records are generally under-used, sources that might shed light on the experience of reading, the reception of particular authors, and the influence of particular books on communities of readers.

In my analysis of the Richmond and New Orleans circulating records, car-ried out in the context of a larger project on Walter Scott's popularity in nine-teenth-century America,[5] I have been able to establish the borrowing patterns of people who read Scott's novels. My research, though, also allows me to specu-late more broadly on the complicated relationship between library borrowing records and reading history. Library history has tended to focus on institutional histories of various libraries, not on the agency of those people who have used libraries, borrowing from a library's collection to suit their own interests. The detailed records from two Southern antebellum libraries reveal the preferences of "real" readers and lead me to two conclusions, one about reading history and one about library history. First, borrowing records, perhaps more than any other source, enable scholars to determine the pace at which patrons read, the "cur-riculum" of reading they fashioned for themselves, and the likelihood that pa-trons who borrowed a book one day and returned it the next read silently to themselves. Second, these records expose a tension between the aims of the library and the uses to which the patron put the library's collections: borrowers did not always play along with the founding principles of an institution nor did they follow the design outlined in catalogues. Library history, then needs to consider the experience of borrowers which, in drawing on a library's collec-tions to create their own world of books, tell us not what the library *intended* to become but what it in fact *did* become for real readers.

"Real" Readers and Library Borrowing Records

One of the important challenges faced by History-of-the-Book scholars is how to determine the experiences and practices of "real" readers. In Robert Darnton's "communications circuit," which he outlines in "What is the History of Books?", readers both end and begin the cycle: readers consume the literary products created by the writer, publisher, and printer, but these acts of consump-tion in turn influence the decisions publishers and writers make about future publications.[6] In "Literary Economics and Literary History," William Charvat, like Darnton, urges literary critics to consider the responses of actual readers to particular texts: "Literary history has been much too busy trying to prove that past writers shouted loud enough to be heard by posterity. We should be more interested in knowing how far their voices carried in their own generation, and—equally important—whether their generation talked back."[7] To highlight the reader's role in shaping literary history, Charvat argues, for example, that the reactions of lyceum audiences to Emerson's early speeches forced him to write more coherent lectures.[8] Like publishers and editors, Charvat suggests, readers influence the literary works that authors create. He admits, however, that it is extraordinarily difficult to find evidence of readers talking back to writers of their own generation. Difficult as it might be to *hear* readers, studying the practices of "real" readers helps us to understand important components of the book trade; these readers are, we must acknowledge, authors' audiences, publishers' markets, booksellers' customers, and libraries' patrons. Without readers, there would be no book trade.

Until recently, literary scholars have tended to approach the study of readers and reading in abstract ways. Literary critics wrote about ideal readers and suggested that each text imagines a reader who will understand all the complexities of a particular literary work. In the 1970s and 1980s, reader-response theories challenged the New Critical position that texts have a self-contained meaning. Work by Jane Tompkins, Stanley Fish, and others argued that the reader's process of understanding the text makes meaning; therefore, because interpretations differ depending on who is reading, the meaning of a text cannot be fixed.[9] Meaning or literary value, in this view, does not reside in a text but rather in readers' responses to that text. Even though this theory marked a shift in how literary critics interpreted texts, reader-response theory did not lead to an investigation of *historical* communities of readers; it produced new theories about texts but not a picture of readers, new insights about interpretive practices but not new knowledge about the actual readers who engaged in such practices.

Admittedly, it is challenging to find these historical or "real" readers. In *Readers in History: Nineteenth-Century American Literature and the Contexts of Response*, James L. Machor writes that

> what remains elusive finally is a clear sense of what the actual reading experiences were for the numerous nineteenth-century readers whose encounters with literature took place, not in public forums, but alone in the bedrooms of middle-class homes in suburban Boston, or in barn lofts in rural Virginia, or between stolen moments of leisure at factory workbenches in Pittsburgh and Chicago.[10]

Finding out the experiences of real readers in Boston, Virginia, and Chicago has been hindered by a lack of sources. In general, librarians and archivists have not preserved the evidence that illuminates the encounters of ordinary readers with texts. The libraries of many famous authors or figures have been preserved intact, but libraries belonging to unknown people have more often been dispersed.[11] Many libraries have also discarded circulating records or marked-up books (full of marginalia), considered "imperfect" and less valuable than books left unmarked. For a historian of reading, though, such lists of circulating records (as I have suggested) and imperfect books offer evidence of readers' involvement in particular books.

Nonetheless, recent scholarship by Janice Radway, Cathy N. Davidson, William J. Gilmore, and Ronald and Mary Zboray, among others, has turned our attention to real readers. These critics take seriously the readers who rapidly consumed romances, penned marginalia in *Charlotte Temple*, and found solace in books during Vermont's cold winters.[12] Using the marginalia in books, interviews with real readers, readers' diaries, commonplace books, library borrowing records, and subscription records, scholars have begun to find evidence of readers' engagement with books. Important to this scholarship is the notion that readers help us understand the place of literature in a particular community. Studies of "real" readers, therefore, allow us to understand how acts of reading shape lives, but, in turn, this scholarship also helps us learn how various nineteenth-century literary institutions (libraries, bookstores, publishing houses) affected reading practices.[13]

What do we know already about the place of books and reading in antebellum culture? The scholarship on antebellum print culture underscores the rapid expansion in the publishing industry that produced an abundance of books for American consumption. Whereas eighteenth-century publishers imported selected books from Britain, publishers in the nineteenth century printed many more books in the United States. For their part, readers had access to more books, and some readers, especially upper-class women who were relieved of some domestic responsibilities in the home, had more leisure time in which to read. For both men and women, reading became an important means of forging community. Research by Ronald and Mary Zboray, for example, describes the ways in which books connected readers to particular communities or were integrated into work lives: women read aloud while sewing or cooking and both men and women read while working in factories.[14] Antebellum middle-class Americans also participated in the new expansion of reading, gathering regularly for parlor social hours to read books aloud.[15] For them and other Americans who now read devotional writings less often and secular works more regularly, reading became a kind of entertainment.[16] Reading gave people something to talk about and eased the tedium of work.

Circulating records from antebellum libraries help us explore the experiences of these elusive "real" readers and "real" reading practices in a few different ways. On the most basic level, these records tell us what people read—or at least intended to read—thus announcing which books were popular and when they were most popular. As Christine Pawley's work has shown, borrowing records also allow us to recreate various "sub-communities" of readers—school friends, families, religious groups, and so on—as we trace the records of friends or siblings who borrowed similar books.[17] Perhaps most important, though, library borrowing records help us gauge, with some precision, people's reading patterns: when a patron checked out a particular book, how long a patron held on to it, and what the patron borrowed next.

The reading patterns that I discovered in the Richmond and New Orleans library records complicate the thesis that by the nineteenth century people always read "extensively," covering a wide range of books and authors. The historian Rolf Engelsing has argued that during the early modern period people read "intensively" and focused solely on one or two texts, which they read over and over again. By the eighteenth century, readings practices had begun to become more extensive as readers began to move more quickly through a whole range of books. David Hall develops a similar argument about American literary culture in "The Uses of Literacy in New England, 1600-1850," showing that, by the nineteenth century, Americans had access to many more books and read more widely than they had earlier.[18] According to the Richmond and New Orleans records, though, readers combined intensive and extensive approaches to reading. Although the most avid readers borrowed a wide variety of books, they had not entirely abandoned intensive reading practices.[19] Many readers borrowed four or five Scott novels in a row, sometimes keeping a title for only two or three days before coming back to borrow another one. They also checked out many of the same Waverley Novels more than once. These patrons read several titles, but they had become "intensive" readers of Scott.

Even though circulating records reveal patterns of reading and promise excellent access to those hard-to-find "real" readers of literary history (those same readers, I should add, who have often been absent from library history), these records also pose challenges for the historian of reading. The most obvious problem is that we cannot tell whether the person who borrowed a book actually read it. As Simon Eliot points out in his introduction to the "Reading Experience Database" on the web, "to own, buy, borrow or steal a book is no proof of wishing to read it let alone proof of having read it."[20] We also do not know what happens to books when they leave a library—whether the "real" reader whose name is in the borrowing ledger is the same person who actually read (or intended to read) the book. Finally, borrowing ledgers do not voice the responses of readers; unlike marginalia or the diaries that Ronald and Mary Zboray have studied, library borrowing records do not illuminate readers' responses to the works they borrowed.[21] Nonetheless, library patrons are important agents in library history, and the evidence left behind in old ledgers is a testament to how they appropriated library collections for themselves.

The Richmond Library Company and the New Orleans Library Society and Lyceum

Patrons, of course, borrow books within particular institutional structures, within particular library cultures. They enter a library building, flip through a catalogue (or browse shelves), and perhaps speak with a librarian before determining which books to check out. Rules and guidelines also attempt to shape the experience a patron might have in a library. Like other libraries from the period, the Richmond Library Company and Lyceum and Library Society took time to outline guidelines for proper library behavior and rationales for the collections these libraries had built. Usually civic-minded and lofty in their goals, these institutions articulated aims for the role their libraries would play in the community and, in the case of the Richmond Library Company, developed a hierarchy for the books included on their shelves.

The Richmond library sought to improve the cultural life of the city, although the institution itself often struggled financially. Opened as the Mercantile Association in 1839, the library became the Richmond Library Company in 1844, because the Association had run a deficit and needed the revenue that new subscribers would bring.[22] At this time, the library attempted to bring together "all classes of citizens in its support" by forming the library company.[23] (The Richmond Library Company, a social library, depended on the support of subscribers and stockholders for its cash.)[24] By 1849, though, the library had gone into debt again; in the early 1850s, the city came to the rescue and began to allocate funds for its support, which helped the institution to thrive. In an effort to rally support for the library, an 1849 broadside announced the importance of the library to the city:

> The people in Richmond are not wanting in city pride, nor in expressions of it. The general credit of every city of any consequence, demands that it should be provided with all those conveniences, appliances and resources which are appropriate to its rank and importance; and by a proper and spasmodic exercise of liberality and enterprise on the part of a people, they may impart to their city an honorable reputation for such things far in advance of its size and population.[25]

In its various incarnations as Mercantile Association and Richmond Library Company, this antebellum library attempted to boost the status and resources of the city and, perhaps not surprisingly, attracted many of the town's wealthy patrons, including lawyers, judges, doctors, professors, and merchants as subscribers and stockholders.

Founded for the students of the public schools in Municipality No. 2, the Lyceum and Library Society in New Orleans was part of the lyceum movement in America and thus endeavored to provide its patrons not only with books but also with other educational opportunities, in the form of lectures. The library served students, of course, and also their teachers, and various life members and members of the board of directors. The ordinance proclaiming the new library, published in the 1858 catalogue, dates back to December 3, 1844, though the library did not open its doors until 1846 and most of the existing records are from the 1850s and 1860s. In this ordinance, the rules for funding the library and for using the building are stringently set forth. Students were to pay up to 25 cents each month, or $3 per year, in order to use the library and would become life members after using the library for three years or paying $9 (whichever came first). While the spending priority, according to the ordinance, was books ("the sum of five thousand dollars shall be paid into the Treasury, to the credit of said Society, and shall be invested by the Directors in books"[26]), the Lyceum and Library Society also promised that

> when ten thousand dollars shall have been invested in books, at least one half of the annual income thereafter, shall be applied to purchasing such chemical and philosophical apparatus as may be necessary to aid in imparting a knowledge of the natural sciences; and for obtaining during eight months of each year, able professors, to lecture weekly on such branches of useful knowledge as may be determined on by the Directors; Provided, That the lecture rooms of the Lyceum shall never be used for any religious or political discussions, and that no person shall be allowed to lecture therein, without the consent of the Directors previously obtained.[27]

Books received promises of funding before professors or equipment, but the plans articulated in the library's 1844 ordinance makes clear that this institution valued sciences and branches of "useful knowledge." As an agency of culture, the Lyceum and Library Society hoped to form students' minds not only with books but also with lectures determined useful by the directors.

Both institutions published catalogues of their collections in the 1850s, and, like the broadsides and ordinances characterizing each library's aims, these catalogues reveal the institutions' values, and, particularly in the case of the Richmond Library Company, how and why they prized particular books. Like all cataloguing systems, the Richmond Library Company's and Lyceum and Library Society's catalogues organize knowledge and in so doing emphasize the relative importance of the various books held by these libraries. For the Richmond Library Company, both a manuscript catalogue (perhaps from the 1840s?) and a published catalogue (1855) describe the reading material available, which included a range of fiction, history, and politics.[28] The design of this 1855 catalogue, according to the cataloguer, Henry B. Michard, was meant to model the development of a "civilization."

> Whether we consider the importance everywhere attributed to the subject of religion or the fact that according to all the accounts we have the origin of every people is coincident with the establishment of religion; it is natural to assign it the first place. As the next step that is taken in the progress of civilization is the formation of the State and making laws, but following out the same analogy, the second place would be for Poli-

tics and Jurisprudence, covering the whole ground of Legislative, Executive, & Judicial action and international relations.
Sciences and arts grow out of the establishment of the state
and mark its advance in power and prosperity. The analogy
already adopted requires then that the next place be allotted to
this division. Next the Literature and Belles Lettres [,] marking the period of the greatest prosperity of a state[,] their place
comes next in succession.[29]

This letter suggests both the range of reading matter the library catalogued but
also how the librarians regarded its mission: readers were to receive an education in the history of culture when they turned the pages of the catalogue or
browsed the shelves. Ranking categories of books—religion occupies first place
and law and jurisprudence take second place—Michard's catalogue relegates
"Literature and Belles Lettres" to the back of the catalogue. Fiction perhaps
represented the height of "prosperity" in any given civilization, but these titles
were not given priority within the catalogue's pages.

The Lyceum and Library Society also published catalogues in the 1850s but
took a more practical approach to organizing its collection. The Society published two catalogues in 1858, one describing the general contents of the library
and the second listing the holdings in the juvenile library. The library also collected French-language books, and a manuscript volume including titles lists of
these books in detail. Unlike the Richmond Library Company's catalogue, however, the Lyceum and Library Society's 1858 catalogue of English works and its
manuscript catalogue of French books depend purely on alphabetical organization, forgoing any design meant to evoke the "development of civilization." At
the beginning of the catalogue, the index lists subjects—arts, belles lettres, dic-
tionaries, foreign works, history, law, medicine, science, statistics, and theology
and religion—and, in most categories, a list of the authors (not titles) is included
under each heading. (In the case of belles lettres, foreign works, and history, the
catalogue omits authors' names and instead details place and time period covered by the books.) The manuscript catalogue of French works also proceeds
alphabetically but emphasizes subjects rather than authors. Finally, published at
the same time as the main library catalogue, the juvenile library catalogue is
more chaotically arranged than either the French catalogue or the main catalogue, lumping all books together and listing them alphabetically by author.
Like the ordinance proclaiming that the library should both spend money on
books and on resources to promote "useful knowledge," the catalogue itself aims
to be useful and practical for its readers. In the process, its alphabetical organization ends up, perhaps inadvertently, giving priority to arts and belles lettres.

Regardless of the status accorded fiction in each catalogue, both the Richmond Library Company and Lyceum and Library Society stocked a fair amount

of novels, including works by Charles Dickens, Susan Warner, Catharine Maria Sedgwick, William Makepeace Thackeray, James Fenimore Cooper, Maria Edgeworth, Washington Irving, Edward Bulwer-Lytton, James Kirke Paulding, and, of course, Walter Scott.[30] Both libraries also housed several works of history including Agnes Strickland's *Lives of the Queens of England*, William Mitford's *The History of Greece*, and Thomas Babington Macaulay's *The History of England*. The Richmond Library Company housed 4,000 titles by 1860, and a full 28 pages of its 1855 catalogue list works of history while nine pages are devoted to fiction. The Lyceum and Library Society had a collection of 10,000 volumes, and devoted 12 pages each of its 1858 catalogue to history and to fiction. The longer section of historical works in the Richmond Library Company's catalogue might owe to the bibliographical citations (publisher, date of publication, place of publication, and so on) included for each title. In any case, these works of fiction and history listed in the catalogues also fill the pages of the libraries' manuscript borrowing ledgers, especially for those readers who became avid readers of Walter Scott.

Manuscript borrowing ledgers record which books listed in the libraries' published catalogues actually circulated among readers: they record how readers used the books on the shelves. The volumes of borrowing ledgers for both the Richmond Library Company and Lyceum and Library Society list the borrowers' names, the titles or accession numbers of the books they borrowed, the dates the books were borrowed, and the dates returned. In the Richmond Library Company ledgers, a note about the patron's status, as either subscriber or stockholder, follows a name. While this information is not directly recorded in the Lyceum and Library Society's borrowing ledgers, the names of life members, board directors, and teachers come first in the ledger and the students' names follow. Ledgers for both libraries appear slightly chaotic (the Richmond Library Company's records, more so than the Lyceum and Library Society's records), as a librarian would run out of space for a particularly avid reader and would continue the entry on a half-filled page elsewhere in the book.[31]

These libraries' catalogues, ordinances, and broadsides outlined the institutions' aims, but borrowing records document the reading program that patrons outlined for themselves. These antebellum libraries, I would argue, did not necessarily succeed in promoting the kind of reading they set out to foster (reading that traced the "development of civilization" or led to the acquisition of "useful knowledge"); their collections did, though, shape patrons' reading in perhaps unintended ways. By giving readers easy access to one author's oeuvre, for not much money ($3 a year, in both Richmond and New Orleans), libraries supplied readers with fiction that they could read quickly at home, knowing as they were reading that another work by the same author could be easily found on the libraries' shelves. That these two libraries stocked all the works by Scott, Edgeworth, Cooper, and Jane Austen, among others, allowed readers to become hooked on a particular writer and to race through every title that writer had published. Whereas an antebellum bookstore, of course, charged for individual books, libraries gave readers access to them at a fixed rate. These library's circulating records thus have led me to speculate that the rapid pace at which library patrons read fiction indicates that they were reading to themselves, not aloud, and that the long list of titles by a single author listed under borrowers' names reveals that these patrons often read one author intensively.

Richmond and New Orleans Libraries and the Practices of Real Readers

My conclusion that patrons focused on one author and most likely read silently stems from my research on readers of Walter Scott.[32] I have, however, also discovered similar patterns for readers of Edgeworth and Cooper (and, to a lesser extent, Austen). Patrons borrowed several novels by Scott in a row, as well as batches of novels by Cooper and Edgeworth, and they read through many volumes of fiction quite rapidly (they sometimes also read volumes of history with similar speed). Because many readers in my sample, as I will detail below, borrowed four or five Scott novels during a two to three week period, I feel more certain that these borrowers read the books, simply because they kept coming back for works by the same author. The intensity with which readers approached reading Scott, Edgeworth, Cooper, among others, suggests that these libraries' comprehensive holdings in fiction and history enabled readers to become dedicated to one author or one historical subject. The Richmond Library Company and the Lyceum and Library Society in New Orleans may not have encouraged readers to study civilization's development or advances in sciences, but the libraries did encourage their patrons, albeit inadvertently, to come back again and again to check out books by the same author.[33]

Both the New Orleans and Richmond circulating records reveal distinct patterns about how patrons read Walter Scott and other historical fiction. Benjamin Cochran's charge records exemplify the pattern I discovered throughout the borrowing records. On June 21, 1848, Cochran, a Richmond Library Company subscriber, borrowed *Waverley* and then returned it three days later, when he checked *Guy Mannering*. He kept *Guy Mannering* until July 5th and upon returning it, borrowed *The Antiquary*. The pattern continued. Every week until August 18th Cochran borrowed a Waverley novel—reading not only the novels mentioned above, but also *Rob Roy*, the first three series of *Tales of My Landlord*, *Ivanhoe*, and *The Monastery*. For the whole summer, Cochran borrowed only Scott novels; he did not check out other books or periodicals from the library. But then on August 25, 1848, he abandoned the Waverley Novels in favor of Edgeworth. Between September 4 and January 15, 1849, he read nine volumes of Edgeworth's works. Cochran's focused, systematic reading pattern suggests both that he read the novels and that he focused on one author.[34] His wife, Amanda Cochran, also read Scott, as well as Cooper, intensively, if less systematically than Benjamin Cochran. From March until May of 1853, Amanda

Cochran read *Waverley, Ivanhoe, Keniwlorth, Peveril of the Peak,* and *Guy Mannering.* Over the course of three years, she also managed to read 21 works by Cooper. While Benjamin Cochran read in a perhaps more orderly way, both Cochrans singled out particular authors from the library's collection and read these authors with great intensity.

The Cochrans were not unusual in their reading habits. Many other Richmond Library Company patrons become equally absorbed in books by one author. John Dooley, a stockholder in the library, read 17 Scott novels during a five-year period. Even though his reading stretched over several years, he did read some of the novels quickly: he raced through *Peveril of the Peak, The Pirate,* and *The Betrothed* in two weeks in the spring of 1854. For the next two months, his reading consisted of Cooper novels—*The Red Rover, The Water-Witch, The Pioneers, The Deerslayer,* and *The Spy.* Dr. T. R. Harrison, also a library stockholder, read several of Scott's novels, including *The Talisman, Quentin Durward, The Monastery, The Abbot, Guy Mannering,* and *The Heart of Mid-Lothian* bewteen April 6 and August 28, 1852.[35] Harrison did not read as quickly as some other readers, but he nonetheless focused most of his reading on one author. These patrons demonstrated their devotion to particular writers, coming back to the library several times to read yet one more book by the same writer whom they had been reading for weeks.

Similar reading patterns emerge in the New Orleans records. The dates in this ledger are more difficult to determine, but in the mid-1850s Albert Greene read a series of Cooper's works in a short period of time. On April 21, he borrowed *Pathfinder*; he returned on April 26 to borrow *The Deerslayer.* Then between April 29 and May 30, he read *The Last of the Mohicans, The Prairie, The Spy, The Pilot, The Water Witch, The Red Rover,* and *The Two Admirals.*[36] On November 11, 1856, Richard Bein borrowed Walter Scott's *Guy Mannering*; on November 17th, he borrowed *Waverley.* Then between December 1, 1856, and February 28, 1857, Bein borrowed (and presumably read) Scott's *Redgauntlet, The Abbot, Woodstock, The Betrothed, Quentin Durward, St. Ronan's Well, Ivanhoe, Antiquary, Kenilworth, Old Mortality,* and *Rob Roy*, checking out books by no other author during this three month period.[37] In 1861, Julia Benedict, read Scott's novels steadily, interspersing her reading of his novels with *Harper's Magazine* and *Robinson Crusoe.* Between April 3rd and August 19th, she read *The Fortunes of Nigel, Anne of Geierstein, St. Ronan's Well, Chronicles of the Canongate, Redgauntlet, Count Robert of Paris, The Abbot, The Monastery,* and *Waverley.*[38]

But Scott was not the only writer who inspired such dedication. The New Orleans reader Frederick Ames, between July 6th and August 17th, devoted his reading entirely to Jane Austen, checking out *Pride and Prejudice, Sense and Sensibility, Mansfield Park, Emma,* and *Northanger Abbey,* one right after the other.[39] Albert Collings read Dickens with similar intensity, he borrowed *Dombey and Son* on December 30, 1856, *David Copperfield* on January 16, 1857, *Martin*

Chuzzlewit on January 26th, and *Oliver Twist* on February 12th. By the summer, though, he turned to Scott, reading three novels in a row.[40] Some New Orleans readers also read works of history with similar intensity. Also in 1856, M. G. Beck, for example, borrowed 11 volumes of *Roman History*, reading them in order, between September 16th and December 4th. The following year, he read three volumes of the *History of Ancient Europe* and four volumes of Gibbon's *The History of the Decline and Fall of the Roman Empire*, again in order.[41] At the Lyceum and Library Society, readers found a small selection of writers included in the library's collection and read those writers intensively. The library's 10,000 volumes and its promised emphasis on "useful knowledge" did not determine patrons' borrowing habits; instead, these readers looked to the library as a place that guaranteed them a steady and certain supply of works by one writer.

As the evidence I have cited above suggests, many patrons read long, complicated novels within a short period of time, and this has led me to speculate that they did not read aloud in family gatherings, but instead read privately. For example, the Richmond Library Company patron Dr. Edward Fisher borrowed *Peveril of the Peak* for only two days and *The Betrothed* and *Waverley* for the same four days. B. B. Minor checked out *Waverley* one day and returned it to the Richmond Library Company the next. Henry Spiller Place, a Richmond patron in the 1850s, borrowed 18 Waverley Novels over the course of year. Place ended up borrowing six novels one day and returning the next.[42] (Perhaps he did not like the novels he returned quickly, but more likely, considering the amount of Scott he borrowed in a little over a year, he read each one quickly and returned to the library right away for another one.) In New Orleans, readers also moved quickly through the novels they borrowed: William Herriday kept *The Spy* for two days, *The Red Rover* for four days, and *The Prairie* for three.[43] The pace at which patrons borrowed novels suggest that they must have read to themselves, because readers would have needed several days, even weeks, to read these two- and three-volume novels aloud to gatherings.

Conclusion

We cannot hear these Richmond and New Orleans readers "talking back" (as William Charvat asks us to), as they walked through the doors of the Richmond Library Company and the Lyceum and Library Society, week after week over the course of years, to borrow books. But circulating records do document how patrons used libraries and demonstrate, quite clearly, that many patrons discovered a corner in a library's collection, stayed there, and read books by one writer intensively before moving on to another author's works. I would argue that the Richmond and New Orleans libraries inadvertently cultivated such absorption by offering readers the promise of so many books by one author— Scott, Edgeworth, Dickens, Cooper, Austen—in one place and for a fixed amount of money. In my sample, patrons did not read according to the plans set forward by the boards of directors of these institutions; they did not read to boost the status of the city, model the development of civilization, or promote useful knowledge. Neither did patrons seem to take their cues from the organization of the libraries' catalogues. Instead, many patrons returned to the same library over and over, drawing on the institution's extensive resources to nurture a new passion for reading one author or reading about one historical subject. We may not have patrons' words but we do have a record of patrons' reading preferences and practices. So the records do, in a fashion, allow readers to speak: they testify to patrons' agency in shaping their own reading experiences through the practice of visiting antebellum libraries.

Notes

I thank the Virginia Historical Society for awarding me an Andrew W. Mellow Fellowship, which allowed me to carry out research on the Richmond Library Company's records. The University of Minnesota's William Stout Fellowship afforded me time to travel to New Orleans to research the Lyceum and Library Society. Some of the evidence from the Richmond borrowing records cited here originally appeared in my article "Walter Scott and the Nineteenth-Century American Literary Marketplace: Antebellum Richmond Readers and the Collected Edition of the Waverley Novels," *The Papers of the Bibliographical Society of America* 93 (December 1999): 495-517.

1. The Virginia Historical Society has preserved several documents relating to the Richmond Library Company (1839-1860), including three ledgers listing books borrowed and returned, a manuscript catalogue, cash books, a published catalogue, business correspondence, and minutes of meetings. The library began as the Mercantile Association in 1839 and became the Richmond Library Company in 1844.

2. The Lyceum and Library Society records, housed in City Archives of the New Orleans Public Library, include three volumes of borrowing records (1854-1867), register of members (1872-1881), inventory of books (1870), catalogue of French works owned by the library (1854), and two published catalogues, the 124-page *Catalogue of the Library of the Lyceum and Library Society* (1858) and the 22-page *Catalogue of the Juvenile Library of the Lyceum and Library Society* (1858). Only pre-1861 materials have been microfilmed.

3. For a brief history of the Richmond Library Company, see E. Lee Shepard, "Two Early Libraries of Richmond," *The Richmond Quarterly* (Summer 1981): 48-52.

4. See Ronald Zboray's chapter "Gender and Boundlessness in Reading Patters" in *A Fictive People: Antebellum Economic Development and the American Reading Public* (New York, 1993), 156-179 and Christine Pawley, *Reading on the Middle Border: The Culture of Print in Late-Nineteenth-Century Osage, Iowa* (Amherst, Mass., 2001), especially pages 61-116.

5. Emily B. Todd, "The Transatlantic Context: Walter Scott and Nineteenth-Century American Literary History," Unpublished dissertation, University of Minnesota, 1999.

6. Robert Darnton, "What is the History of Books?" in *Reading in America: Literature & Social History*, ed. Cathy N. Davidson (Baltimore, 1989) 27-52.

7. William Charvat, *The Profession of Authorship in America*, ed. Matthew Bruccoli (1968; Amherst, Mass., 1992), 283-297; quotation appears on pages 283-284.

8. William Charvat, *The Profession of Authorship in America*, 296-297.

9. For a helpful overview of reader-response scholarship see Jane Tompkins, ed. *Reader-Response Criticism: From Formalism to Post-Structuralism* (Baltimore, 1980).

10. James L. Machor, ed. *Readers in History: Nineteenth-Century American Literature and the Contexts of Response* (Baltimore, 1993), xxi.

11. The Thomas Dowse library at the Massachusetts Historical Society is an excellent example of a library belonging to an upper-class Bostonian that has been preserved in its entirety. It now fills an entire room on the second floor of the Massachusetts Historical Society; Dowse owned first editions of the Waverley Novels, which he had bound uniformly.

12. See Cathy N. Davidson, *Revolution and the Word: The Rise of the Novel in America* (New York, 1986); William J. Gilmore, *Reading Becomes a Necessity of Life: Material and Cultural Life in Rural New England, 1780-1835* (Knoxville, 1989); Janice Radway, *Reading the Romance: Women, Patriarchy, and Popular Literature* (Chapel Hill, 1984); and Ronald J. Zboray

and Mary Saracino Zboray, "Reading and Everyday Life in Antebellum Boston: The Diary of Daniel F. and Mary D. Child," *Libraries & Culture* 32 (Summer 1997): 285-323; "'Have You Read . . .': Real Readers and Their Responses in Antebellum Boston and Its Region," *Nineteenth-Century Literature* 52 (September 1997): 139-162; "Books, Reading, and the World of Goods in Antebellum New England," *American Quarterly* 48 (December 1996): 587-622, among other articles.

13. It is important to remember, of course, that it is difficult to *learn* about historical readers. Almost everything we learn is based on inference—based on interpretations of library borrowing records, marginalia, and diary entries, for instance. "Real" readers are always constructed by book historians, based on the limited archival materials.

14. Ronald and Mary Saracino Zboray, "The Experience of Reading in Antebellum New England: Part III. Reception. Chapter 3. Habits. Section C. Allied Activities." Unpublished paper delivered at the Massachusetts Historical Society, February 4, 1999. Thanks to the Zborays for their permission to cite this unpublished work.

15. Joan Hedrick, *Harriet Beecher Stowe: A Life* (New York, 1995) 76-88.

16. William B. Warner nicely reframes the history of the novel by reminding us that it should be seen within the context of the history of entertainment. See *Licensing Entertainment: The Elevation of Novel Reading in Britain, 1684-1750* (Berkeley, 1998).

17. Pawley, *Reading on the Middle Border*, 111-116.

18. For a summary of Rolf Engelsing's theory of reading, published in "Die Perioden der Lesergeschichte in der Nezeit: Das statistische Ausmass und die soziokulturelle Bedeutung der Lekture," *Archiv fur Geschichte des Buchwesens* 10 (1969): cols 944-1002, see Robert Darnton's "First Steps Toward a History of Reading" in *Kiss of Lamourette: Reflections in Cultural History* (New York, 1990), 154-187. On page 166, Darnton draws the parallel between Hall's and Engelsing's theories. See David D. Hall, "The Uses of Literacy in New England, 1600 to 1850" in *Cultures of Print: Essays in the History of the Book* (Amherst, Mass., 1996), 36-78. For another important work on the history of reading, see Roger Chartier, *The Order of Books: Readers, Authors, and Libraries in Europe between the Fourteenth and Eighteenth Centuries*, trans. Lydia G. Cochrane (Stanford, Calif., 1994), especially pages 1-23.

19. Robert Darnton also suggests that "[r]eading did not evolve in one direction, extensiveness." See "First Steps Toward a History of Reading," 166.

20. Simon Eliot, "The Reading Experience Database; or what are we to do about the history of reading" (http:/www2.open.ac.uk/arts/RED).

21. Ronald J. Zboray and Mary Saracino Zboray have studied extensively diaries and letters of antebellum New Englanders in order to determine these readers' experiences of reading. See, for example, their articles "Reading and Everyday Life in Antebellum Boston: The Diary of Daniel F. and Mary D. Child," *Libraries & Culture* 32 (Summer 1997): 285-323 and "'Have You Read . . .': Real Readers and Their Responses in Antebellum Boston and Its Region," *Nineteenth-Century Literature* 52 (September 1997): 139-162.

22. For an overview of the library's history, see E. Lee Shepard, "Two Early Libraries of Richmond," *The Richmond Quarterly* 4 (Summer 1981): 48-52.

23. See "Statement in Behalf of the Richmond Library Company."

24. For more information on social libraries, see Jesse H. Shera, *Foundations of the Public Library: The Origins of the Public Library Movement in New England 1629-1855* (Chicago, 1949). See also Paul Kaufman, *Libraries and their Users: Collected Papers in Library History* (London, 1969), especially "The Community Library: A Chapter in English Social History," 188-228.

25. "Statement in Behalf of the Richmond Library Company."

26. *Catalogue of the Library of The Lyceum and Library Society, First District, City of New Orleans* (New Orleans, 1858), iii.

27. *Ibid.*, iii-iv.

28. For more details about the organization of the catalogue, see a letter by the library's cataloguer, Henry B. Michard, to George Nicholson Johnson, April 18, 1855, Virginia Historical Society, Mss2M5822al.

29. *Ibid.*

30. There are discrepancies between the borrowing records and the library's catalogue. For example, Susan Warner's *Wide, Wide World* shows up in the borrowing records, but it is not listed in the 1855 catalogue.

31. These library borrowing records therefore differ from the ones Ronald J. Zboray analyzes in *A Fictive People*. His chapter entitled "Gender and Boundlessness in Reading Patterns," though, is a model for my work in this paper.

32. I do not analyze the possible reasons for Scott's particular popularity in the South here, because I am more interested in discussing how to use these library records to illuminate reading practices. For more on Scott in the South, please see Grace Warren Landrum, "Sir Walter Scott and His Literary Rivals in the Old South," *American Literature* 2 (November 1930): 256-276. G. Harrison Orians, "Walter Scott, Mark Twain, and the Civil War," *South Atlantic Quarterly* 40

(Autumn 1941): 342-359, and Rollin G. Osterweis, *Romanticism and Nationalism in the Old South* (1949; Baton Rouge, 1967) 48-49. In *Rethinking the South: Essays in Intellectual History* (Baltimore, 1988), Michael O'Brien argues that the detailed research needed to accurately determine Scott's reception in the South simply has not been done (53). The evidence I supply here begins to give such evidence, but more systematic work will need to be done to understand the nature of Scott's popularity in the South.

33. For a full study of the Richmond Library Company patrons' reading of Scott, please see my article, "Walter Scott and the Nineteenth-Century American Literary Marketplace: Antebellum Richmond Readers and the Collected Editions of the Waverley Novels" *The Papers of the Bibliographical Society of America* 93 (December 1999): 495-517. At the Virginia Historical Society, I sampled the records of over 250 readers from the span of the library's history, and I recorded the titles of the novels by Scott, Edgeworth, and Cooper, and I also recorded the titles of the books and periodicals patrons borrowed before and after Scott. I sampled the records of all the women who borrowed books during this period. My sample for the Lyceum and Library Society in New Orleans was smaller (about 40 readers). In my study of the Richmond library, I recorded the number of transactions for each reader, the titles of each work by Scott, Cooper, and Edgeworth borrowed, the books or periodicals readers borrowed before and after Scott, and the dates the books were checked out and returned. My goal was to discover not only how many people read Scott and which novels they read, but also to think about what led them to Scott and which books they turned to after Scott. After spending time with the records, I also became interested in the pattern I detected in my research. All of this information is now on an Excel database. Finally, I should note that in *A Fictive People*, Ronald J. Zboray mentions parenthetically that patrons of the New York Society Library in his sample read Cooper in clusters (170).

34. Benjamin Cochran, 1848, Richmond Library Company borrowing records, Virginia Historical Society.

35. John Dooley, 1848-1856, 444, and T. R. Harrison, 1850-1853, 3, Richmond Library Company borrowing records, Virginia Historical Society.

36. Albert Greene, 1850s, Lyceum and Library Society borrowing records, New Orleans Public Library.

37. Richard Bein, 1856, Lyceum and Library Society borrowing records, New Orleans Public Library.

38. Julia Benedict, 1860, Lyceum and Library Society borrowing records, New Orleans Public Library.

39. Frederick Ames, [1856], Lyceum and Library Society borrowing records, New Orleans Public Library.

40. Albert Collings, [1856], Lyceum and Library Society borrowing records, New Orleans Public Library.

41. M. G. Beck, 1856, Lyceum and Library Society borrowing records, New Orleans Public Library.

42. Edward Fisher, 1852, 255; B. B. Minor, 1849-1852, 259; Henry Spiller Place, 1853-1855; Richmond Library Company borrowing records, Virginia Historical Society.

43. William Herriday, [1850s], Lyceum and Library Society, New Orleans Public Library.

(continued from p. 4)

memoration. He has published articles on architecture, a contemporary African masquerade, and Bugs Bunny.

Ari Kelman is a Ph.D. candidate in the American Studies Program at New York University, where he is writing his dissertation about the culture of Yiddish language radio in New York, 1923-1955.

Christine Pawley teaches at the School of Library and Information Science at The University of Iowa. Her book, *Reading on the Middle Border: The Culture of Print in Late Nineteenth-Century Osage, Iowa*, was published by the University of Massachusetts Press in 2001. She is currently researching the history of print culture in Cold War Wisconsin, focusing particularly on the Door-Kewaunee Regional Library Demonstration of 1950-1952.

Jean Preer is Associate Professor at the School of Library and Information Science of The Catholic University of America. She earned an MLS degree at the University of California at Berkeley, and a law degree and a Ph.D. in American Civilization at George Washington University. Her doctoral dissertation was published by Greenwood Press as *Lawyers v. Educators: Black Colleges and Desegregation in Public Higher Education.* She spent the 2000-2001 as a Visiting Scholar at the School of Library and Information Studies of the University of Wisconsin-Madison, researching the American Heritage Project of the American Library Association as part of a study tentatively titled *Informed Citizenry: Public Libraries, Discussion and Democracy, 1936 to 1956.*

Emily B. Todd, assistant professor in the Department of English at Westfield State College, has her Ph.D. from the University of Minnesota, where she wrote a dissertation, "The Transatlantic Context: Walter Scott and Nineteenth-Century American Literary History." She is a recipient of the Virginia Library History Award for her article, "Walter Scott and the Nineteenth-Century American Literary Marketplace," in the Decembr 1999 issue of *Papers of the Biographical Society of America.*

Mary Saracino Zboray is an independent scholar residing in Pittsburgh, Pennsylvania. She co-authored with Ronald J. Zboray *A Handbook for the Study of Book History in the United States* (Library of Congress, 2000), along with articles and essays on common readers, authors, and women's political culture in antebellum New England.

Ronald J. Zboray is Associate Professor of Communication at the University of Pittsburgh. In addition to his co-authored work with Mary Saracino Zboray, he has produced *A Fictive People: Antebellum Economic Development* and the *American Reading Public* (Oxford University Press, 1993) and numerous articles and essays on antebellum authorship, reading, and publishing.

American Studies

A tri-annual interdisciplinary journal sponsored by the Mid-America American Studies Association, the University of Kansas, and the Hall Center for the Humanities.

2000 special double issue available for $18.00

American Studies: Globalization, Transnationalism, and The End of the American Century

Editors: David M. Katzman and Norman R. Yetman

1999 special summer issue, *American Studies: A Critical Retrospective*

Order Form
(please copy and send)

_____ Please send me the 2000 special double issue for $18.00.

_____ Please send me the 1999 special summer issue for $10.00.

_____ I would like to enroll as a 2002 member of MAASA for $20.00.

2002 MAASA membership rates: Individual $20.00, Institutional $35.00, Students $8.00, Emeritus $14.00. Individual subscription includes three issues and the MAASA Newsletter. International subscribers please add $12.00 for postage. Make checks payable to MAASA. Send to Managing Editor, American Studies , 1445 Jayhawk Blvd., Rm. 2120, University of Kansas, Lawrence, KS 66045.